THE STATE OF THE WORLD'S CHILDREN 2014 IN NUMBERS

EVERY CHILD COUNTS

**Revealing disparities,
advancing children's rights**

CONTENTS

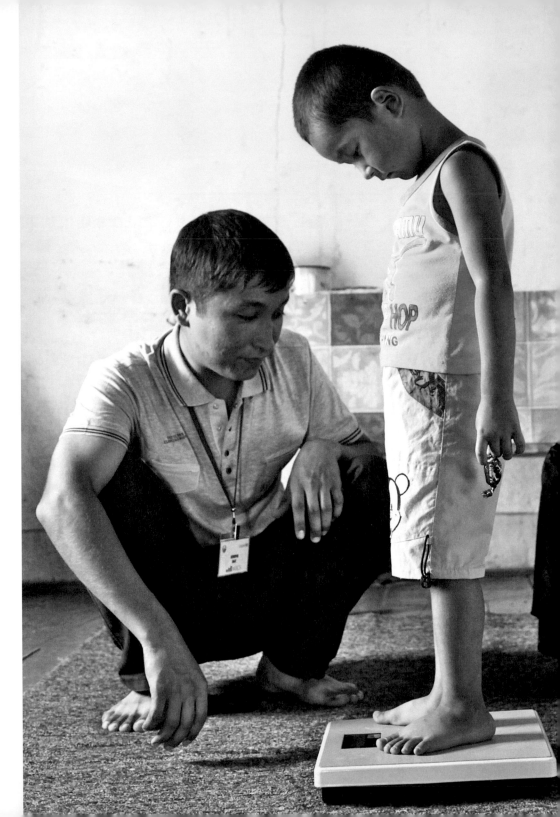

Introduction

Thirty years have passed since *The State of the World's Children* began to publish tables of standardized global and national statistics aimed at providing a detailed picture of children's circumstances.

Much has changed in the decades since the first indicators of child well-being were presented. But the basic idea has not: Credible data about children's situations are critical to the improvement of their lives – and indispensable to realizing the rights of every child.

Data continue to support advocacy and action on behalf of the world's 2.2 billion children, providing governments with facts on which to base decisions and actions to improve children's lives. And new ways of collecting and using data will help target investments and interventions to reach the most vulnerable children.

Data do not, of themselves, change the world. They make change possible – by identifying needs, supporting advocacy, and gauging progress. What matters most is that decision-makers use the data to make positive change, and that the data are available for children and communities to use in holding duty-bearers to account.

◀ Erlan, 3, has his height and weight recorded in the Konlikul District, Uzbekistan.
© UNICEF/NYHQ2011-1680/Giacomo Pirozzi

Lives behind the numbers

Consider the tables that follow this essay: the rows and columns of numbers, the array of fine print. Here, reduced to stark symbols, are the present and future of nations: children. As your eyes move from column to column, some of the many facets of their lives unfold. The numbers tell stories about the circumstances in which children are born and cared for, grow and learn, work and connect with others, and make their way in the world.

Pick a country, any country. What proportion of births is registered, and how many children are thus granted an official identity and the rights that flow from it – rights to services, protection, the exercise of citizenship?

How many children die within a year of being born, and how many never live to see their fifth birthday? How long can those who do survive expect to live? Are they receiving essential vaccines and medicines to protect them against the diseases that prey on the young and vulnerable? Are they getting the nourishment they need for their bodies and minds to thrive? Do they have clean water for drinking and washing, and access to safe, hygienic toilets?

What percentage of children enter primary school, and how many make it to secondary school? How many are put to work or married while still children? Do they enter adolescence equipped with the knowledge to protect themselves against HIV?

The data show that tremendous progress has been made during the past few decades:

- About 90 million children who would have died if mortality rates had stuck at their 1990 level have, instead, lived past the age of 5.[1]

- Deaths from measles among children under 5 years of age fell from 482,000 in 2000 to 86,000 in 2012, thanks in large part to immunization coverage, which increased from 16 per cent in 1980 to 84 per cent in 2012.[2]

- Improvements in nutrition have led to a 37 per cent drop in stunting since 1990.[3]

- Primary school enrolment has increased, even in the least developed countries: Whereas in 1990 only 53 per cent of children in those countries gained school admission, by 2011 the rate had improved to 81 per cent.[4]

- Nearly 1.9 billion people have gained access to improved sanitation since 1990.[5]

But the tables also bear witness to ongoing violations of children's rights:

- Some 6.6 million children under 5 years of age died in 2012, mostly from preventable causes, their fundamental right to survive and develop unrealized.

- Fifteen per cent of the world's children[6] engage in child labour that compromises their right to protection from economic exploitation and infringes on their right to learn and play.

The world's poorest children are

2.7X

less likely than the richest ones to have a skilled attendant at their birth

- Eleven per cent of girls are married before they turn 15,[7] jeopardizing their rights to health, education and protection.

- The right to freedom from cruel and degrading punishment is violated whenever children are subjected to violent discipline at home or in school.

The tables also reveal gaps and inequities, showing that gains and deprivations are unevenly distributed. Children's chances differ depending on whether their country is a rich or a

All rights, every child

In creating the Convention on the Rights of the Child (CRC), the international community has recognized that children are people who have rights that must be respected equally to those of adults.

Four main principles form the core of the CRC:
- Non-discrimination or universality (article 2): All children have rights, regardless of race, colour, sex, language, religion, political or other opinion, national, ethnic or social origin, property, disability, birth or other status.

- Best interests (article 3): The child's best interests must be a primary consideration in all decisions affecting her or him.

- Life, survival and development (article 6): All children have a right to life, and to survive and develop – physically, mentally, spiritually, morally, psychologically and socially – to their full potential.

- Respect for the views of the child (article 12): Children have the right to express themselves freely on matters that affect them, and to have their views taken seriously.

◄ A newborn in Wau Hospital in Western Bahr al Ghazal State, South Sudan.
© UNICEF/NYHQ2011-0453crop/Veronique de Viguerie

poor one; whether they are born girls or boys, into families rich or poor; or whether they live in the countryside or the city – and there, too, whether they live in well-to-do areas or impoverished neighbourhoods.

Of the roughly 18,000 children under 5 years old who die every day, a disproportionate number are from parts of cities or the countryside that are cut off from services because of poverty or geography. Many could be saved by proven means and at little cost.

Although diarrhoea can be treated effectively and inexpensively with

By articulating children's rights and obliging States Parties to respect, protect and fulfil them, the CRC provides a strong impetus for the collection, analysis and dissemination of data.

In order to survive and develop to their full potential, children need health care, nutritious food, education that nurtures their minds and equips them with useful knowledge and skills, freedom from violence and exploitation, and the time and space to play. The right to life, survival and development thus points to a wide range of indicators that must be measured in order to make sure that this right is realized.

Combating discrimination and inequity entails identifying children who are discriminated against and excluded from services and opportunities. To this end, the Committee on the Rights of the Child, the body charged with tracking implementation of the CRC, has urged that data be disaggregated by age, sex, urban and rural residence, membership in minority or indigenous groups, ethnicity, religion, disability and 'any other category considered appropriate.'[8]

The Committee has further emphasized that it is not enough to collect data. In order to identify problems and inform policies, the data also need to be analysed, disseminated to the public and used to assess progress in realizing children's rights.[9]

The CRC's guarantee of the right to be heard requires that adults who make decisions affecting children's lives listen to children deeply and seriously, giving due respect and consideration to their views. Children therefore need safe, meaningful opportunities to participate in research, as well as access to the fruits of data collection and analysis.

39%

of rural households in the Niger have access to improved drinking water, compared with 100% of urban households

oral rehydration salts, children from the richest homes who become ill with diarrhoea are up to four times more likely to be treated than children from the poorest homes.[10] And while improved drinking water has become available to 2.1 billion more people worldwide since 1990,[11] this progress has bypassed many residents of rural areas. They account for less than half of the world's population but make up 83 per cent of those still deprived of a reliable source of safe drinking water.

Data that reveal disparities masked by aggregate figures can help to direct interventions that can reach the unreached and right the wrong of exclusion. The more precisely aid and opportunity can be focused, the greater the potential impact.

Data for children's rights

The world will commemorate the 25th anniversary of the Convention on the Rights of the Child (CRC) in November 2014, and the culmination of the

Millennium Development Goals (MDGs) in 2015. Both will be occasions to celebrate the progress made for children and to recommit to reaching the millions of children whose rights are not yet fulfilled.

Data have played a key role in achieving that progress and are essential in identifying the most disadvantaged of the world's 2.2 billion children, understanding the barriers they confront, and designing and monitoring initiatives that make it possible for every child to realize her or his rights.

Evidence has both reflected and galvanized commitment to children's rights. It has spurred not only greater awareness of the realities that confront children but also improvement in those realities.

The importance of data won new recognition when the United Nations General Assembly adopted the CRC on 20 November 1989. In addition to codifying children's rights and promising to fulfil them, States Parties to the Convention

(Continued on page 10)

Topics covered in Multiple Indicator Cluster Surveys (MICS)

Developed in the early 1990s by UNICEF and conducted by national authorities, Multiple Indicator Cluster Surveys (MICS) are the largest source of statistical information on children. Each survey is made up of discrete modules on specific topics. Countries can choose which modules to use based on relevance to their situation. Survey methods are standardized, so data can be compared over time and across countries. Data are disaggregated by sex, education, wealth, residence or other factors to reveal disparities.

The surveys have been designed to provide a manageable framework with which to monitor progress towards global goals. Each survey typically samples around 10,000 households and includes interviews with women and men aged 15–49 years, as well as mothers and caretakers of all children under age 5. The number of topics covered has increased substantially over the years as demand for data has grown.

For more information on MICS, please visit
<http://www.childinfo.org/mics.html>

MICS TOPICS

MICS 5 — 51
MICS 4 — 49
MICS 3 — 41
MICS 2 — 25
MICS 1 — 15

2015

DIETARY RECALL ZINC
LIFE SATISFACTION
CHILDREN LEFT BEHIND PLACE FOR HANDWASHING
MASS MEDIA · INFORMATION AND COMMUNICATION TECHNOLOGIES
POSTNATAL/NEONATAL CARE
INDOOR RESIDUAL SPRAYING TOBACCO AND ALCOHOL USE
ECD OUTCOMES C-SECTION
BIRTH HISTORIES
MATERNAL MORTALITY MALE CIRCUMCISION
MARRIAGE/UNION SEXUAL BEHAVIOR
LITERACY FGM/C ITNs POLYGYNY IPTP
HOUSEHOLD CHARACTERISTICS
ATTITUDES TOWARD DOMESTIC VIOLENCE UNMET NEED
CHILD DISCIPLINE
EDUCATIONAL ATTENDANCE
BIRTH REGISTRATION ATTENDANCE TO ECD PROGRAMMES
CHILD LABOUR ARI SYMPTOMS
AND TREATMENT
CONTRACEPTION ANTENATAL CARE PREVALENCE AND CONTENT
HIV/AIDS, KNOWLEDGE, ATTITUDES, TESTING
ORPHANHOOD AND LIVING ARRANGEMENTS BIRTH WEIGHT
DELIVERY CARE MALARIA
CHILD DISABILITY DIARRHOEA AND TREATMENT
EARLY CHILDBEARING SUPPLEMENTARY FEEDING
BREASTFEEDING +
IMMUNIZATION TETANUS TOXOID
ANTHROPOMETRY
VITAMIN A WATER AND SANITATION MORTALITY
SALT IODIZATION/TESTING
KNOWLEDGE OF ILLNESS SYMPTOMS
SOLID FUELS

1995

ADVANCES IN DATA

Mobile phone technologies allow a quicker response to disease outbreaks.

MICS and Demographic Health Surveys (DHS) are piloting a water quality module that will test households' water for *E. coli*.

Objective measurements, such as **blood tests,** help monitor the prevalence of health conditions.

New approaches

New tools and partnerships are yielding new ways to collect and share data and, in some cases, are testing old assumptions.

In the absence of cost-effective, periodic and standardized water quality testing, the World Health Organization and UNICEF made 'use of an improved water source' a proxy for sustainable access to safe drinking water. The presence of a protected well makes it more likely that the water is safe – but until recently there was no way to be sure. Now that new, rapid, low-cost water quality testing kits are available, MICS and Demographic Health Surveys (DHS) are piloting a water quality module that will actually test households' water for *E. coli*. [12]

Similarly, household surveys use objective measurements to produce more accurate estimates of the prevalence of HIV and other health conditions. Previously, HIV prevalence was estimated mostly from sentinel surveillance systems that monitored pregnant women in antenatal care. In 2001, the Mali DHS included HIV testing – allowing prevalence estimates to be drawn from a nationally representative, population-based sample (now including men). This led the Joint United Nations Programme on HIV/AIDS (UNAIDS) and governments to adjust their official HIV prevalence estimates, and also improved understanding of the social, demographic and behavioural aspects of the pandemic. [13]

Mobile phone technologies are cutting the time it takes to assess and respond to situations affecting children. M-Trac, a health management information system in Uganda, uses text messages sent by health workers to alert public health officials to outbreaks of disease and to let them know how much medicine is on hand at health facilities so they can anticipate and resolve any shortages. Uganda also is home to Ureport, a text message-based means by which members of the public can lodge anonymous complaints about service delivery.

Other efforts seek to extract useful information from satellite imagery, traffic sensors, social media, the blogosphere, online searches, mobile banking, hotline usage and other contributors to the hubbub of modern life. Numerous initiatives are exploring ways to mine such 'big data' for nuggets that can inform policymakers about people's well-being and help them to pinpoint vulnerabilities.

Different tools and methods will suit different purposes. Innovations in real-time data collection may not be suited to the job of monitoring global commitments, which requires nationally representative data collected in a standard format for comparison across countries and over time. But experiments like those above have the potential to solve problems at the local level.

A girl drinks from a tap in the Za'atari camp for Syrian refugees, Jordan.
© UNICEF/NYHQ2013-0667/Shehzad Noorani

4%

of the poorest
Tanzanians are
registered at birth,
compared to
56% of the richest

(Continued from page 6)
obligated themselves to report regularly
on the state of their children. The following
September, when the CRC entered into
force, leaders at the World Summit for
Children set specific goals to improve the
survival, development, education and
protection of children by the year 2000.[14]
In 2001, global goal-setting gained further
affirmation and scope with the adoption
of the eight MDGs, each with specific
targets that would require monitoring
through 2015.

These landmarks in international public
policy constituted an unprecedented
expression of commitment to children's
rights. They also required data –
comparable between countries and over
time – in order to monitor progress and
prospects. UNICEF was charged with
charting global progress toward the
health-related MDGs.

Many actors contribute to the monitoring
effort, including national authorities,
multilateral organizations and inter-
agency groups, universities and non-
governmental organizations. For its part,
UNICEF developed Multiple Indicator

Cluster Surveys (MICS), which are
conducted by national statistical offices.

The importance of monitoring cannot
be overstated: It measures the extent to
which commitments made on the political
stage are honoured in the homes, clinics,
schools and streets where children live.
With reliable data, disseminated effectively
and used judiciously, monitoring makes it
impossible for the denial of rights to
go unnoticed.

Telling untold stories

Being counted makes children visible,
and this act of recognition makes it
possible to address their needs and
advance their rights.

In the Democratic Republic of the Congo,
for example, the 2010 MICS found that
only 28 per cent of births had been
registered. Rapid surveys modelled on
UNICEF's Monitoring Results for Equity
Systems framework further revealed that
the denial of the right to an official identity
led to more deprivations – denying access
to health, education and other services.

Action plans developed and implemented with community involvement led to a surge in birth registration – in one district, from 6 per cent in June 2012 to 41 per cent in December 2012. Pregnant women also benefited: 58 per cent received at least four antenatal care visits, up from 16 per cent six months earlier.[15]

But not all children are being counted, and not to be counted only perpetuates invisibility and voicelessness. This puts children at greater risk. Groups commonly undercounted or overlooked include children living in institutions or temporary housing, children in detention, children living and working on the street, children with disabilities, trafficked children,

Syrian refugee children in art class in the Ramtha Facility, Jordan.
© UNICEF/NYHQ2012-0197/Giacomo Pirozzi

migrant children, internally displaced and refugee children, and children from ethnic minorities living in remote areas or following a nomadic or pastoralist way of life.[16]

Many children in these categories experience intersecting forms of discrimination and deprivation. Data collected must be further broken down to reveal how marginalization on account of disability, detention or migration, for example, is also affected by such factors as wealth, sex or where a child lives.

Efforts are being made to extend data collection to cover children previously excluded. UNICEF and its partners in the

Numbers and narratives

Quantitative data consist of numbers that can represent anything from the proportion of children entering school to the prevalence of a given disease or the distribution of knowledge about how young people can reduce their risk of exposure to HIV. Qualitative data come from in-depth interviews, observations or visuals such as photographs or maps.

Quantitative data produce such bedrock indicators as 'wealth', which includes information about household members' religion, ethnicity and occupation; the number of rooms in their dwelling; the materials from which its floor, roof and walls are made; whether it has electricity, a bed, a table or a bicycle; and whether the household owns land or livestock. This complex indicator serves as the basis for the wealth quintiles that are used to analyse disparities in children's enjoyment of the full spectrum of rights.[17]

Quantitative and qualitative data complement each other, enabling a detailed and nuanced appreciation of children's realities. Take, for example, Young Lives, a long-term study of childhood poverty in Ethiopia, India, Peru and Viet Nam. It combines household surveys of 12,000 children (conducted every three years) with case studies that use interviews, children's diaries and child-led neighbourhood tours to delve into topics ranging from children's socio-economic status and access to services, to how children spend their time, what they think has shaped their current situation, how they feel about it and what goals they aspire to.

Alongside the aggregate picture of children's circumstances that emerges from the household survey data, the qualitative data from the case studies are woven into narratives that highlight specific issues affecting children's lives from an individual child's perspective.

Washington Group on Disability Statistics, for example, are developing tools to help identify children with disabilities and the deprivations they face.[18]

Other overlooked issues – such as early childhood development, the importance of which went largely unrecognized by policymakers until recently – also demand closer attention. Research in neurobiology has shown that disadvantages in early childhood can haunt a person into adulthood: poor health and nutrition in early life can impair a child's ability to learn and, consequently, to earn a living.[19]

Data on early childhood development, the topic of Table 14, have accumulated steadily since MICS started surveying households on the subject in 2000. Even so, reliable data are still available for only about one-third as many countries as are data on the relatively well-established topics covered in other tables.

The sensitive nature of some issues – violence against children, for instance, or such harmful traditional practices as female genital mutilation/cutting –

complicates data collection. Great care must be taken to ensure the safety of the children who are the subjects of or participants in research.

In 2011, the Committee on the Rights of the Child noted the lack of data on the root causes of violence against children.[20] Researchers are working to fill the gaps: Governments, UNICEF and others are developing and conducting national and multi-country studies. Examples include recent surveys in Cambodia, Haiti, Kenya,[21] Malawi, the United Republic of Tanzania[22] and Zimbabwe. Many more countries are waiting to conduct their own surveys on violence against children.

New data have also been collected on female genital mutilation/cutting. In 2013, UNICEF published the first report summarizing and analysing data from the 29 countries where the practice is most prevalent, in addition to presenting new data on girls younger than 15.[23] In so doing, it presented work that could be used to respond to a United Nations General Assembly resolution of the previous year demanding intensified

(Continued on page 16)

In Ukraine,
rich (99%) and poor (93%)
children are about equally likely to have books at home

"We need to be
heard because the
neighbourhood needs
a lot of help."

— Katherine, 17, on why adolescents
   took part in a digital mapping
   project in Argentina.

Children drive change

Children are the experts on their own lives. They can contribute valuable knowledge to validate and enrich the evidence base – if only they have a chance to be heard. They can also use knowledge that they obtain through research to effect change in their communities.

Take the example of Kundapura Taluk, in India's Karnataka state, where a dozen children drowned in unprotected irrigation areas during the 2012 monsoon. The Concerned for Working Children (CWC), a non-governmental child rights organization, reports that these deaths prompted children who survived the rains to map danger zones within the community. In the process, the children discovered that many ponds and ditches had been dug without the local government's knowledge alongside paths frequented by children. Their findings led to the introduction of new mandatory guidelines on the use of safety enclosures, signboards and other low-cost ways to secure irrigation ponds. No further accidents were reported in 2012, and when the rains returned in 2013, not a single accident was reported in the community of more than 377,000 people.

Innovations in data collection are opening new avenues for children's participation. UNICEF, the Massachusetts Institute of Technology, Public Laboratory for Open Technology and Science, and Innovative Support to Emergencies, Diseases and Disasters are developing a mapping platform that enables real-time data collection using web and mobile applications. Young people in low-income communities of Rio de Janeiro, Brazil, and Port-au-Prince, Haiti, have used mobile phones loaded with a Geographic Information System application to take geotagged photos documenting neighbourhood problems. In Rio, their vigilance has led to the removal of piled-up garbage and the repair of a bridge. Work by adolescents in Rio and in Port-au-Prince is ongoing, and in late 2013 the programme was expanded to Buenos Aires, Argentina.[24]

These examples represent significant victories for children. Children are using data to improve their own situation as well as the infrastructure and services used by their community as a whole. In the process, they are learning the power of evidence and gaining the confidence to advocate for their own rights.

These examples involve serious but relatively straightforward issues. Other issues, like abuse, can be fraught with difficulty, and they highlight the need for safeguards. Although children are agents of knowledge and change when they participate in research, they are also vulnerable and dependent. They need to feel – and to be – safe and listened to. Adults involved in participatory research therefore have an obligation to ensure children's safety and privacy. Children who disclose abuse must not be exposed to retribution by perpetrators, and children who have experienced traumatic events must not be pushed to talk about them more than is strictly necessary. Risks are worth taking only if the results benefit the child.

◄ Adolescents prepare to take a geotagged photo of abandoned cars in Port-au-Prince, Haiti.
© UNICEF/NYHQ2012-0915/Marco Dormino

In Burkina Faso, 76% of girls and women 15–49 years old have undergone FGM/C, but only 9% favour continuation of the practice[26]

▲ A health worker talks with a woman who is breastfeeding her daughter at a health centre in Cobán Municipality, Guatemala.
© UNICEF/NYHQ2012-2245/Susan Markisz

(Continued from page 13)

global efforts to eliminate the practice. The resolution specifically called for data to be collected using unified methods and standards.[25]

Progress has made it possible to expand the scope of research. As more children are living past their fifth birthdays, and as many families and countries have become better off, research is looking beyond survival and basic health to encompass the many factors that contribute to children's development and the quality of their lives.

Evidence for action

The rights and well-being of children must be at the heart of the goals and targets that the international community sets for the post-MDG era.

Whether worthy targets are set and achieved will depend on many factors – not the least of these being whether development decision-makers heed the evidence and listen seriously to poor or otherwise marginalized children and communities.

Fortunately for decision-makers, the crucial evidence is being provided by household surveys, which cover large numbers of people and use methods capable of generating reliable, standardized, comparable data based on people's actual experiences. Increasingly, children and young people are participating in research and the advocacy that it makes possible.

Children and their communities have the right to be provided with information

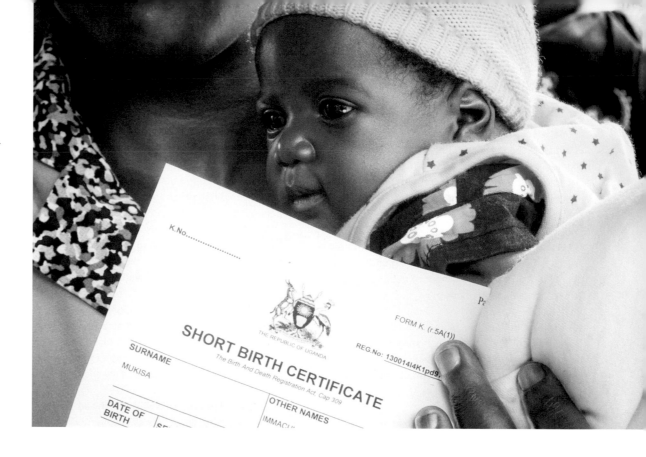

A mother displays her child's birth certificate generated by Mobile Vital Records System at Mulago hospital, Uganda.
© UNICEF/UGDA201300588/ Michele Sibiloni

about their lives and to participate in decision-making that affects them. These rights to information and participation are ends in themselves. They also make development programmes more effective. Data provide evidence on which to base decisions and with which to evaluate action. Information and participation enable people to demand change and hold duty-bearers to account.

Overcoming exclusion begins with inclusive data. To improve the reach, availability and reliability of data on the deprivations with which children and their families contend, the tools of collection and analysis are constantly being modified – and new ones are being developed. This will require sustained investment and commitment.

Data show that progress is being made but that disparities in children's circumstances persist. Data are identifying the children at greatest risk – those least visible and furthest from society's reach. It is up to decision-makers at all levels, from officialdom to the grass roots, to make sure that every child is granted the opportunity to fully enjoy her or his rights.

A selection of indicators and what they tell us about children's lives

1 Underweight/Stunting/Wasting: Well-nourished children perform better in school, grow into healthy adults and, in turn, give their own children a better start in life. Malnourished children are identified by assessing whether they are of a healthy weight for their age, a healthy height for their age and a healthy weight for their height.

2 Use of insecticide-treated nets: These nets are crucial to preventing malaria. Sleeping under them every night can cut the number of deaths by about 20% among children under 5.

3 Violent discipline: Many parents and caregivers still use physical punishment or psychological aggression as a way to correct children's 'misbehaviour'. Such practices violate children's human rights.

4 Use of improved drinking water sources and sanitation facilities: People have a right to an adequate supply of safe drinking water and sanitation. The lack of these contributes to deaths and illness, especially among children. Each day, on average, more than 1,400 children die from diarrhoeal diseases because of contaminated drinking water, lack of sanitation and poor hygiene.

5 Birth registration: Every child has the right to an identity. Those who go unregistered may not be able to claim the services and protections due to them on an equal basis with other children.

6 Immunization coverage: Immunization against diphtheria, pertussis, tetanus, childhood tuberculosis, polio and measles has saved millions of lives, protected countless children from illness and disability, and contributed to reducing poverty. It is one of the most important and cost-effective public health interventions.

7 Exclusive breastfeeding: Breastmilk alone is the perfect food for all infants in the first six months of life. The practice of exclusive breastfeeding provides much more than an ideal food source: exclusively breastfed infants are much less likely to die from diarrhoea, acute respiratory infections and other diseases; and exclusive breastfeeding has been found to support infants' immune systems and protect from chronic diseases later in life such as obesity and diabetes.

8 Care for pneumonia and diarrhoea: These diseases are leading killers of children. Of the estimated 6.6 million deaths among children under 5 in 2012, 17% were due to pneumonia and 9% to diarrhoea. The death toll is highly concentrated in the poorest regions and countries and among the most disadvantaged children within these societies. Yet treatments are inexpensive and effective.

9 Comprehensive knowledge of HIV: Young people aged 15–24 accounted for about one third of new HIV infections in 2012. Young people have the right to knowledge with which to protect themselves.

10 Skilled attendant at birth: Insufficient care during pregnancy and delivery was largely responsible for nearly 300,000 maternal deaths in 2010 and almost 3 million deaths among children less than a month old in 2012. In order to ensure the best possible outcome for both mother and child, a skilled doctor, nurse or midwife should attend the birth.

11 Primary and secondary school enrolment: Despite decades of commitments made and reaffirmed, some 57 million primary school-aged children were out of school in 2011, denied their right to a quality education. Only 64% of boys and 61% of girls of secondary school age are enrolled in secondary school worldwide, and 36% and 30%, respectively, in the least developed countries.

12 Youth literacy and Adult literacy rate: Basic reading, writing and numeracy skills are essential to individual well-being and societal development.

13 Child labour: Many children work to help their families in ways that are neither harmful nor exploitative. But millions of others are put to work in ways that interfere with their education, drain their childhood of joy and crush their right to normal physical and mental development.

14 Use of mass media: Mass media provide information and opportunities for children and young people to express ideas and connect with others. They can also expose children to inappropriate content and unwelcome contact.

15 Adolescent pregnancy: Pregnancy can harm adolescent girls' health and future prospects. Less likely to finish school or to obtain work that allows them to become economically independent, adolescent mothers – along with their children – can become trapped in poverty.

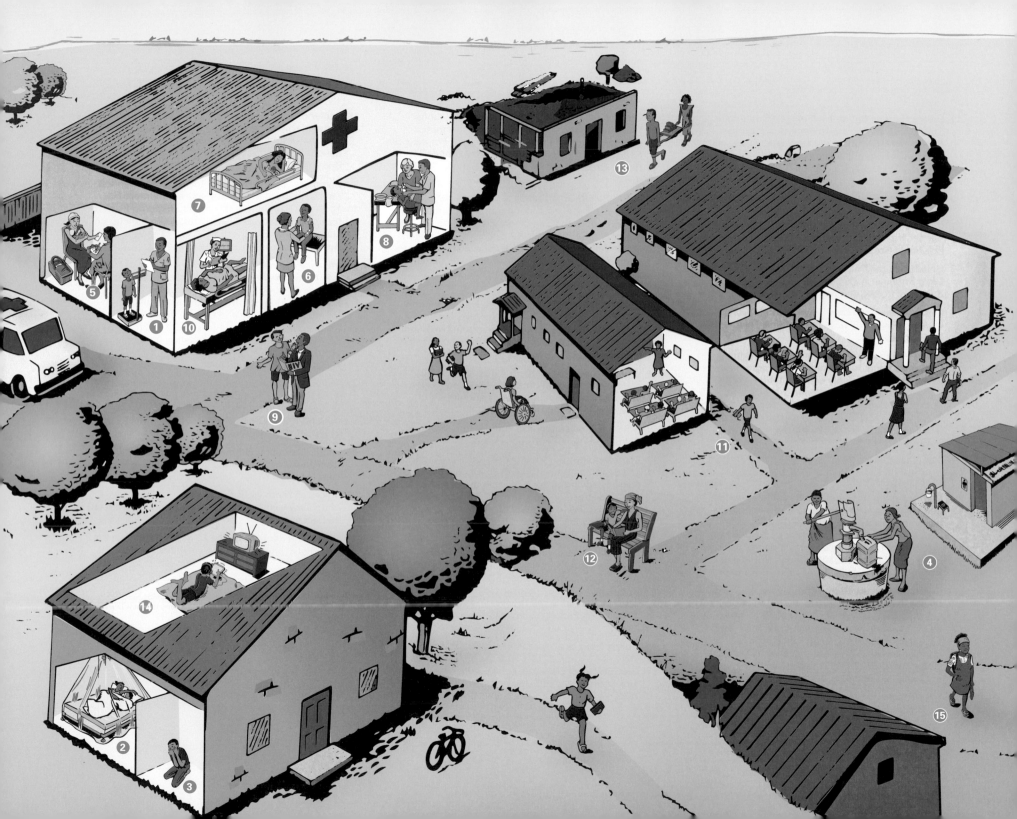

REFERENCES

1 United Nations Children's Fund, *Committing to Child Survival: A Promise Renewed, Progress Report 2013*, UNICEF, New York, 2013, p. 12, <http://www.unicef.org/publications/files/APR_Progress_Report_2013_9_Sept_2013.pdf>, accessed 18 December 2013.

2 UNICEF analysis based on UN Inter-agency Group for Child Mortality Estimation (IGME), 2013, drawing on provisional analyses by the World Health Organization and Child Epidemiology Reference Group (CHERG), 2013.

3 United Nations Children's Fund, *Committing to Child Survival: A Promise Renewed, Progress Report 2013*, UNICEF, New York, 2013, p. 27.

4 Report of the Secretary-General on the work of the Organization, A/68/1, United Nations, New York, 2013, p. 34.

5 World Health Organization and United Nations Children's Fund Joint Monitoring Programme (JMP) for Water Supply and Sanitation, *Progress on Sanitation and Drinking-Water: 2013 Update,* World Health Organization and UNICEF, Geneva, 2013, p. 4, <http://www.wssinfo.org/fileadmin/user_upload/resources/JMPreport2013.pdf>, accessed 18 December 2013.

6 Figure excludes China.

7 Figure excludes China.

8 Committee on the Rights of the Child, General guidelines regarding the form and contents of periodic reports to be submitted by States Parties under article 44, paragraph 1(b), of the Convention, 11 October 1996, <http://www.childoneurope.org/issues/crc_committee/su06-General-Guidelines-for-Periodic-Reports.pdf>, accessed 18 December 2013.

9 Committee on the Rights of the Child, Convention on the Rights of the Child General Comment No. 5 (2003): General measures of implementation of the Convention on the Rights of the Child (arts. 4, 42 and 44, para. 6), p. 12 (48), 27 November 1993, <http://daccess-dds-ny.un.org/doc/UNDOC/GEN/G03/455/14/PDF/G0345514.pdf?OpenElement>, accessed 18 December 2013.

10 United Nations Children's Fund, *Committing to Child Survival: A Promise Renewed, Progress Report 2013,* UNICEF, New York, 2013, p. 25.

11 World Health Organization and United Nations Children's Fund Joint Monitoring Programme (JMP) for Water Supply and Sanitation, *Progress on Sanitation and Drinking-Water: 2013 Update,* World Health Organization and UNICEF, Geneva, 2013, p. 8.

12 World Health Organization and United Nations Children's Fund Joint Monitoring Programme for Water Supply and Sanitation, *Progress on Drinking Water and Sanitation: 2012 Update,* World Health Organization and UNICEF, Geneva, 2012, p. 25, <http://www.wssinfo.org/fileadmin/user_upload/resources/JMP-report-2012-en.pdf>, accessed 18 December 2013.

13 ICF International, HIV Prevalence Estimates from the Demographic and Health Surveys: Updated July 2012, ICF International, Calverton, Maryland, 2012, p. 1, <http://www.measuredhs.com/pubs/pdf/OD65/OD65.pdf>, accessed 18 December 2013.

14 World Declaration on the Survival, Protection and Development of Children, 1990, <http://www.unicef.org/wsc/declare.htm>, accessed 19 November 2013.

15 United Nations Children's Fund, Democratic Republic of the Congo submission.

16 Martorano, Bruno, Luisa Natali, Chris de Neubourg and Jonathan Bradshaw (2013). 'Child well-being in advanced economies in the late 2000s,' Working Paper 2013-01, UNICEF Office of Research, Florence, p. 40, <http://www.unicef-irc.org/publications/pdf/iwp_2013_1.pdf>, accessed 18 December 2013.

17 See, for example, Shea O. Rutstein, 'The DHS Wealth Index: Approaches for Rural and Urban Areas', DHS Working Paper, Macro International Inc., Calverton, Maryland, October 2008, <http://www.measuredhs.com/publications/publication-wp60-working-papers.cfm>, accessed 7 January 2014.

18 United Nations Children's Fund, *The State of the World's Children 2013: Children with Disabilities,* UNICEF, New York, 2013, p. 68, <http://www.unicef.org/sowc2013>, accessed 18 December 2013.

19 Center on the Developing Child, Harvard University, <http://developingchild.harvard.edu/index.php/resources/multimedia/interactive_features/biodevelopmental-framework/>, accessed 18 December 2013.

20 Committee on the Rights of the Child, Convention on the Rights of the Child General Comment No. 13 (2011): The right of the child to freedom from all forms of violence, pp. 6–7, <http://www2.ohchr.org/english/bodies/crc/docs/CRC.C.GC.13_en.pdf>, 11 April 2011, accessed 18 December 2013.

21 *Violence against Children in Kenya: findings from a 2010 national survey,* Nairobi, Kenya: United Nations Children's Fund Kenya Country Office, Division of Violence Prevention, National Center for Injury Prevention and Control, U.S. Centers for Disease Control and Prevention, and the Kenya National Bureau of Statistics, 2012, <http://www.unicef.org/esaro/VAC_in_Kenya.pdf>, accessed 18 December 2013.

22 *Violence against Children in Tanzania: findings from a national survey 2009,* Dar es Salaam, 2011, <http://www.unicef.org/media/files/VIOLENCE_AGAINST_CHILDREN_IN_TANZANIA_REPORT.pdf>, accessed 18 December 2013.

23 United Nations Children's Fund, *Female Genital Mutilation/Cutting: a statistical overview,* UNICEF, New York, 2013.

24 Voices of Youth website, <http://www.voicesofyouth.org/en/maps>, accessed 18 December 2013.

25 Resolution adopted by the United Nations General Assembly, 'Intensifying global efforts for the elimination of female genital mutilations', A/RES/67/146, 20 December 2012.

26 United Nations Children's Fund, *Female Genital Mutilation/Cutting: a statistical overview,* UNICEF, New York, 2013.

Statistical Tables

Economic and social statistics on the countries and areas of the world, with particular reference to children's well-being.

Overview

This reference guide presents the most recent key statistics on child survival, development and protection for the world's countries, areas and regions.

The statistical tables in this volume support UNICEF's focus on progress and results towards internationally agreed-upon goals and compacts relating to children's rights and development. UNICEF is the lead agency responsible for monitoring the child-related goals of the Millennium Declaration as well as the Millennium Development Goals (MDGs) and indicators. UNICEF is also a key partner in the United Nations' work on monitoring these targets and indicators.

Efforts have been made to maximize the comparability of statistics across countries and time. Nevertheless, data used at the country level may differ in terms of the methods used to collect data or arrive at estimates, and in terms of the populations covered. Furthermore, data presented here are subject to evolving methodologies, revisions of time series data (e.g., immunization, maternal mortality ratios) and changing regional classifications. Also, data comparable from one year to the next are unavailable for some indicators. It is therefore not advisable to compare data from consecutive editions of *The State of the World's Children.*

The numbers presented in this reference guide are available online at <www.unicef.org/sowc2014> and via the UNICEF global statistical databases at <www.childinfo.org>. Please refer to these websites for the latest tables and for any updates or corrigenda subsequent to printing.

General note on the data

Data presented in the following statistical tables are derived from the UNICEF global databases and are accompanied by definitions, sources and, where necessary, additional footnotes. The tables draw on inter-agency estimates and nationally representative household surveys such as Multiple Indicator Cluster Surveys (MICS) and Demographic and Health Surveys (DHS). In addition, data from other United Nations organizations have been used.

Data presented in this year's statistical tables generally reflect information available as of August 2013. More detailed information on methodology and data sources is available at <www.childinfo.org>.

This volume includes the latest population estimates and projections from *World Population Prospects: The 2012 revision* and *World Urbanization Prospects: The 2011 revision* (United Nations Department of Economic and Social Affairs, Population Division). Data quality is likely to be adversely affected for countries that have recently suffered disasters, especially where basic country infrastructure has been fragmented or where major population movements have occurred.

Multiple Indicator Cluster Surveys (MICS): UNICEF supports countries in collecting reliable and globally mapped data through MICS. Since 1995, about 250 surveys have been conducted in more than 100 countries and areas. The fifth round of MICS, involving over 40 surveys to date, is under way.

MICS are among the largest sources of data for monitoring progress towards internationally agreed-upon development goals for children, including the MDGs. More information is available at <www.childinfo.org/mics.html>.

Child mortality estimates

Each year, in *The State of the World's Children,* UNICEF reports a series of mortality estimates for children – including the annual neonatal mortality rate, infant mortality rate, the under-five mortality rate (total, male and female) and the number of under-five deaths – for at least two reference years. These figures represent the best estimates available at the time of printing and are based on the work of the United Nations Inter-agency Group for Child Mortality Estimation (IGME), which includes UNICEF, the World Health Organization (WHO), the World Bank and the United Nations Population Division. IGME mortality estimates are updated annually through a detailed review of all newly available data points, which often results in adjustments to previously reported estimates. As a result, consecutive editions of *The State of the World's Children* should not be used for analysing mortality trends over time. Comparable global and regional under-five mortality estimates for the period 1970–2012 are presented on page 23. Country-specific mortality indicators for 1970–2012, based on the most recent IGME estimates, are presented in Table 10 (for the years 1970, 1990, 2000 and 2012) and are available at <www.childinfo.org> and <www.childmortality.org>.

Under-five mortality rate (per 1,000 live births)

UNICEF Region	1970	1975	1980	1985	1990	1995	2000	2005	2010	2012
Sub-Saharan Africa	242	216	199	185	177	170	155	130	106	98
Eastern and Southern Africa	209	190	186	172	163	155	139	111	85	77
West and Central Africa	274	245	217	203	195	189	174	151	127	118
Middle East and North Africa	202	165	126	90	71	61	50	41	32	30
South Asia	211	193	170	149	129	111	94	78	65	60
East Asia and Pacific	114	92	75	63	58	51	41	30	23	20
Latin America and Caribbean	118	102	84	67	54	43	32	25	23	19
CEE/CIS	97	74	68	55	47	47	36	27	21	19
Least developed countries	238	227	209	188	172	156	138	114	93	85
World	**145**	**128**	**116**	**99**	**90**	**85**	**75**	**63**	**52**	**48**

Under-five deaths (millions)

UNICEF Region	1970	1975	1980	1985	1990	1995	2000	2005	2010	2012
Sub-Saharan Africa	3.1	3.2	3.4	3.5	3.8	4.0	4.1	3.8	3.4	3.2
Eastern and Southern Africa	1.3	1.4	1.5	1.6	1.7	1.7	1.7	1.5	1.3	1.2
West and Central Africa	1.7	1.7	1.7	1.8	2.0	2.2	2.2	2.2	2.0	2.0
Middle East and North Africa	1.3	1.1	1.0	0.8	0.6	0.5	0.4	0.4	0.3	0.3
South Asia	5.8	5.6	5.5	5.1	4.7	4.0	3.4	2.8	2.2	2.1
East Asia and Pacific	4.7	3.5	2.3	2.5	2.5	1.6	1.2	0.9	0.7	0.6
Latin America and Caribbean	1.2	1.1	0.9	0.8	0.6	0.5	0.4	0.3	0.2	0.2
CEE/CIS	0.6	0.5	0.5	0.4	0.4	0.3	0.2	0.1	0.1	0.1
Least developed countries	3.3	3.4	3.5	3.6	3.5	3.5	3.4	3.0	2.6	2.4
World	**17.1**	**15.3**	**13.8**	**13.2**	**12.6**	**10.9**	**9.7**	**8.2**	**7.0**	**6.6**

UNDER-FIVE MORTALITY RANKINGS

The following list ranks countries and areas in descending order of their estimated 2012 under-five mortality rate (U5MR), a critical indicator of the well-being of children. Countries and areas are listed alphabetically in the tables on the following pages.

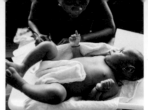

HIGHEST UNDER-5 MORTALITY RATE

Countries and areas	Under-5 mortality rate (2012) Value	Rank	Countries and areas	Under-5 mortality rate (2012) Value	Rank	Countries and areas	Under-5 mortality rate (2012) Value	Rank
Sierra Leone	182	1	Sudan	73	33	Guyana	35	68
Angola	164	2	Ghana	72	36	Iraq	34	70
Chad	150	3	Lao People's Democratic Republic	72	36	Guatemala	32	71
Somalia	147	4	Malawi	71	38	Indonesia	31	72
Democratic Republic of the Congo	146	5	Uganda	69	39	Morocco	31	72
Central African Republic	129	6	Ethiopia	68	40	Solomon Islands	31	72
Guinea-Bissau	129	6	Papua New Guinea	63	41	Philippines	30	75
Mali	128	8	Gabon	62	42	Tuvalu	30	75
Nigeria	124	9	Kiribati	60	43	Democratic People's Republic of Korea	29	77
Niger	114	10	Senegal	60	43	Mongolia	28	78
Côte d'Ivoire	108	11	Yemen	60	43	Dominican Republic	27	79
Burundi	104	12	Madagascar	58	46	Kyrgyzstan	27	79
South Sudan	104	12	Tajikistan	58	46	Niue	25	81
Burkina Faso	102	14	Timor-Leste	57	48	Nicaragua	24	82
Guinea	101	15	India	56	49	Ecuador	23	83
Equatorial Guinea	100	16	Rwanda	55	50	Honduras	23	83
Lesotho	100	16	United Republic of Tanzania	54	51	Saint Vincent and the Grenadines	23	83
Afghanistan	99	18	Botswana	53	52	State of Palestine	23	83
Congo	96	19	Sao Tome and Principe	53	52	Viet Nam	23	83
Togo	96	19	Turkmenistan	53	52	Cabo Verde	22	88
Cameroon	95	21	Eritrea	52	55	Fiji	22	88
Benin	90	22	Myanmar	52	55	Paraguay	22	88
Mozambique	90	22	Bhutan	45	57	Egypt	21	91
Zimbabwe	90	22	South Africa	45	57	Palau	21	91
Zambia	89	25	Nepal	42	59	Suriname	21	91
Pakistan	86	26	Bangladesh	41	60	Trinidad and Tobago	21	91
Mauritania	84	27	Bolivia (Plurinational State of)	41	60	Algeria	20	95
Djibouti	81	28	Cambodia	40	62	Georgia	20	95
Swaziland	80	29	Uzbekistan	40	62	Jordan	19	97
Comoros	78	30	Micronesia (Federated States of)	39	64	Kazakhstan	19	97
Haiti	76	31	Namibia	39	64	Panama	19	97
Liberia	75	32	Marshall Islands	38	66	Barbados	18	100
Gambia	73	33	Nauru	37	67	Belize	18	100
Kenya	73	33	Azerbaijan	35	68	Colombia	18	100

ABOUT 18,000 CHILDREN UNDER FIVE YEARS OLD STILL DIE EVERY DAY.

LOWEST UNDER-5 MORTALITY RATE

Countries and areas	Under-5 mortality rate (2012) Value	Rank
Iran (Islamic Republic of)	18	100
Peru	18	100
Republic of Moldova	18	100
Saint Lucia	18	100
Samoa	18	100
Vanuatu	18	100
Albania	17	109
Bahamas	17	109
Jamaica	17	109
Armenia	16	112
El Salvador	16	112
Mexico	16	112
Tunisia	16	112
Libya	15	116
Mauritius	15	116
Syrian Arab Republic	15	116
Venezuela (Bolivarian Republic of)	15	116
Argentina	14	120
Brazil	14	120
China	14	120
Grenada	14	120
Turkey	14	120
Dominica	13	125
Seychelles	13	125
Thailand	13	125
Tonga	13	125
Bulgaria	12	129
Oman	12	129
Romania	12	129
Cook Islands	11	132
Kuwait	11	132
Maldives	11	132
Ukraine	11	132
Antigua and Barbuda	10	136

Countries and areas	Under-5 mortality rate (2012) Value	Rank
Bahrain	10	136
Costa Rica	10	136
Russian Federation	10	136
Sri Lanka	10	136
Chile	9	141
Latvia	9	141
Lebanon	9	141
Malaysia	9	141
Saint Kitts and Nevis	9	141
Saudi Arabia	9	141
Brunei Darussalam	8	147
Slovakia	8	147
United Arab Emirates	8	147
Bosnia and Herzegovina	7	150
Malta	7	150
Qatar	7	150
Serbia	7	150
The former Yugoslav Republic of Macedonia	7	150
United States	7	150
Uruguay	7	150
Cuba	6	157
Hungary	6	157
Montenegro	6	157
New Zealand	6	157
Australia	5	161
Belarus	5	161
Canada	5	161
Croatia	5	161
Greece	5	161
Lithuania	5	161
Poland	5	161
Spain	5	161
United Kingdom	5	161

Countries and areas	Under-5 mortality rate (2012) Value	Rank
Austria	4	170
Belgium	4	170
Czech Republic	4	170
Denmark	4	170
Estonia	4	170
France	4	170
Germany	4	170
Ireland	4	170
Israel	4	170
Italy	4	170
Monaco	4	170
Netherlands	4	170
Portugal	4	170
Republic of Korea	4	170
Switzerland	4	170
Andorra	3	185
Cyprus	3	185
Finland	3	185
Japan	3	185
Norway	3	185
San Marino	3	185
Singapore	3	185
Slovenia	3	185
Sweden	3	185
Iceland	2	194
Luxembourg	2	194
Holy See	–	–
Liechtenstein	–	–

Regional classification

Averages presented at the end of each of the 14 statistical tables are calculated using data from countries and areas as classified below.

Sub-Saharan Africa
Eastern and Southern Africa; West and Central Africa; Djibouti; Sudan

Eastern and Southern Africa
Angola; Botswana; Burundi; Comoros; Eritrea; Ethiopia; Kenya; Lesotho; Madagascar; Malawi; Mauritius; Mozambique; Namibia; Rwanda; Seychelles; Somalia; South Africa; South Sudan; Swaziland; Uganda; United Republic of Tanzania; Zambia; Zimbabwe

West and Central Africa
Benin; Burkina Faso; Cabo Verde; Cameroon; Central African Republic; Chad; Congo; Côte d'Ivoire; Democratic Republic of the Congo; Equatorial Guinea; Gabon; Gambia; Ghana; Guinea; Guinea-Bissau; Liberia; Mali; Mauritania; Niger; Nigeria; Sao Tome and Principe; Senegal; Sierra Leone; Togo

Middle East and North Africa
Algeria; Bahrain; Djibouti; Egypt; Iran (Islamic Republic of); Iraq; Jordan; Kuwait; Lebanon; Libya; Morocco; Oman; Qatar; Saudi Arabia; State of Palestine; Sudan; Syrian Arab Republic; Tunisia; United Arab Emirates; Yemen

South Asia
Afghanistan; Bangladesh; Bhutan; India; Maldives; Nepal; Pakistan; Sri Lanka

East Asia and Pacific
Brunei Darussalam; Cambodia; China; Cook Islands; Democratic People's Republic of Korea; Fiji; Indonesia; Kiribati; Lao People's Democratic Republic; Malaysia; Marshall Islands; Micronesia (Federated States of); Mongolia; Myanmar; Nauru; Niue; Palau; Papua New Guinea; Philippines; Republic of Korea; Samoa; Singapore; Solomon Islands; Thailand; Timor-Leste; Tonga; Tuvalu; Vanuatu; Viet Nam

Latin America and Caribbean
Antigua and Barbuda; Argentina; Bahamas; Barbados; Belize; Bolivia (Plurinational State of); Brazil; Chile; Colombia; Costa Rica; Cuba; Dominica; Dominican Republic; Ecuador; El Salvador; Grenada; Guatemala; Guyana; Haiti; Honduras; Jamaica; Mexico; Nicaragua; Panama; Paraguay; Peru; Saint Kitts and Nevis; Saint Lucia; Saint Vincent and the Grenadines; Suriname; Trinidad and Tobago; Uruguay; Venezuela (Bolivarian Republic of)

CEE/CIS
Albania; Armenia; Azerbaijan; Belarus; Bosnia and Herzegovina; Bulgaria; Croatia; Georgia; Kazakhstan; Kyrgyzstan; Montenegro; Republic of Moldova; Romania; Russian Federation; Serbia; Tajikistan; the former Yugoslav Republic of Macedonia; Turkey; Turkmenistan; Ukraine; Uzbekistan

Least developed countries/areas
(Classified as such by the United Nations High Representative for the Least Developed Countries, Landlocked Developing Countries and Small Island Developing States [UN-OHRLLS]). Afghanistan; Angola; Bangladesh; Benin; Bhutan; Burkina Faso; Burundi; Cambodia; Central African Republic; Chad; Comoros; Democratic Republic of the Congo; Djibouti; Equatorial Guinea; Eritrea; Ethiopia; Gambia; Guinea; Guinea-Bissau; Haiti; Kiribati; Lao People's Democratic Republic; Lesotho; Liberia; Madagascar; Malawi; Mali; Mauritania; Mozambique; Myanmar; Nepal; Niger; Rwanda; Samoa; Sao Tome and Principe; Senegal; Sierra Leone; Solomon Islands; Somalia; South Sudan; Sudan; Timor-Leste; Togo; Tuvalu; Uganda; United Republic of Tanzania; Vanuatu; Yemen; Zambia

Notes on specific tables
TABLE 2. NUTRITION

Underweight, stunting, wasting and overweight: UNICEF, WHO and the World Bank have continued a process to harmonize anthropometric data used for computation and estimation of regional and global averages and trend analysis. As part of this process, regional and global averages for underweight (moderate and severe), stunting, wasting and overweight prevalences are derived from a model described in M. de Onis et al., 'Methodology for Estimating Regional and Global Trends of Child Malnutrition' (*International Journal of Epidemiology*, vol. 33, 2004, pp. 1260–1270). Owing to differences in data sources (i.e., new empirical data are incorporated as made available) and estimation methodology, these regional average prevalence estimates may not be comparable to the averages published in previous editions of *The State of the World's Children.*

Vitamin A supplementation: Emphasizing the importance for children of receiving two annual doses of vitamin A (spaced 4–6 months apart), this report presents only full coverage of vitamin A supplementation. In the absence of a direct method to measure this indicator, full coverage is reported as the lower coverage estimate from rounds 1 and 2 in a given year.

TABLE 3. HEALTH

Water and sanitation: The drinking water and sanitation coverage estimates in this report come from the WHO/UNICEF Joint Monitoring Programme for Water Supply and Sanitation (JMP). These are the official United Nations estimates for measuring progress towards the MDG target for drinking water and sanitation. Full details of the JMP methodology can be found at <www.childinfo.org> and <www.wssinfo.org>. As the JMP estimates use linear regression applied to data from all available household sample surveys and censuses, and additional data become available between each issue of estimates, subsequent JMP estimates should not be compared.

Immunization: This report presents WHO and UNICEF estimates of national immunization coverage. These are official United Nations estimates for measuring progress towards the MDG indicator for measles-containing vaccine coverage. Since 2000, the estimates are updated once annually in July, following a consultation process wherein countries are provided draft reports for review and comment. As the system incorporates new empirical data, each annual revision supersedes prior data releases, and coverage levels from earlier revisions are not comparable. A more detailed explanation of the process can be found at <www.childinfo.org/immunization_ countryreports.html>.

Diarrhoea treatment: The table includes diarrhoea treatment with oral rehydration salts (ORS). ORS is a key commodity for child survival and therefore it is crucial to monitor its coverage. This replaces the indicator used in previous years, diarrhoea treatment with oral rehydration therapy and continued feeding, which will continue to be available at <www.childinfo.org>.

Regional averages for the six reported antigens are computed as follows:
* For BCG, regional averages include only those countries where BCG is included in the national routine immunization schedule.
* For DPT, polio, measles, HepB and Hib vaccines, regional averages include all countries.
* For protection at birth (PAB) from tetanus, regional averages include only the countries where maternal and neonatal tetanus is endemic.

TABLE 4. HIV/AIDS
In 2013, the Joint United Nations Programme on HIV/AIDS (UNAIDS) released new global, regional and country-level HIV and AIDS estimates for 2012 that reflect key changes in WHO HIV treatment guidelines for adults and children and for prevention of mother-to-child transmission of HIV, in addition to improvements in assumptions of the probability of HIV transmission from mother to child and net survival rates for infected children. Furthermore, there are also more reliable data available from population-based surveys, expanded national sentinel surveillance systems and programme service statistics in a number of countries. Based on the refined methodology, UNAIDS has retrospectively generated new estimates of HIV prevalence, the number of people living with HIV and those needing treatment, AIDS-related deaths, new HIV infections and the number of children whose

parents have died due to all causes including AIDS for past years. Only new estimates should be used for trend analysis. The new HIV and AIDS estimates included in this table are also published in the UNAIDS *Report on the Global AIDS Epidemic, 2013*. Overall, the global and regional figures published in *The State of the World's Children 2014 In Numbers* are not comparable to estimates previously published. More information on HIV and AIDS estimates, methodology and updates can be found at <www.unaids.org>.

TABLE 8. WOMEN

Maternal mortality ratio (adjusted): The table presents the 'adjusted' maternal mortality ratios for the year 2010, as published in 2012 by the Maternal Mortality Estimation Inter-agency Group (MMEIG), composed of WHO, UNICEF, the United Nations Population Fund (UNFPA) and the World Bank, together with independent technical experts. To derive these estimates, the inter-agency group used a dual approach: making adjustments to correct misclassification and underreporting in existing estimates of maternal mortality from civil registration systems, and using a model to generate estimates for countries without reliable national-level estimates of maternal mortality. These 'adjusted' estimates should not be compared with previous inter-agency estimates. The full report – with complete country and regional estimates for the years 1990, 1995, 2000, 2005 and 2010, in addition to details on the methodology – can be found at <www.childinfo.org/maternal_mortality.html>.

TABLE 9. CHILD PROTECTION

Birth Registration: Changes in the definition of birth registration were made from the second and third rounds of MICS (MICS2 and MICS3) to the fourth round (MICS4). In order to allow for comparability with later rounds, data from MICS2 and MICS3 on birth registration were recalculated according to the MICS4 indicator definition. Therefore, the recalculated data presented here may differ from estimates included in MICS2 and MICS3 national reports.

Child labour: Data from the fourth round of MICS (MICS4, 2009–2012) included in the table have been recalculated according to the indicator definition used in MICS3 surveys, to ensure cross-country comparability. In this definition, the activities of fetching water or collecting firewood are classified as household chores rather than

as an economic activity. Under this approach, a child aged 5–14 would have to be engaged in fetching water or collecting firewood for at least 28 hours per week to be considered as a child labourer.

Female genital mutilation/cutting (FGM/C): Data on the prevalence of FGM/C among girls aged 0–14 were recalculated for technical reasons and may differ from that presented in original DHS and MICS country reports. For further details, refer to *Female Genital Mutilation/Cutting: A statistical overview and exploration of the dynamics of change*, UNICEF, New York, 2013.

Violent discipline: Estimates used in UNICEF publications and in MICS country reports prior to 2010 were calculated using household weights that did not take into account the last-stage selection of children for the administration of the child discipline module in MICS surveys. (A random selection of one child aged 2–14 is undertaken for the administration of the child discipline module.) In January 2010, it was decided that more accurate estimates are produced by using a household weight that takes the last-stage selection into account. MICS3 data were recalculated using this approach. All UNICEF publications produced after 2010, including *The State of the World's Children 2014 In Numbers*, use the revised estimates.

TABLE 10. THE RATE OF PROGRESS

The under-five mortality rate (U5MR) is used as the principal indicator of progress in child well-being. In 1970, about 17.1 million children under 5 years old were dying every year. In 2012, by comparison, the estimated number of children who died before their fifth birthday stood at 6.6 million – highlighting a significant long-term decline in the global number of under-five deaths.

U5MR has several advantages as a gauge of child well-being:
- First, U5MR measures an end result of the development process rather than an 'input' such as school enrolment level, per capita calorie availability or number of doctors per thousand population – all of which are means to an end.

- Second, U5MR is known to be the result of a wide variety of inputs: for example, antibiotics to treat pneumonia; insecticide-treated mosquito nets to prevent malaria; the nutritional well-being and health knowledge of mothers; the level of immunization and oral rehydration therapy use; the availability of maternal and child health services, including antenatal care; income and food availability in the family; the availability of safe drinking water and basic sanitation; and the overall safety of the child's environment.

• Third, U5MR is less susceptible to the fallacy of the average than, for example, per capita gross national income (GNI). This is because the natural scale does not allow the children of the rich to be one thousand times more likely to survive, even if the human-made scale does permit them to have one thousand times as much income. In other words, it is much more difficult for a wealthy minority to affect a nation's U5MR, and this indicator therefore presents a more accurate, if far from perfect, picture of the health status of the majority of children and of society as a whole.

The speed of progress in reducing U5MR can be assessed by calculating its annual rate of reduction (ARR). Unlike the comparison of absolute changes, ARR measures relative changes that reflect differences compared with the starting value.

As lower levels of under-five mortality are reached, the same absolute reduction represents a greater percentage reduction. ARR therefore shows a higher rate of progress for a 10-point absolute

reduction, for example, if that reduction happens at a lower level of under-five mortality versus a higher level over the same time period. A 10-point decrease in U5MR from 100 in 1990 to 90 in 2012 represents a reduction of 10 per cent, corresponding to an ARR of about 0.5 per cent, whereas the same 10-point decrease from 20 to 10 over the same period represents a reduction of 50 per cent, or an ARR of 3.2 per cent. (A negative value for the percentage reduction indicates an increase in U5MR during the period specified.)

When used in conjunction with gross domestic product (GDP) growth rates, U5MR and its rate of reduction can therefore give a picture of the progress being made by any country, area or region, over any period of time, towards the satisfaction of some of the most essential human needs.

As Table 10 shows, there is no fixed relationship between the ARR of U5MR and the annual rate of growth in per capita GDP. Comparing these two indicators helps shed light on the relationship between economic advances and human development.

Finally, the table gives the total fertility rate for each country and area and the corresponding ARR. It is clear that many of the nations that have achieved significant reductions in their U5MR have also achieved significant reductions in fertility.

Explanation of symbols
The following symbols are common across all tables:

- Data are not available.
x Data refer to years or periods other than those specified in the column heading. Such data are not included in the calculation of regional and global averages, unless otherwise noted.
y Data differ from the standard definition or refer to only part of a country. If they fall within the noted reference period, such data are included in the calculation of regional and global averages.

* Data refer to the most recent year available during the period specified in the column heading.
** Excludes China.

Sources and years for specific data points are available at <www.childinfo.org>. Symbols that appear in specific tables are explained in the footnotes to those tables.

TABLE 1 | BASIC INDICATORS

Countries and areas	Under-5 mortality rank	Under-5 mortality rate (U5MR) 1990	Under-5 mortality rate (U5MR) 2012	U5MR by sex 2012 male	U5MR by sex 2012 female	Infant mortality rate (under 1) 1990	Infant mortality rate (under 1) 2012	Neonatal mortality rate 2012	Total population (thousands) 2012	Annual no. of births (thousands) 2012	Annual no. of under-5 deaths (thousands) 2012	GNI per capita (US$) 2012	Life expectancy at birth (years) 2012	Total adult literacy rate (%) 2008–2012*	Primary school net enrolment ratio (%) 2008–2011*
Afghanistan	18	176	99	102	95	120	71	36	29,825	1,053	103	570 x	61	–	–
Albania	109	43	17	18	15	37	15	8	3,162	40	1	4,090	77	97	–
Algeria	95	50	20	22	18	42	17	12	38,482	946	20	4,110 x	71	73 x	98
Andorra	185	8	3	4	3	7	3	1	78	–	0	d	–	–	–
Angola	2	213	164	171	156	126	100	45	20,821	934	148	4,580	51	70	86
Antigua and Barbuda	136	24	10	11	9	20	9	6	89	1	0	12,640	76	99	86
Argentina	120	28	14	16	13	24	13	8	41,087	695	10	c	76	98	–
Armenia	112	49	16	18	15	42	15	10	2,969	41	1	3,720	74	100	–
Australia	161	9	5	5	4	8	4	3	23,050	305	2	59,570	82	–	97
Austria	170	10	4	4	4	8	3	2	8,464	80	0	48,160	81	–	–
Azerbaijan	68	93	35	38	32	74	31	15	9,309	168	6	6,050	71	100	87
Bahamas	109	23	17	18	16	20	14	8	372	6	0	21,280 x	75	–	98
Bahrain	136	23	10	10	9	20	8	4	1,318	20	0	16,050 x	76	95	–
Bangladesh	60	144	41	44	38	100	33	24	154,695	3,150	127	840	70	58	–
Barbados	100	18	18	20	17	16	17	10	283	4	0	d	75	–	95
Belarus	161	17	5	6	5	14	4	3	9,405	103	1	6,530	70	100	92
Belgium	170	10	4	5	4	8	3	2	11,060	129	1	44,990	80	–	99
Belize	100	43	18	20	16	35	16	9	324	8	0	4,180 x	74	–	97
Benin	22	181	90	93	85	109	59	28	10,051	371	32	750	59	29 x	92
Bhutan	57	131	45	49	40	92	36	21	742	15	1	2,420	68	53 x	89
Bolivia (Plurinational State of)	60	123	41	45	38	85	33	19	10,496	273	11	2,220	67	91	91
Bosnia and Herzegovina	150	18	7	7	6	16	6	4	3,834	34	0	4,650	76	98	90
Botswana	52	48	53	58	49	38	41	29	2,004	48	3	7,720	47	85	87
Brazil	120	62	14	16	13	52	13	9	198,656	3,009	42	11,630	74	90	–
Brunei Darussalam	147	12	8	9	7	9	7	4	412	7	0	d	78	95	–
Bulgaria	129	22	12	13	11	18	11	7	7,278	70	1	6,870	73	98	100
Burkina Faso	14	202	102	108	97	102	66	28	16,460	683	66	670	56	29 x	63
Burundi	12	164	104	111	98	100	67	36	9,850	443	43	240	54	87	–
Cabo Verde	88	62	22	25	20	47	19	10	494	10	0	3,810	75	85	94
Cambodia	62	116	40	44	35	85	34	18	14,865	386	14	880	72	74	98
Cameroon	21	135	95	101	89	84	61	28	21,700	820	74	1,170	55	71	94
Canada	161	8	5	6	5	7	5	4	34,838	391	2	50,970	81	–	–
Central African Republic	6	171	129	135	122	113	91	41	4,525	156	19	490	50	57	69
Chad	3	209	150	157	142	114	89	40	12,448	579	82	740	51	35	–
Chile	141	19	9	10	8	16	8	5	17,465	246	2	14,280	80	99	93
China	120	54	14	15	13	42	12	9	1,377,065	18,455	258	5,740	75	95	100 z
Colombia	100	35	18	20	16	29	15	11	47,704	912	16	6,990	74	94	90
Comoros	30	124	78	83	72	87	58	31	718	26	2	840	61	76	–
Congo	19	100	96	101	91	65	62	32	4,337	165	15	2,550	58	–	93
Cook Islands	132	25	11	12	9	21	9	6	21	–	0	–	–	–	98

TABLE 1 | BASIC INDICATORS >>

TABLE 1

Countries and areas	Under-5 mortality rank	Under-5 mortality rate (U5MR) 1990	Under-5 mortality rate (U5MR) 2012	U5MR by sex 2012 male	U5MR by sex 2012 female	Infant mortality rate (under 1) 1990	Infant mortality rate (under 1) 2012	Neonatal mortality rate 2012	Total population (thousands) 2012	Annual no. of births (thousands) 2012	Annual no. of under-5 deaths (thousands) 2012	GNI per capita (US$) 2012	Life expectancy at birth (years) 2012	Total adult literacy rate (%) 2008–2012*	Primary school net enrolment ratio (%) 2008–2011*
Costa Rica	136	17	10	11	9	14	9	7	4,805	74	1	8,740	80	96	–
Côte d'Ivoire	11	152	108	116	99	104	76	40	19,840	731	75	1,220	50	57	61
Croatia	161	13	5	5	4	11	4	3	4,307	41	0	13,290	77	99	96
Cuba	157	13	6	6	5	11	4	3	11,271	108	1	c	79	100	98
Cyprus	185	11	3	4	3	10	3	2	1,129	13	0	26,000	80	99	99
Czech Republic	170	15	4	4	3	13	3	2	10,660	118	0	18,130	78	–	–
Democratic People's Republic of Korea	77	44	29	32	26	33	23	16	24,763	356	10	a	70	100	–
Democratic Republic of the Congo	5	171	146	154	137	112	100	44	65,705	2,839	391	220	50	61x	–
Denmark	170	9	4	4	3	7	3	3	5,598	64	0	59,770	79	–	96
Djibouti	28	119	81	86	75	93	66	31	860	24	2	b	61	–	52
Dominica	125	17	13	14	12	14	12	9	72	–	0	6,460	–	–	98
Dominican Republic	79	60	27	30	24	46	23	15	10,277	218	6	5,470	73	90	92
Ecuador	83	56	23	26	20	44	20	10	15,492	328	8	5,190	76	92	99
Egypt	91	86	21	22	20	63	18	12	80,722	1,898	40	3,000	71	74	98
El Salvador	112	59	16	18	14	46	14	6	6,297	128	2	3,580	72	84	96
Equatorial Guinea	16	182	100	106	94	123	72	34	736	26	3	13,560	53	94	59
Eritrea	55	150	52	57	47	92	37	18	6,131	230	11	450	62	69	37
Estonia	170	20	4	4	3	17	3	2	1,291	14	0	15,830	74	100	97
Ethiopia	40	204	68	74	62	121	47	29	91,729	3,084	205	410	63	39 x	87
Fiji	88	31	22	25	20	26	19	10	875	18	0	4,200	70	–	99
Finland	185	7	3	3	3	6	2	2	5,408	61	0	46,940	80	–	98
France	170	9	4	5	4	7	3	2	63,937	792	3	41,750	82	–	99
Gabon	42	92	62	67	57	60	42	25	1,633	53	3	10,070	63	89	–
Gambia	33	170	73	78	68	80	49	28	1,791	77	5	510	59	51	70
Georgia	95	35	20	22	17	30	18	15	4,358	59	1	3,280	74	100	98
Germany	170	9	4	5	4	7	3	2	82,800	699	3	44,010	81	–	100
Ghana	36	128	72	77	66	80	49	28	25,366	794	56	1,550	61	71	84
Greece	161	13	5	5	4	11	4	3	11,125	110	1	23,260	81	97	99
Grenada	120	22	14	15	12	18	11	7	105	2	0	7,110	73	–	97
Guatemala	71	80	32	35	29	60	27	15	15,083	474	15	3,120	72	76	98
Guinea	15	241	101	106	96	142	65	34	11,451	428	41	460	56	25	83
Guinea-Bissau	6	206	129	139	119	122	81	46	1,664	63	8	550	54	55	75
Guyana	68	60	35	40	31	46	29	19	795	16	1	3,410	66	85	83
Haiti	31	144	76	82	69	100	57	25	10,174	265	20	760	63	49 x	–
Holy See	–	–	–	–	–	–	–	–	1	–	–	–	–	–	100
Honduras	83	59	23	26	20	46	19	12	7,936	208	5	2,070	74	85	97
Hungary	157	19	6	7	6	17	5	4	9,976	98	1	12,390	74	99	98
Iceland	194	6	2	3	2	5	2	1	326	5	0	38,710	82	–	99
India	49	126	56	54	59	88	44	31	1,236,687	25,642	1,414	1,530	66	63 x	99

TABLE 1 | BASIC INDICATORS >>

Countries and areas	Under-5 mortality rank	Under-5 mortality rate (U5MR)		U5MR by sex 2012		Infant mortality rate (under 1)		Neonatal mortality rate 2012	Total population (thousands) 2012	Annual no. of births (thousands) 2012	Annual no. of under-5 deaths (thousands) 2012	GNI per capita (US$) 2012	Life expectancy at birth (years) 2012	Total adult literacy rate (%) 2008–2012*	Primary school net enrolment ratio (%) 2008–2011*
		1990	2012	male	female	1990	2012								
Indonesia	72	84	31	35	27	62	26	15	246,864	4,736	152	3,420	71	93	99
Iran (Islamic Republic of)	100	56	18	19	17	44	15	11	76,424	1,454	26	c	74	85	100
Iraq	70	53	34	38	31	42	28	19	32,778	1,037	35	5,870	69	78	–
Ireland	170	9	4	4	4	8	3	2	4,576	71	0	38,970	81	–	100
Israel	170	12	4	5	4	10	3	2	7,644	156	1	28,930 x	82	–	97
Italy	170	10	4	4	4	8	3	2	60,885	563	2	33,840	82	99	99
Jamaica	109	30	17	19	15	25	14	11	2,769	50	1	5,140	73	87	82
Japan	185	6	3	3	3	5	2	1	127,250	1,071	3	47,870	83	–	100
Jordan	97	37	19	20	18	30	16	12	7,009	192	4	4,720	74	96	91
Kazakhstan	97	54	19	22	16	46	17	10	16,271	340	6	9,730	66	100	100
Kenya	33	98	73	78	68	64	49	27	43,178	1,535	108	840	61	72 x	84
Kiribati	43	94	60	65	55	68	46	22	101	2	0	2,260	69	–	–
Kuwait	132	16	11	12	10	14	10	6	3,250	67	1	44,730 x	74	94	98
Kyrgyzstan	79	71	27	30	23	58	24	14	5,474	148	4	990	67	99	96
Lao People's Democratic Republic	36	163	72	77	66	112	54	27	6,646	181	14	1,260	68	73 x	97
Latvia	141	20	9	9	8	17	8	5	2,060	23	0	14,180	72	100	96
Lebanon	141	33	9	10	9	27	8	5	4,647	62	1	9,190	80	90 x	97
Lesotho	16	85	100	107	92	68	74	45	2,052	57	6	1,380	49	76	75
Liberia	32	248	75	80	69	165	56	27	4,190	150	11	370	60	43 x	41
Libya	116	43	15	17	14	37	13	9	6,155	130	2	c	75	90	–
Liechtenstein	–	–	–	–	–	–	–	–	37	–	–	d	–	–	99
Lithuania	161	17	5	6	5	14	4	2	3,028	34	0	13,850	72	100	94
Luxembourg	194	9	2	2	2	7	2	1	524	6	0	76,960	80	–	95
Madagascar	46	159	58	62	54	97	41	22	22,294	781	44	430	64	64	–
Malawi	38	244	71	76	66	143	46	24	15,906	639	43	320	55	61	97
Malaysia	141	17	9	9	8	14	7	5	29,240	516	4	9,800	75	93	–
Maldives	132	94	11	12	9	68	9	6	338	8	0	5,750	78	98 x	95
Mali	8	253	128	134	122	130	80	42	14,854	705	83	660	55	33	67
Malta	150	11	7	7	6	10	6	5	428	4	0	19,760	80	92 x	94
Marshall Islands	66	49	38	42	33	39	31	16	53	–	0	4,140	–	–	99
Mauritania	27	128	84	92	76	82	65	34	3,796	131	11	1,110	61	59	75
Mauritius	116	23	15	17	13	20	13	9	1,240	14	0	8,570	73	89	–
Mexico	112	46	16	18	15	37	14	7	120,847	2,269	37	9,740	77	94	99
Micronesia (Federated States of)	64	55	39	42	35	43	31	16	103	2	0	3,310	69	–	–
Monaco	170	8	4	4	4	6	3	2	38	–	0	d	–	–	–
Mongolia	78	107	28	33	22	76	23	10	2,796	64	2	3,160	67	97	99
Montenegro	157	17	6	6	6	15	6	4	621	7	0	6,940	75	98	92
Morocco	72	80	31	34	28	63	27	18	32,521	739	23	2,940	71	67	96
Mozambique	22	233	90	94	85	155	63	30	25,203	995	84	510	50	51	90

TABLE 1 | BASIC INDICATORS >>

TABLE 1

Countries and areas	Under-5 mortality rank	Under-5 mortality rate (U5MR) 1990	Under-5 mortality rate (U5MR) 2012	U5MR by sex 2012 male	U5MR by sex 2012 female	Infant mortality rate (under 1) 1990	Infant mortality rate (under 1) 2012	Neonatal mortality rate 2012	Total population (thousands) 2012	Annual no. of births (thousands) 2012	Annual no. of under-5 deaths (thousands) 2012	GNI per capita (US$) 2012	Life expectancy at birth (years) 2012	Total adult literacy rate (%) 2008–2012*	Primary school net enrolment ratio (%) 2008–2011*
Myanmar	55	106	52	58	47	76	41	26	52,797	922	48	a	65	93	–
Namibia	64	73	39	43	35	49	28	18	2,259	60	2	5,670	64	76x	86
Nauru	67	58	37	41	33	45	30	21	10	–	0	–	–	–	–
Nepal	59	142	42	44	39	99	34	24	27,474	593	24	700	68	57	–
Netherlands	170	8	4	5	4	7	3	3	16,714	180	1	48,250	81	–	100
New Zealand	157	11	6	6	5	9	5	3	4,460	63	0	30,620 x	81	–	99
Nicaragua	82	66	24	27	22	50	21	12	5,992	139	3	1,650	75	78 x	94
Niger	10	326	114	117	110	137	63	28	17,157	858	91	370	58	29x	64
Nigeria	9	213	124	129	118	126	78	39	168,834	7,028	827	1,430	52	51	58
Niue	81	14	25	28	22	12	21	12	1	–	0	–	–	–	–
Norway	185	9	3	3	3	7	2	2	4,994	62	0	98,860	81	–	99
Oman	129	39	12	13	10	32	10	7	3,314	72	1	19,120 x	76	87	98
Pakistan	26	138	86	90	82	106	69	42	179,160	4,604	409	1,260	66	55	72
Palau	91	34	21	23	19	30	15	10	21	–	0	9,860	–	–	–
Panama	97	32	19	21	16	26	16	9	3,802	75	1	9,910	77	94	98
Papua New Guinea	41	89	63	68	58	65	48	24	7,167	210	13	1,790	62	62	–
Paraguay	88	46	22	24	20	36	19	12	6,687	160	3	3,290	72	94	84
Peru	100	79	18	20	16	56	14	9	29,988	600	11	5,880	75	90 x	97
Philippines	75	59	30	33	26	41	24	14	96,707	2,383	69	2,470	69	95	89
Poland	161	17	5	5	5	15	4	3	38,211	411	2	12,670	76	100	97
Portugal	170	15	4	4	3	12	3	2	10,604	94	0	20,580	80	95	99
Qatar	150	21	7	8	7	18	6	4	2,051	22	0	78,720 x	78	96	95
Republic of Korea	170	7	4	4	4	6	3	2	49,003	470	2	22,670	81	–	99
Republic of Moldova	100	32	18	20	16	27	15	9	3,514	43	1	2,070	69	99	91
Romania	129	38	12	14	11	31	11	8	21,755	224	3	8,420	74	98	88
Russian Federation	136	26	10	12	9	22	9	6	143,170	1,690	17	12,700	68	100	96
Rwanda	50	151	55	59	51	92	39	21	11,458	410	24	560 x	64	66	99
Saint Kitts and Nevis	141	29	9	10	8	23	7	7	54	–	0	13,330	–	–	87
Saint Lucia	100	22	18	19	16	18	15	10	181	3	0	6,530	75	–	88
Saint Vincent and the Grenadines	83	25	23	25	21	21	21	15	109	2	0	6,380	72	–	98
Samoa	100	30	18	19	16	25	15	7	189	5	0	3,220	73	99	93
San Marino	185	11	3	4	3	10	3	1	31	–	0	d	–	–	92
Sao Tome and Principe	52	104	53	58	49	67	38	20	188	7	0	1,320	66	70	99
Saudi Arabia	141	47	9	9	8	37	7	5	28,288	565	5	18,030 x	75	87	97
Senegal	43	142	60	65	55	71	45	24	13,726	524	30	1,040	63	50	79
Serbia	150	28	7	7	6	24	6	4	9,553	94	1	5,280	74	98	94
Seychelles	125	17	13	14	12	14	11	8	92	2	0	11,640	73	92	–
Sierra Leone	1	257	182	190	173	153	117	50	5,979	222	39	580	45	43	–
Singapore	185	8	3	3	3	6	2	1	5,303	53	0	47,210	82	96	–
Slovakia	147	18	8	8	7	16	6	4	5,446	58	0	17,170	75	–	–

TABLE 1 | BASIC INDICATORS >>

Countries and areas	Under-5 mortality rank	Under-5 mortality rate (U5MR)		U5MR by sex 2012		Infant mortality rate (under 1)		Neonatal mortality rate 2012	Total population (thousands) 2012	Annual no. of births (thousands) 2012	Annual no. of under-5 deaths (thousands) 2012	GNI per capita (US$) 2012	Life expectancy at birth (years) 2012	Total adult literacy rate (%) 2008–2012*	Primary school net enrolment ratio (%) 2008–2011*
		1990	2012	male	female	1990	2012								
Slovenia	185	10	3	3	3	9	3	2	2,068	21	0	22,710	79	100	98
Solomon Islands	72	39	31	34	28	31	26	14	550	17	1	1,130	67	–	88
Somalia	4	177	147	154	141	107	91	46	10,195	452	65	a	55	–	–
South Africa	57	61	45	49	40	47	33	15	52,386	1,102	50	7,610	56	93	90
South Sudan	12	251	104	109	98	149	67	36	10,838	396	40	650	55	–	–
Spain	161	11	5	5	4	9	4	3	46,755	493	2	30,110	82	98	100
Sri Lanka	136	21	10	10	9	18	8	6	21,098	383	4	2,920	74	91	93
State of Palestine	83	43	23	24	21	35	19	13	4,219	130	3	b	73	95	90
Sudan	33	128	73	79	67	80	49	29	37,195	1,263	89	1,450	62	–	–
Suriname	91	51	21	23	18	43	19	12	535	10	0	8,480	71	95	93
Swaziland	29	71	80	85	75	54	56	30	1,231	37	3	2,860	49	88	–
Sweden	185	7	3	3	3	6	2	2	9,511	114	0	56,210	82	–	99
Switzerland	170	8	4	5	4	7	4	3	7,997	82	0	82,730	82	–	100
Syrian Arab Republic	116	38	15	17	14	31	12	9	21,890	529	8	2,610 x	75	84	100
Tajikistan	46	105	58	64	52	82	49	23	8,009	265	15	860	67	100	98
Thailand	125	38	13	15	11	31	11	8	66,785	702	9	5,210	74	94 x	90
The former Yugoslav Republic of Macedonia	150	37	7	8	7	33	7	6	2,106	23	0	4,690	75	97	98
Timor-Leste	48	171	57	62	52	129	48	24	1,114	40	2	3,670	67	58	91
Togo	19	143	96	102	89	89	62	33	6,643	245	22	500	56	60	94
Tonga	125	23	13	14	11	20	11	7	105	3	0	4,240	73	99 x	–
Trinidad and Tobago	91	33	21	23	19	29	18	15	1,337	20	0	14,400	70	99	97
Tunisia	112	51	16	17	15	40	14	10	10,875	189	3	4,150	76	79	99
Turkey	120	74	14	16	13	55	12	9	73,997	1,268	18	10,830	75	94	99
Turkmenistan	52	90	53	60	45	72	45	22	5,173	111	6	5,550	65	100	–
Tuvalu	75	58	30	33	27	45	25	13	10	–	0	6,070	–	–	–
Uganda	39	178	69	75	62	107	45	23	36,346	1,591	103	440	59	73	94
Ukraine	132	20	11	12	9	17	9	5	45,530	495	6	3,500	68	100	92
United Arab Emirates	147	17	8	9	8	14	7	5	9,206	131	1	36,040 x	77	90 x	–
United Kingdom	161	9	5	5	4	8	4	3	62,783	771	4	38,250	80	–	100
United Republic of Tanzania	51	166	54	58	50	101	38	21	47,783	1,898	98	570	61	68	98
United States	150	11	7	8	6	9	6	4	317,505	4,226	29	50,120	79	–	96
Uruguay	150	23	7	8	7	20	6	4	3,395	49	0	13,510	77	98	100
Uzbekistan	62	74	40	45	34	61	34	14	28,541	623	25	1,720	68	99	93
Vanuatu	100	35	18	20	16	29	15	9	247	7	0	3,080	71	83	–
Venezuela (Bolivarian Republic of)	116	30	15	17	13	25	13	9	29,955	601	9	12,470	74	96	95
Viet Nam	83	51	23	26	20	36	18	12	90,796	1,440	33	1,400	76	93	99
Yemen	43	125	60	64	56	88	46	27	23,852	752	43	1,110 x	63	65	76
Zambia	25	192	89	94	83	114	56	29	14,075	608	50	1,350	57	61 x	97
Zimbabwe	22	74	90	96	83	50	56	39	13,724	439	39	680	58	84	–

TABLE 1

TABLE 1 | BASIC INDICATORS

Countries and areas	Under-5 mortality rank	Under-5 mortality rate (U5MR) 1990	Under-5 mortality rate (U5MR) 2012	U5MR by sex 2012 male	U5MR by sex 2012 female	Infant mortality rate (under 1) 1990	Infant mortality rate (under 1) 2012	Neonatal mortality rate 2012	Total population (thousands) 2012	Annual no. of births (thousands) 2012	Annual no. of under-5 deaths (thousands) 2012	GNI per capita (US$) 2012	Life expectancy at birth (years) 2012	Total adult literacy rate (%) 2008–2012*	Primary school net enrolment ratio (%) 2008–2011*
SUMMARY INDICATORS#															
Sub-Saharan Africa		177	98	103	92	107	64	32	913,135	34,734	3,245	1,397	56	59	77
Eastern and Southern Africa		163	77	82	71	101	51	28	441,512	15,780	1,170	1,729	59	66	87
West and Central Africa		195	118	124	112	115	76	37	433,568	17,667	1,985	1,071	54	52	68
Middle East and North Africa		71	30	32	28	53	24	15	425,055	10,223	306	–	71	79	90
South Asia		129	60	59	60	92	47	32	1,650,019	35,448	2,082	1,440	67	62	93
East Asia and Pacific		58	20	22	19	44	17	11	2,074,608	30,975	632	5,592	74	94	97
Latin America and Caribbean		54	19	21	17	43	16	10	604,436	10,951	206	9,212	75	92	95
CEE/CIS		47	19	21	17	38	16	9	408,336	5,889	112	8,727	70	98	96
Least developed countries		172	85	90	79	107	58	30	878,097	29,287	2,388	779	61	58	81
World		90	48	50	46	63	35	21	7,040,823	138,314	6,553	10,132	71	84	91

For a complete list of countries and areas in the regions, subregions and country categories, see page 26.

DEFINITIONS OF THE INDICATORS

Under-5 mortality rate – Probability of dying between birth and exactly 5 years of age, expressed per 1,000 live births.

Infant mortality rate – Probability of dying between birth and exactly 1 year of age, expressed per 1,000 live births.

Neonatal mortality rate – Probability of dying during the first 28 completed days of life, expressed per 1,000 live births.

GNI per capita – Gross national income (GNI) is the sum of value added by all resident producers, plus any product taxes (less subsidies) not included in the valuation of output, plus net receipts of primary income (compensation of employees and property income) from abroad. Gross national income per capita is GNI divided by midyear population. Gross national income per capita in US dollars is converted using the World Bank Atlas method.

Life expectancy at birth – Number of years newborn children would live if subject to the mortality risks prevailing for the cross section of population at the time of their birth.

Total adult literacy rate – Percentage of population aged 15 years and over who can both read and write with understanding a short simple statement on his/her everyday life.

Primary school net enrolment ratio – Number of children enrolled in primary or secondary school who are of official primary school age, expressed as a percentage of the total number of children of official primary school age. Because of the inclusion of primary-school-aged children enrolled in secondary school, this indicator can also be referred to as a primary adjusted net enrolment ratio.

MAIN DATA SOURCES

Under-5 and infant mortality rates – United Nations Inter-agency Group for Child Mortality Estimation (UNICEF, World Health Organization, United Nations Population Division and the World Bank).

Neonatal mortality rate – World Health Organization, using civil registrations, surveillance systems and household surveys.

Total population and births – United Nations Population Division.

Under-5 deaths – United Nations Inter-agency Group for Child Mortality Estimation (UNICEF, World Health Organization, United Nations Population Division and the World Bank).

GNI per capita – The World Bank.

Life expectancy at birth – United Nations Population Division.

Total adult literacy rate and primary school net enrolment ratio – UNESCO Institute for Statistics (UIS).

NOTES

a low-income country (GNI per capita is $1,035 or less).

b lower-middle-income country (GNI per capita is $1,036 to $4,085).

c upper-middle-income country (GNI per capita is $4,086 to $12,615).

d high-income country (GNI per capita is $12,616 or more).

– Data not available.

x Data refer to years or periods other than those specified in the column heading. Such data are not included in the calculation of regional and global averages.

z Data provided by the Chinese Ministry of Education. The UNESCO Institute for Statistics dataset does not currently include net enrolment rates for China.

* Data refer to the most recent year available during the period specified in the column heading.

TABLE 2 | NUTRITION

Countries and areas	Low birthweight (%) 2008–2012*	Early initiation of breastfeeding (%)	Exclusive breastfeeding <6 months (%)	Introduction of solid, semi-solid or soft foods 6–8 months (%)	Breastfeeding at age 2 (%)	Underweight (%) moderate and severe⊖	Underweight (%) severe	Stunting (%) moderate and severe⊖	Wasting (%) moderate and severe⊖	Overweight (%) moderate and severe⊖	Vitamin A supplementation, full coverage△ (%) 2012	Iodized salt consumption (%) 2008–2012*
				2008–2012*				2008–2012*				
Afghanistan	–	–	–	29 x	54 x	33 x	12 x	59 x	9 x	5 x	–	20
Albania	4	43	39	78	31	5	2	19	9	22	–	76
Algeria	6 x	50 x	7 x	39 x,y	22 x	3 x	1 x	15 x	4 x	13 x	–	61 x
Andorra	–	–	–	–	–	–	–	–	–	–	–	–
Angola	12 x	55 x	11 x	77 x	37 x	16 x	7 x	29 x	8 x	–	44	45 x
Antigua and Barbuda	5 x	–	–	–	–	–	–	–	–	–	–	–
Argentina	7	–	54	–	28 x	2 x	0 x	8 x	1 x	10 x	–	–
Armenia	8	36	35	75	23	5	1	19	4	15	–	97 x
Australia	7 x	–	–	–	–	–	–	–	–	–	–	–
Austria	7 x	–	–	–	–	–	–	–	–	–	–	–
Azerbaijan	10 x	32 x	12 x	83 x	16 x	8 x	2 x	25 x	7 x	13 x	90 w	54 x
Bahamas	11 x	–	–	–	–	–	–	–	–	–	–	–
Bahrain	–	–	–	–	–	–	–	–	–	–	–	–
Bangladesh	22 x	47	64	62	90	36	10	41	16	2	99	82 y
Barbados	12	–	–	–	–	–	–	–	–	–	–	–
Belarus	4 x	21 x	9 x	38 x	4 x	1 x	1 x	4 x	2 x	10 x	–	–
Belgium	–	–	–	–	–	–	–	–	–	–	–	–
Belize	11	62	15	69	35	6	1	19	3	8	–	–
Benin	15 x	50	33	76 y	92	21	8	45	16	18	99	86
Bhutan	10	59	49	67	66	13	3	34	6	8	43	96 x,y
Bolivia (Plurinational State of)	6	64	60	83	40	4	1	27	1	9	41	89 y
Bosnia and Herzegovina	3	42	19	71	12	2	1	9	2	17	–	62 x,y
Botswana	13 x	40 x	20 x	46 x,y	6 x	11 x	4 x	31 x	7 x	11 x	–	65 x
Brazil	8	68	41	70 x,y	25 x	2 x	–	7 x	2 x	7 x	–	96 x,y
Brunei Darussalam	–	–	–	–	–	–	–	–	–	–	–	–
Bulgaria	9	–	–	–	–	–	–	–	–	–	–	100 x
Burkina Faso	14	42	38	57	80	24	6	33	11	2	99	96 y
Burundi	13	74	69	70 y	79	29	8	58	6	3	–	96 y
Cabo Verde	6 x	73 x	60 x	80 x,y	13 x	–	–	–	–	–	–	75
Cambodia	11	66	74	88	43	28	7	40	11	2	98	83 y
Cameroon	11 x	20 x	20	63 x	24	15	5	33	6	7	88	49 x,y
Canada	6 x	–	–	–	–	–	–	–	–	–	–	–
Central African Republic	14	44	34	60	32	24	8	41	7	2	83	65
Chad	20	29	3	46	59	30	13	39	16	3	0	54
Chile	6	–	63 x	–	–	–	–	–	–	–	–	–
China	3	41	28	43 y	–	4	–	10	2	7	–	97 y
Colombia	6 x	49 x	43	86	33	3	1	13	1	5	–	–
Comoros	25 x	25 x	–	34 x,y	45 x	15	4	30	11	9	–	82 x
Congo	13 x	39 x	19 x	78 x,y	21 x	11 x	3 x	30 x	8 x	3	–	82 x

TABLE 2 | NUTRITION >>

TABLE 2

Countries and areas	Low birthweight (%) 2008–2012*	Early initiation of breastfeeding (%)	Exclusive breastfeeding <6 months (%)	Introduction of solid, semi-solid or soft foods 6–8 months (%)	Breastfeeding at age 2 (%)	Underweight (%) moderate and severe⊖	Underweight (%) severe	Stunting (%) moderate and severe⊖	Wasting (%) moderate and severe⊖	Overweight (%) moderate and severe⊖	Vitamin A supplementation, full coverage△ (%) 2012	Iodized salt consumption (%) 2008–2012*
				2008–2012*				2008–2012*				
Cook Islands	3x	–	–	–	–	–	–	–	–	–	–	–
Costa Rica	7	–	19x	92	40	1	–	6	1	8	–	–
Côte d'Ivoire	17x	31	12	64	38	15	3	30	8	3	99	84x,y
Croatia	5	–	–	–	–	–	–	–	–	–	–	–
Cuba	5	77	49	77	17	–	–	–	–	–	–	88x
Cyprus	–	–	–	–	–	–	–	–	–	–	–	–
Czech Republic	7x	–	–	–	–	–	–	–	–	–	–	–
Democratic People's Republic of Korea	6	18	65x	31x,y	36	15	3	28	4	–	99	25y
Democratic Republic of the Congo	10	43	37	52	53	24	8	43	9	5	84	59
Denmark	5x	–	–	–	–	–	–	–	–	–	–	–
Djibouti	10x	55x	1x	35x	18x	23	5	31	10	8	88	0x
Dominica	10	–	–	–	–	–	–	–	–	–	–	–
Dominican Republic	11x	69x	8x	88x	14	3x	0x	10x	2x	8	–	19x
Ecuador	8	–	40x	76x,y	23x	6x	1x	29x	2x	5x	–	–
Egypt	13	43x	53	70	35	6	1	29	7	21	62	79
El Salvador	9	33	31	80	54	6	1	19	1	6	81	62x
Equatorial Guinea	13x	–	24x	–	–	11x	5x	35x	3x	8x	–	33x
Eritrea	14x	78x	52x	43x,y	62x	35x	13x	44x	15x	2x	38	68x
Estonia	4x	–	–	–	–	–	–	–	–	–	–	–
Ethiopia	20x	52	52	49	82	29	9	44	10	2	31	15y
FIJI	10x	57x	40x	–	–	–	–	–	–	–	–	–
Finland	4x	–	–	–	–	–	–	–	–	–	–	–
France	–	–	–	–	–	–	–	–	–	–	–	–
Gabon	14x	32	6	62x,y	4	6	1	17	3	7	2	36x
Gambia	10	52	34	34	31	17	4	23	10	2	46	22
Georgia	5	69	55	43y	17	1	1	11	2	20	–	100
Germany	–	–	–	–	–	–	–	–	–	–	–	–
Ghana	11	46	46	75	37	13	3	23	6	3	17	35
Greece	–	–	–	–	–	–	–	–	–	–	–	–
Grenada	9x	–	–	–	–	–	–	–	–	–	–	–
Guatemala	11	56	50	71y	46	13	–	48	1	5	14	76x
Guinea	12x	40x	48	32y	–	16	4	35	5	4	99	41
Guinea-Bissau	11	55	38	43	65	18	5	32	6	3	95	12
Guyana	14	43x	33	81	49	11	2	18	5	6	–	11
Haiti	23	47	40	87	31	11	3	22	5	4	54	18
Holy See	–	–	–	–	–	–	–	–	–	–	–	–
Honduras	10	64	31	83x	43	7	1	23	1	5	58	–
Hungary	9x	–	–	–	–	–	–	–	–	–	–	–

TABLE 2 | NUTRITION >>

Countries and areas	Low birthweight (%) 2008–2012*	Early initiation of breastfeeding (%)	Exclusive breastfeeding <6 months (%)	Introduction of solid, semi-solid or soft foods 6–8 months (%)	Breastfeeding at age 2 (%)	Underweight (%) moderate and severe⊖	Underweight (%) severe	Stunting (%) moderate and severe⊖	Wasting (%) moderate and severe⊖	Overweight (%) moderate and severe⊖	Vitamin A supplementation, full coverage△ (%) 2012	Iodized salt consumption (%) 2008–2012*
				2008–2012*				2008–2012*				
Iceland	4x	–	–	–	–	–	–	–	–	–	–	–
India	28x	41	46x	56x	77x	43x	16x	48x	20x	2x	59	71
Indonesia	9x	29	42	85x	55	18	5	36	13	12	73	62x,y
Iran (Islamic Republic of)	7x	56x	23x	68x,y	58x	–	–	–	–	–	–	99x,y
Iraq	13	43	20	36	23	9	4	23	7	12	–	29
Ireland	–	–	–	–	–	–	–	–	–	–	–	–
Israel	8x	–	–	–	–	–	–	–	–	–	–	–
Italy	–	–	–	–	–	–	–	–	–	–	–	–
Jamaica	12x	62x	15x	36x	24x	3	–	5	4	4	–	–
Japan	8x	–	–	–	–	–	–	–	–	–	–	–
Jordan	13x	39x	23	83x	13	3	1	8	2	4	–	88x,y
Kazakhstan	5	68	32	49	26	4	1	13	4	1	–	85
Kenya	8	58	32	85	54	16	4	35	7	5	66	98
Kiribati	–	–	69	–	82	–	–	–	–	–	–	–
Kuwait	–	–	–	–	–	–	–	–	–	–	–	–
Kyrgyzstan	5x	65x	32x	60x	26x	5	1	23	1	4	–	76x
Lao People's Democratic Republic	15	30x	26x	41x	48x	27	7	44	6	2	47	80y
Latvia	5x	–	–	–	–	–	–	–	–	–	–	–
Lebanon	12	–	15	35x,y	15	–	–	–	–	–	–	71
Lesotho	11	53	54	68	35	13	2	39	4	7	–	84
Liberia	14	67x	29x	–	–	15	2	42	3	5	13	–
Libya	–	–	–	–	–	4x	–	21x	4x	22x	–	–
Liechtenstein	–	–	–	–	–	–	–	–	–	–	–	–
Lithuania	4x	–	–	–	–	–	–	–	–	–	–	–
Luxembourg	8x	–	–	–	–	–	–	–	–	–	–	–
Madagascar	16	72	51	86	61	36x	–	50	15x	–	88	53
Malawi	14	95	71	86	77	13	3	47	4	8	60	97y
Malaysia	11	–	–	–	–	12	2	17	12	5	–	18
Maldives	11	64	48	91	68	17	3	19	11	7	–	44x
Mali	18	57	20	27	46	19	5	28	9	1	93	79x
Malta	6x	–	–	–	–	–	–	–	–	–	–	–
Marshall Islands	18x	73x	31x	77x	53x	–	–	–	–	–	–	–
Mauritania	35	81	46	61y	47	20	4	23	12	1	99	23
Mauritius	14x	–	21x	–	–	–	–	–	–	–	–	–
Mexico	9	18	19	27	–	3	–	14	2	10	–	91x
Micronesia (Federated States of)	18x	–	–	–	–	–	–	–	–	–	–	–
Monaco	–	–	–	–	–	–	–	–	–	–	–	–
Mongolia	5	71	66	66	65	3	1	15	2	11	54	70

TABLE 2 | NUTRITION >>

Countries and areas	Low birthweight (%) 2008–2012*	Early initiation of breastfeeding (%)	Exclusive breastfeeding <6 months (%)	Introduction of solid, semi-solid or soft foods 6–8 months (%)	Breastfeeding at age 2 (%)	Underweight (%) moderate and severe⊖	Underweight (%) severe	Stunting (%) moderate and severe⊖	Wasting (%) moderate and severe⊖	Overweight (%) moderate and severe⊖	Vitamin A supplementation, full coverage△ (%) 2012	Iodized salt consumption (%) 2008–2012*
Montenegro	4 x	25 x	19 x	35 x,y	13 x	2 x	1 x	7 x	4 x	16 x	–	71 x
Morocco	15 x	52 x	31 x	52 x,y	15 x	3	2 x	15	2	11	–	21 x
Mozambique	17	77	43	90	52	15	4	43	6	7	20	45 y
Myanmar	9	76	24	76	65	23	6	35	8	3	86	93
Namibia	16 x	71 x	24 x	91 x	28 x	17 x	4 x	29 x	8 x	5 x	46	63 x
Nauru	27 x	76 x,y	67 x	65 x	65 x	5 x	1 x	24 x	1 x	3 x	–	–
Nepal	18	45	70	66	93	29	8	41	11	2	95	80
Netherlands	–	–	–	–	–	–	–	–	–	–	–	–
New Zealand	6 x	–	–	–	–	–	–	–	–	–	–	–
Nicaragua	8	76 x	31 x	76 x,y	43 x	6 x	1 x	22 x	1 x	6 x	7	97 x
Niger	27 x	42	23	65 y	50	36	13	44	18	2	98	32
Nigeria	15	23	15	33	35	24	9	36	10	3	78	52
Niue	0 x	–	–	–	–	–	–	–	–	–	–	–
Norway	5 x	–	–	–	–	–	–	–	–	–	–	–
Oman	10	85 x	–	91 x,y	73 x	9	1	10	7	2	–	69 x,y
Pakistan	32 x	29 x	37 x	36 x,y	55 x	32	12	44	15	6	99	69
Palau	–	–	–	–	–	–	–	–	–	–	–	–
Panama	10 x	–	–	–	–	4	–	19	1	–	–	–
Papua New Guinea	11 x	–	56 x	76 x,y	72 x	18 x	5 x	44 x	5 x	4 x	15	92 x
Paraguay	6	47	24	67 y	14	3 x	–	18 x	1 x	7 x	–	93
Peru	8 x	51	71	82	55	4	1	20	0	10	–	91
Philippines	21	54	34	90	34	22	–	32	7	4	90	45 x
Poland	6 x	–	–	–	–	–	–	–	–	–	–	–
Portugal	8 x	–	–	–	–	–	–	–	–	–	–	–
Qatar	–	–	–	–	–	–	–	–	–	–	–	–
Republic of Korea	4 x	–	–	–	–	–	–	–	–	–	–	–
Republic of Moldova	6 x	65 x	46 x	18 x,y	2 x	3 x	1 x	10 x	5 x	9 x	–	60 x
Romania	8 x	–	16 x	41 x,y	–	4 x	1 x	13 x	4 x	8 x	–	74 x
Russian Federation	6 x	–	–	–	–	–	–	–	–	–	–	35 x,y
Rwanda	7	71	85	79	84	11	2	44	3	7	3	99
Saint Kitts and Nevis	8	–	–	–	–	–	–	–	–	–	–	100 x,y
Saint Lucia	11	–	–	–	–	–	–	–	–	–	–	–
Saint Vincent and the Grenadines	8	–	–	–	–	–	–	–	–	–	–	–
Samoa	10	88	51	71 y	74	–	–	–	–	–	–	–
San Marino	–	–	–	–	–	–	–	–	–	–	–	–
Sao Tome and Principe	10	35 x	51	74	20	13	3	29	11	11	34	86
Saudi Arabia	–	–	–	–	–	–	–	–	–	–	–	–
Senegal	19	48	39	67 y	51	18	5	27	10	3	–	47
Serbia	6	8	14	84	15	2	1	7	4	16	–	32 x

STATISTICAL TABLES 39

TABLE 2 | NUTRITION >>

Countries and areas	Low birthweight (%) 2008–2012*	Early initiation of breastfeeding (%)	Exclusive breastfeeding <6 months (%)	Introduction of solid, semi-solid or soft foods 6–8 months (%)	Breastfeeding at age 2 (%)	Underweight (%) moderate and severe⊖	Underweight (%) severe	Stunting (%) moderate and severe⊖	Wasting (%) moderate and severe⊖	Overweight (%) moderate and severe⊖	Vitamin A supplementation, full coverageᐃ (%) 2012	Iodized salt consumption (%) 2008–2012*
				2008–2012*				2008–2012*				
Seychelles	–	–	–	–	–	–	–	–	–	–	–	–
Sierra Leone	11	45	32	25	48	22	8	44	9	10	99	63
Singapore	8x	–	–	–	–	3x	0x	4x	4x	3x	–	–
Slovakia	7x	–	–	–	–	–	–	–	–	–	–	–
Slovenia	–	–	–	–	–	–		–	–	–	–	–
Solomon Islands	13x	75x	74x	80x,y	67x	12x	2x	33x	4x	3x	–	–
Somalia		26x	9x	16x	35x	32x	12x	42x	13x	5	–	1x
South Africa	–	61x	8x	49x,y	31x	9x	–	33x	6x	19x	–	–
South Sudan	–	–	45	21	38	28	12	31	23	5	70	54
Spain	–	–	–	–	–	–	–	–	–	–	–	–
Sri Lanka	17x	80x	76x	87x,y	84x	21x	4x	17x	15x	1	90	92x,y
State of Palestine	9	–	27x	–	–	4	1	11	3	–	–	86x
Sudan	–	–	41	51	40	32	13	35	16	–	83	10
Suriname	14	45	3	47	15	6	1	9	5	4	–	–
Swaziland	9	55	44	66	11	6	1	31	1	11	33	52
Sweden	–	–	–	–	–	–	–	–	–	–	–	–
Switzerland	–	–	–	–	–	–	–	–	–	–	–	–
Syrian Arab Republic	10	46	43	–	25	10	–	28	12	18	–	79x
Tajikistan	10x	61x	25x	41x	34x	12	4	26	10	6	97	62
Thailand	7	50x	15	–	–	7x	1x	16x	5x	8x	–	47x
The former Yugoslav Republic of Macedonia	6	21	23	41	13	1	0	5	2	12	–	94x,y
Timor-Leste	12x	82	52	82	33	45	15	58	19	5	59	60x
Togo	11	46	62	44	64	17	4	30	5	2	64	32
Tonga	3x	–	–	–	–	–	–	–	–	–	–	–
Trinidad and Tobago	10	41x	13x	83x	22x	–	–	–	–	–	–	28x
Tunisia	7	87x	6x	61x,y	15x	2	1	10	3	14	–	97x
Turkey	11	39	42	68x,y	22	2	0	12	1	–	–	69
Turkmenistan	4x	60x	11x	54x	37x	8x	2x	19x	7x	–	–	87x
Tuvalu	6x	15x	35x	40x,y	51x	2x	0x	10x	3x	6x	–	–
Uganda	12	53	63	67	46	14	3	33	5	3	70	99y
Ukraine	4x	41x	18x	86x	6x	–	–	–	–	–	–	18x
United Arab Emirates	6	–	–	–	–	–	–	–	–	–	–	–
United Kingdom	8x	–	–	–	–	–	–	–	–	–	–	–
United Republic of Tanzania	8	49	50	92	51	16	4	42	5	5	95	59
United States	8x	–	–	–	–	1x	0x	3x	0x	7x	–	–
Uruguay	9	59	65	35x,y	27	5x	2x	15x	2x	10x	–	–
Uzbekistan	5x	67x	26x	47x	38x	4x	1x	19x	4x	13x	99	53x
Vanuatu	10x	72x	40x	68x	32x	11x	2x	26x	6x	5x	–	23x

TABLE 2 | NUTRITION

TABLE 2

Countries and areas	Low birthweight (%) 2008–2012*	Early initiation of breastfeeding (%)	Exclusive breastfeeding <6 months (%)	Introduction of solid, semi-solid or soft foods 6–8 months (%)	Breastfeeding at age 2 (%)	Underweight (%) moderate and severe⊖	Underweight (%) severe	Stunting (%) moderate and severe⊖	Wasting (%) moderate and severe⊖	Overweight (%) moderate and severe⊖	Vitamin A supplementation, full coverage△ (%) 2012	Iodized salt consumption (%) 2008–2012*
				2008–2012*				2008–2012*				
Venezuela (Bolivarian Republic of)	8	–	–	–	–	4x	–	16x	5x	6x	–	–
Viet Nam	5	40	17	50	19	12	2	23	4	4	98w	45
Yemen	–	30x	12x	76x,y	–	43x	19x	58x	15x	5x	11	30x
Zambia	11x	57x	61x	94x	42x	15x	3x	45x	5x	8x	–	77x
Zimbabwe	11	65	31	86	20	10	2	32	3	6	61	94y

SUMMARY INDICATORS#

Countries and areas	Low birthweight (%)	Early initiation of breastfeeding (%)	Exclusive breastfeeding <6 months (%)	Introduction of solid, semi-solid or soft foods 6–8 months (%)	Breastfeeding at age 2 (%)	Underweight moderate and severe	Underweight severe	Stunting moderate and severe	Wasting moderate and severe	Overweight moderate and severe	Vitamin A supplementation	Iodized salt consumption
Sub-Saharan Africa	13	45	36	56	50	21	7	38	9	6	68	54
Eastern and Southern Africa	11	60	52	72	61	18	5	39	7	5	56	61
West and Central Africa	14	35	25	45	44	22	8	37	11	6	77	53
Middle East and North Africa	–	–	–	–	–	7	–	18	8	11	–	–
South Asia	28	41	49	57	78	32	15	38	16	4	69	71
East Asia and Pacific	6	41	30	51	45**	5	4**	12	4	5	81**	91
Latin America and Caribbean	9	49	39	–	–	3	–	11	1	7	–	–
CEE/CIS	–	–	–	–	–	2	–	11	1	15	–	–
Least developed countries	13	53	48	63	64	23	7	37	10	5	70	60
World	15	43	38	55	58**	15	9**	25	8	7	70**	76

For a complete list of countries and areas in the regions, subregions and country categories, see page 26.

DEFINITIONS OF THE INDICATORS

Low birthweight – Percentage of infants weighing less than 2,500 grams at birth.

Early initiation of breastfeeding – Percentage of infants who are put to the breast within one hour of birth.

Exclusive breastfeeding <6 months – Percentage of children aged 0–5 months who are fed exclusively with breast milk in the 24 hours prior to the survey.

Introduction of solid, semi-solid or soft foods (6–8 months) – Percentage of children aged 6–8 months who received solid, semi-solid or soft foods in the 24 hours prior to the survey.

Breastfeeding at age 2 – Percentage of children aged 20–23 months who received breast milk in the 24 hours prior to the survey.

Underweight – Moderate and severe: Percentage of children aged 0–59 months who are below minus two standard deviations from median weight-for-age of the World Health Organization (WHO) Child Growth Standards; Severe: Percentage of children aged 0–59 months who are below minus three standard deviations from median weight-for-age of the WHO Child Growth Standards.

Stunting – Moderate and severe: Percentage of children aged 0–59 months who are below minus two standard deviations from median height-for-age of the WHO Child Growth Standards.

Wasting – Moderate and severe: Percentage of children aged 0–59 months who are below minus two standard deviations from median weight-for-height of the WHO Child Growth Standards.

Overweight – Moderate and severe: Percentage of children aged 0–59 months who are above two standard deviations from median weight-for-height of the WHO Child Growth Standards.

Vitamin A supplementation, full coverage – The estimated percentage of children aged 6–59 months reached with 2 doses of vitamin A supplements.

Iodized salt consumption – Percentage of households consuming adequately iodized salt (15 parts per million or more).

MAIN DATA SOURCES

Low birthweight – Demographic and Health Surveys (DHS), Multiple Indicator Cluster Surveys (MICS), other national household surveys, data from routine reporting systems, UNICEF and WHO.

Breastfeeding – DHS, MICS, other national household surveys and UNICEF.

Underweight, stunting, wasting and overweight – DHS, MICS, other national household surveys, WHO and UNICEF.

Vitamin A supplementation – UNICEF.

Iodized salt consumption – DHS, MICS, other national household surveys and UNICEF.

NOTES

– Data not available.

w Identifies countries with national vitamin A supplementation programmes targeted towards a reduced age range. Coverage figure is reported as targeted.

x Data refer to years or periods other than those specified in the column heading. Such data are not included in the calculation of regional and global averages, with the exception of 2005–2006 data from India. Estimates from data years prior to 2000 are not displayed.

y Data differ from the standard definition or refer to only part of a country. If they fall within the noted reference period, such data are included in the calculation of regional and global averages.

△ Full coverage with vitamin A supplements is reported as the lower percentage of 2 annual coverage points (i.e., lower point between round 1 (January–June) and round 2 (July–December) of 2012).

* Data refer to the most recent year available during the period specified in the column heading.

** Excludes China.

⊖ Regional averages for underweight (moderate and severe), stunting (moderate and severe), wasting (moderate and severe) and overweight (moderate and severe) are estimated using statistical modeling of data from the UNICEF-WHO-World Bank Joint Global Nutrition Database, 2012 revision (completed July 2013). The severe underweight indicator was not included in this exercise; regional averages for this indicator are based on a population-weighted average calculated by UNICEF.

TABLE 3 | HEALTH

Countries and areas	Use of improved drinking water sources (%) 2011			Use of improved sanitation facilities (%) 2011			Routine EPI vaccines financed by government (%) 2012	Immunization coverage (%) 2012							Newborns protected against tetanus (%)	Pneumonia 2008–2012*		Diarrhoea 2008–2012*	Malaria 2008–2012*		
	total	urban	rural	total	urban	rural	2012	BCG	DPT1[6]	DPT3[6]	Polio3	MCV	HepB3	Hib3		Care-seeking for children with symptoms of pneumonia (%)	Antibiotic treatment for children with symptoms of pneumonia (%)	Treatment with oral rehydration salts (ORS) (%)	Antimalarial treatment for children with fever (%)	Children sleeping under ITNs (%)	Households with at least one ITN (%)
Afghanistan	61	85	53	28	46	23	5	75	86	71	71	68	71	71	60	61	64	53	–	–	–
Albania	95	95	94	94	95	93	–	99	99	99	99	99	99	99	87	70	60	54	–	–	–
Algeria	84	85	79	95	98	88	100	99	99	95	95	95	95	95	90	53 x	59 x	19 x	–	–	–
Andorra	100	100	100	100	100	100	–	–	99	99	99	98	97	98	–	–	–	–	–	–	–
Angola	53	66	35	59	86	19	100	87	99	91	88	97	91	91	72	–	–	–	28	26	35
Antigua and Barbuda	98	98	98	91	91	91	100	–	99	98	97	98	98	98	–	–	–	–	–	–	–
Argentina	99	100	95	96	96	98	100	99	94	91	90	94	91	91	–	–	–	–	–	–	–
Armenia	99	100	98	90	96	81	65	96	99	95	96	97	95	95	–	57	36	33	–	–	–
Australia	100	100	100	100	100	100	100	–	92	92	92	94	92	92	–	–	–	–	–	–	–
Austria	100	100	100	100	100	100	–	–	93	83	83	76	83	83	–	–	–	–	–	–	–
Azerbaijan	80	88	71	82	86	78	–	82	81	75	78	66	46	91	–	36 x	–	21 x	1 x	1 x	–
Bahamas	96	96	96	–	–	–	100	–	99	98	99	91	96	98	92	–	–	–	–	–	–
Bahrain	100	100	100	99	99	99	100	–	99	99	99	99	99	99	94	–	–	–	–	–	–
Bangladesh	83	85	82	55	55	55	37	95	99	96	96	96	96	96	94	35	71	78	1	–	–
Barbados	100	100	100	–	–	–	–	–	93	87	88	90	88	88	–	–	–	–	–	–	–
Belarus	100	100	99	93	92	97	47	98	98	98	98	98	97	22	–	94	76	45	–	–	–
Belgium	100	100	100	100	100	100	–	–	99	99	99	96	98	98	–	–	–	–	–	–	–
Belize	99	97	100	90	93	87	100	98	99	98	98	96	98	98	88	82	44 x	23	–	–	–
Benin	76	85	69	14	25	5	17	94	88	85	85	72	85	85	93	31	–	50	38	71	80
Bhutan	97	100	96	45	74	29	14	95	97	97	97	95	97	97	89	74	49	61	–	–	–
Bolivia (Plurinational State of)	88	96	72	46	57	24	75	87	85	80	79	84	80	80	76	51	64	35	–	–	–
Bosnia and Herzegovina	99	100	98	96	100	92	–	96	95	92	87	94	92	87	–	87	76	36	–	–	–
Botswana	97	99	93	64	78	42	–	99	98	96	99	94	96	96	92	14 x	–	49 x	–	–	–
Brazil	97	100	84	81	87	48	100	99	99	94	97	99	97	95	93	50 x	–	–	–	–	–
Brunei Darussalam	–	–	–	–	–	–	–	99	96	90	90	99	99	90	95	–	–	–	–	–	–
Bulgaria	99	100	99	100	100	100	100	97	96	95	95	94	95	95	–	–	–	–	–	–	–
Burkina Faso	80	96	74	18	50	6	39	96	94	90	90	87	90	90	88	56	47	21	35	47	57
Burundi	74	82	73	50	45	51	7	98	99	96	94	93	96	96	85	55	43	38	17	45	52
Cabo Verde	89	91	86	63	74	45	–	99	99	90	90	96	90	90	92	–	–	–	–	–	–
Cambodia	67	90	61	33	76	22	25	99	97	95	95	93	95	95	91	64	39	34	0	4 x	5 x
Cameroon	74	95	52	48	58	36	13	81	94	85	85	82	85	85	85	30	45	17	23	21	36
Canada	100	100	99	100	100	99	–	–	98	95	99	98	70	95	–	–	–	–	–	–	–
Central African Republic	67	92	51	34	43	28	2	74	69	47	47	49	47	47	66	30	31	16	34	36	47
Chad	50	71	44	12	31	6	24	63	64	45	56	64	45	45	43	26	31	13	43	10	42
Chile	98	100	90	99	100	89	100	92	90	90	90	90	90	90	–	–	–	–	–	–	–
China	92	98	85	65	74	56	–	99	99	99	99	99	99	–	–	–	–	–	–	–	–
Colombia	93	100	72	78	82	65	100	89	92	92	91	94	92	91	79	64	–	54	–	–	3 x
Comoros	–	–	97	–	–	–	8	76	91	86	85	85	86	86	85	38	–	38	28	41	59
Congo	72	95	32	18	19	15	11	92	90	85	85	80	85	85	83	52	–	35	25	26	27
Cook Islands	100	100	100	95	95	95	–	98	98	98	98	97	98	98	–	–	–	–	–	–	–

TABLE 3 | HEALTH >>

TABLE 3

Countries and areas	Use of improved drinking water sources (%) 2011			Use of improved sanitation facilities (%) 2011			Routine EPI vaccines financed by government (%) 2012	Immunization coverage (%)							Newborns protected against tetanus[1] (%)	Pneumonia		Diarrhoea	Malaria		
	total	urban	rural	total	urban	rural	2012	BCG	DPT1[8]	DPT3[8]	Polio3	MCV	HepB3	Hib3	2012	Care-seeking for children with symptoms of pneumonia (%)	Antibiotic treatment for children with symptoms of pneumonia (%)	Treatment with oral rehydration salts (ORS) (%)	Antimalarial treatment for children with fever (%)	Children sleeping under ITNs (%)	Households with at least one ITN (%)
										2012						2008–2012*		2008–2012*	2008–2012*		
Costa Rica	96	100	91	94	95	92	100	78	92	91	90	90	91	90	–	–	–	–	–	–	–
Côte d'Ivoire	80	91	68	24	36	11	26	99	98	94	94	85	94	94	82	38	19 x	17	18	37	67
Croatia	99	100	97	98	99	98	100	99	97	96	96	95	98	96	–	–	–	–	–	–	–
Cuba	94	96	86	92	94	87	99	99	96	96	98	99	96	96	–	97	70	51	–	–	–
Cyprus	100	100	100	100	100	100	–	–	99	99	99	86	96	96	–	–	–	–	–	–	–
Czech Republic	100	100	100	100	100	100	–	–	99	99	99	98	99	99	–	–	–	–	–	–	–
Democratic People's Republic of Korea	98	99	97	82	88	73	–	98	97	96	99	99	96	32	93	80	88	74	–	–	–
Democratic Republic of the Congo	46	80	29	31	29	31	11	78	86	72	76	73	72	72	70	40	42	27	39	38	51
Denmark	100	100	100	100	100	100	–	–	97	94	94	90	–	94	–	–	–	–	–	–	–
Djibouti	92	100	67	61	73	22	0	87	85	81	81	83	81	81	79	62 x	43 x	62 x	1	20	30
Dominica	–	96	–	–	–	–	100	98	98	97	99	99	97	97	–	–	–	–	–	–	–
Dominican Republic	82	82	81	82	86	74	–	99	92	85	85	79	74	70	90	68	42	32	–	–	–
Ecuador	92	96	82	93	96	86	100	99	99	99	99	94	98	99	85	–	–	–	–	–	–
Egypt	99	100	99	95	97	93	100	95	94	93	93	93	93	–	86	73	58	28	–	–	–
El Salvador	90	94	81	70	79	53	100	90	92	92	92	93	92	92	90	67	51	58	–	–	–
Equatorial Guinea	–	–	–	–	–	–	–	73	65	33	39	51	–	–	75	–	–	29 x	49 x	1 x	–
Eritrea	–	–	–	–	–	4	3	99	99	99	99	99	99	99	94	44 x	–	45 x	13	49	71
Estonia	99	99	97	98	100	94	–	97	96	94	94	94	94	94	–	–	–	–	–	–	–
Ethiopia	49	97	39	21	27	19	8	80	80	61	70	66	61	61	68	27	7	26	26	30	47
Fiji	96	100	92	87	92	82	100	99	99	99	99	99	99	99	94	–	–	–	–	–	–
Finland	100	100	100	100	100	100	–	–	99	99	99	97	–	99	–	–	–	–	–	–	–
France	100	100	100	100	100	100	–	–	99	99	99	89	74	98	–	–	–	–	–	–	–
Gabon	88	95	41	33	33	30	100	98	86	82	80	71	82	82	75	68	50	26	26	39	36
Gambia	89	92	85	68	70	65	16	98	99	98	98	95	98	98	92	69	70	39	30	33	51
Georgia	98	100	96	93	96	91	57	95	94	92	93	93	92	92	–	74 x	56 x	40 x	–	–	–
Germany	100	100	100	100	100	100	–	–	97	93	95	97	86	94	–	–	–	–	–	–	–
Ghana	86	92	80	13	19	8	11	98	92	92	91	88	92	92	88	41	56	35	53	39	48
Greece	100	100	99	99	99	97	–	–	99	99	99	99	98	94	–	–	–	–	–	–	–
Grenada	–	–	–	–	–	–	100	–	99	97	98	94	97	97	–	–	–	–	–	–	–
Guatemala	94	99	89	80	88	72	100	94	98	96	93	96	96	96	85	64 x	–	37	–	–	–
Guinea	74	90	65	18	32	11	0	84	86	59	57	58	59	59	80	37	–	34	28	26	47
Guinea-Bissau	72	94	54	19	33	8	–	94	92	80	78	69	76	76	80	52	35	19	51	36	53
Guyana	95	98	93	84	88	82	57	98	99	97	97	99	97	97	90	65	18	50	6	24	26
Haiti	64	77	48	26	34	17	–	75	81	60	60	58	–	–	76	38	46	53	3	12	19
Holy See	–	–	–	–	–	–	–	–	–	–	–	–	–	–	–	–	–	–	–	–	–
Honduras	89	96	81	81	86	74	45	90	88	88	88	93	88	88	94	64	60	60	0	–	–
Hungary	100	100	100	100	100	100	100	99	99	99	99	99	–	99	–	–	–	–	–	–	–
Iceland	100	100	100	100	100	100	100	–	97	89	89	90	–	89	–	–	–	–	–	–	–
India	92	96	89	35	60	24	100	87	88	72	70	74	70	–	87	69 x	13 x	26 x	8 x	–	–
Indonesia	84	93	76	59	73	44	–	81	91	64	69	80	64	–	85	75	39	39	1	3 x	3 x

TABLE 3 | HEALTH >>

Countries and areas	Use of improved drinking water sources (%) 2011			Use of improved sanitation facilities (%) 2011			Routine EPI vaccines financed by government (%) 2012	Immunization coverage (%) 2012							Newborns protected against tetanus^ (%)	Pneumonia		Diarrhoea	Malaria		
	total	urban	rural	total	urban	rural	2012	BCG	DPT1§	DPT3§	Polio3	MCV	HepB3	Hib3		Care-seeking for children with symptoms of pneumonia (%) 2008–2012*	Antibiotic treatment for children with symptoms of pneumonia (%)	Treatment with oral rehydration salts (ORS) (%) 2008–2012*	Antimalarial treatment for children with fever (%)	Children sleeping under ITNs (%) 2008–2012*	Households with at least one ITN (%)
Iran (Islamic Republic of)	95	98	90	100	100	99	100	99	99	99	99	98	98	–	95	76	63	61	–	–	–
Iraq	85	94	67	84	86	80	–	90	87	69	70	69	77	46	85	74	67	23	1 x	0 x	–
Ireland	100	100	100	99	100	98	–	42	98	95	95	92	95	95	–	–	–	–	–	–	–
Israel	100	100	100	100	100	100	–	–	96	94	95	96	97	93	–	–	–	–	–	–	–
Italy	100	100	100	–	–	–	–	–	99	97	97	90	97	96	–	–	–	–	–	–	–
Jamaica	93	97	89	80	78	82	100	96	99	99	99	93	99	99	80	75 x	52 x	40 x	–	–	–
Japan	100	100	100	100	100	100	–	95	99	98	99	96	–	–	–	–	–	–	–	–	–
Jordan	96	97	90	98	98	98	100	96	98	98	98	98	98	98	90	77	79 x	20	–	–	–
Kazakhstan	95	99	90	97	97	98	–	95	99	99	98	96	95	97	–	81	87	62	–	–	–
Kenya	61	83	54	29	31	29	–	84	89	83	82	93	83	83	73	56	50	39	23	47	56
Kiribati	66	87	50	39	51	30	–	95	94	94	92	91	94	94	–	81	51	62	–	–	–
Kuwait	99	99	99	100	100	100	–	97	99	98	98	99	98	98	95	–	–	–	–	–	–
Kyrgyzstan	89	96	85	93	94	93	–	98	96	96	94	98	96	96	–	62 x	45 x	35	–	–	–
Lao People's Democratic Republic	70	83	63	62	87	48	2	81	87	79	78	72	79	79	80	54	57	42	2	43	50
Latvia	98	100	96	–	–	–	100	97	95	92	92	90	91	91	–	–	–	–	–	–	–
Lebanon	100	100	100	–	100	–	100	–	84	82	77	80	84	82	–	74 x	–	44 x	–	–	–
Lesotho	78	91	73	26	32	24	–	95	93	83	91	85	83	83	83	66	–	51	–	–	–
Liberia	74	89	60	18	30	7	8	85	86	77	77	80	77	77	91	62 x	–	53 x	57	37	50
Libya	–	–	–	97	97	96	–	99	99	98	98	98	98	98	–	–	–	–	–	–	–
Liechtenstein	–	–	–	–	–	–	–	–	–	–	–	–	–	–	–	–	–	–	–	–	–
Lithuania	–	98	–	–	95	–	–	98	97	93	93	93	93	93	–	–	–	–	–	–	–
Luxembourg	100	100	100	100	100	100	–	–	99	99	99	96	95	99	–	–	–	–	–	–	–
Madagascar	48	78	34	14	19	11	4	78	96	86	86	69	86	86	78	42	–	17	20	77	80
Malawi	84	95	82	53	50	53	–	99	99	96	95	90	96	96	89	70	30 x	69	33	56	55
Malaysia	100	100	99	96	96	95	–	99	99	99	99	95	98	99	90	–	–	–	–	–	–
Maldives	99	100	98	98	97	98	–	99	99	99	99	98	99	–	95	22 x	–	57	–	–	–
Mali	65	89	53	22	35	14	12	89	85	74	74	59	74	74	89	42	44	11	32	46	77
Malta	100	100	100	100	100	100	100	–	99	99	99	93	93	99	–	–	–	–	–	–	–
Marshall Islands	94	93	97	76	84	55	2	97	97	80	80	78	80	67	–	–	–	38 x	–	–	–
Mauritania	50	52	48	27	51	9	15	95	95	80	80	75	80	80	80	43	30	19	20	19	46
Mauritius	100	100	100	91	92	90	100	99	99	98	98	99	98	98	95	–	–	–	–	–	–
Mexico	94	96	89	85	87	77	–	–	99	99	99	99	99	99	88	–	–	52	–	–	–
Micronesia (Federated States of)	89	95	88	55	83	47	–	78	97	81	81	91	82	66	–	–	–	–	–	–	–
Monaco	100	100	–	100	100	–	–	89	99	99	99	99	99	99	–	–	–	–	–	–	–
Mongolia	85	100	53	53	64	29	75	99	99	99	99	99	99	99	–	87	73	31	–	–	–
Montenegro	98	100	95	90	92	87	–	95	98	94	94	90	90	94	–	89 x	57 x	16 x	–	–	–
Morocco	82	98	61	70	83	52	–	99	99	99	99	99	99	99	89	70	–	23 x	–	–	–
Mozambique	47	78	33	19	41	9	30	91	91	76	73	82	76	76	83	50	12	55	30	36	51
Myanmar	84	94	79	77	84	74	56	87	89	85	87	84	38	–	93	69	34	61	–	11	–

TABLE 3 | HEALTH >>

TABLE 3

Countries and areas	Use of improved drinking water sources (%) 2011 total	urban	rural	Use of improved sanitation facilities (%) 2011 total	urban	rural	Routine EPI vaccines financed by government (%) 2012	BCG	DPT1	DPT3	Polio3	MCV	HepB3	Hib3	Newborns protected against tetanus (%)	Pneumonia Care-seeking for children with symptoms of pneumonia (%) 2008–2012*	Antibiotic treatment for children with symptoms of pneumonia (%)	Diarrhoea Treatment with oral rehydration salts (ORS) (%) 2008–2012*	Malaria Antimalarial treatment for children with fever (%) 2008–2012*	Children sleeping under ITNs (%)	Households with at least one ITN (%)
Namibia	93	99	90	32	57	17	100	90	89	84	84	76	84	84	83	53 x	–	63 x	20	34	54
Nauru	96	96	–	66	66	–	100	99	98	79	79	96	79	79	–	69 x	47 x	23 x	–	–	–
Nepal	88	91	87	35	50	32	45	96	90	90	90	86	90	90	82	50	7	39	1	–	–
Netherlands	100	100	100	100	100	100	100	–	99	97	97	96	–	97	–	–	–	–	–	–	–
New Zealand	100	100	100	–	–	–	–	–	94	93	93	92	93	93	–	–	–	–	–	–	–
Nicaragua	85	98	68	52	63	37	19	98	99	98	99	99	98	98	81	58 x	–	59 x	2 x	–	–
Niger	50	100	39	10	34	4	–	97	80	74	78	73	74	74	84	58	–	44	19	20	61
Nigeria	61	75	47	31	33	28	–	60	47	41	59	42	41	10	60	40	45	26	45	16	40
Niue	99	99	99	100	100	100	0	99	99	98	98	99	98	99	–	–	–	–	–	–	–
Norway	100	100	100	100	100	100	100	–	99	95	95	94	–	95	–	–	–	–	–	–	–
Oman	92	95	85	97	97	95	–	99	99	98	99	99	97	98	91	–	–	–	–	–	–
Pakistan	91	96	89	47	72	34	–	87	88	81	75	83	81	81	75	69 x	50 x	41 x	3 x	–	0 x
Palau	95	97	86	100	100	100	–	–	99	89	89	91	89	89	–	–	–	–	–	–	–
Panama	94	97	86	71	77	54	100	99	99	85	87	98	85	85	–	–	–	–	–	–	–
Papua New Guinea	40	89	33	19	57	13	81	84	85	63	70	67	63	63	70	63 x	–	–	–	–	–
Paraguay	–	99	–	–	–	–	100	93	96	87	83	91	87	87	85	–	–	–	–	–	–
Peru	85	91	66	72	81	38	100	95	99	95	94	94	95	95	85	59	48	31	–	–	–
Philippines	92	93	92	74	79	69	83	88	90	86	86	85	70	23	76	50	42	47	0	–	–
Poland	–	100	–	–	96	–	100	93	99	99	96	98	98	99	–	–	–	–	–	–	–
Portugal	100	100	100	100	100	100	100	99	99	98	98	97	98	98	–	–	–	–	–	–	–
Qatar	100	100	100	100	100	100	100	97	94	92	92	97	92	92	–	–	–	–	–	–	–
Republic of Korea	98	100	88	100	100	100	–	99	99	99	99	99	99	–	–	–	–	–	–	–	–
Republic of Moldova	96	99	93	86	89	83	–	99	97	92	92	91	94	90	–	60 x	–	33 x	–	–	–
Romania	–	99	–	–	–	–	100	99	96	89	92	94	96	92	–	–	–	–	–	–	–
Russian Federation	97	99	92	70	74	59	–	96	97	97	98	98	97	18	–	–	–	–	–	–	–
Rwanda	69	80	66	61	61	61	8	99	99	98	98	97	98	98	85	50	13	29	11	70	82
Saint Kitts and Nevis	98	98	98	–	–	–	100	95	99	97	98	95	98	98	–	–	–	–	–	–	–
Saint Lucia	94	98	93	65	70	64	–	99	99	98	98	99	98	98	–	–	–	–	–	–	–
Saint Vincent and the Grenadines	95	95	95	–	–	–	100	97	98	96	96	94	96	97	–	–	–	–	–	–	–
Samoa	98	97	98	92	93	91	100	96	99	92	95	85	99	99	–	–	–	68	–	–	–
San Marino	–	–	–	–	–	–	–	–	98	96	96	87	96	96	–	–	–	–	–	–	–
Sao Tome and Principe	97	99	94	34	41	23	8	99	98	96	96	92	96	96	–	75	60	49	8	56	61
Saudi Arabia	97	97	97	100	100	100	100	99	98	98	98	98	98	98	–	–	–	–	–	–	–
Senegal	73	93	59	51	68	39	27	97	97	92	89	84	92	92	91	50	–	22	8	35	63
Serbia	99	99	99	97	98	96	–	98	91	91	93	87	97	90	–	90	82	36	–	–	–
Seychelles	96	96	96	97	97	97	60	99	98	98	98	98	99	98	–	–	–	–	–	–	–
Sierra Leone	57	84	40	13	22	7	–	97	94	84	81	80	84	84	87	74	58	73	62	30	36
Singapore	100	100	–	100	100	–	–	99	98	96	96	95	96	–	–	–	–	–	–	–	–
Slovakia	100	100	100	100	100	100	–	90	99	99	99	99	99	99	–	–	–	–	–	–	–
Slovenia	100	100	99	100	100	100	–	–	98	96	96	95	–	96	–	–	–	–	–	–	–
Solomon Islands	79	93	76	29	81	15	46	83	94	90	86	85	90	90	85	73 x	23 x	38 x	19 x	40 x	49 x

TABLE 3 | HEALTH >>

Countries and areas	Use of improved drinking water sources (%) 2011			Use of improved sanitation facilities (%) 2011			Routine EPI vaccines financed by government (%) 2012	Immunization coverage (%)							Newborns protected against tetanus¹ (%)	Pneumonia		Diarrhoea	Malaria		
	total	urban	rural	total	urban	rural	2012	BCG	DPT1ᴮ	DPT3ᴮ	Polio3	MCV	HepB3	Hib3	2012	Care-seeking for children with symptoms of pneumonia (%) 2008–2012*	Antibiotic treatment for children with symptoms of pneumonia (%)	Treatment with oral rehydration salts (ORS) (%) 2008–2012*	Antimalarial treatment for children with fever (%) 2008–2012*	Children sleeping under ITNs (%)	Households with at least one ITN (%)
Somalia	30	66	7	24	52	6	0	37	52	42	47	46	–	–	64	13 x	32 x	13 x	8 x	11 x	12 x
South Africa	91	99	79	74	84	57	100	84	70	68	69	79	73	68	77	65 x	–	40 x	–	–	–
South Sudan	57	63	55	9	16	7	0	77	79	59	64	62	–	–	–	48	33	39	51	25	34
Spain	100	100	100	100	100	100	–	–	99	97	97	97	96	97	–	–	–	–	–	–	–
Sri Lanka	93	99	92	91	83	93	–	99	99	99	99	99	99	99	95	58 x	–	50 x	0 x	3 x	5 x
State of Palestine	82	82	82	94	95	93	–	98	98	97	98	98	98	97	–	65	71	31	–	–	–
Sudan	55	66	50	24	44	13	1	92	99	92	92	85	92	92	74	56	66	22	65	30 x	25
Suriname	92	97	81	83	90	66	–	–	94	84	84	73	84	84	93	76	71	42	0	43	61
Swaziland	72	93	67	57	63	55	–	98	97	95	92	88	95	95	86	58	61	57	2	2	10
Sweden	100	100	100	100	100	100	–	24	99	98	98	97	–	98	–	–	–	–	–	–	–
Switzerland	100	100	100	100	100	100	–	–	95	95	96	92	–	95	–	–	–	–	–	–	–
Syrian Arab Republic	90	93	87	95	96	94	100	82	68	45	52	61	43	45	94	77 x	71 x	50 x	–	–	–
Tajikistan	66	92	57	95	95	94	16	97	96	94	96	94	94	94	–	63	41 x	60	2 x	1 x	2 x
Thailand	96	97	95	93	89	96	100	99	99	99	99	98	98	–	91	84 x	65 x	57 x	–	–	–
The former Yugoslav Republic of Macedonia	100	100	99	91	97	83	–	94	97	96	97	97	96	96	–	93 x	74 x	62	–	–	–
Timor-Leste	69	93	60	39	68	27	26	71	69	67	66	62	67	–	81	71	45	71	6	41	41
Togo	59	90	40	11	26	3	25	97	94	84	84	72	84	84	81	32	41	11	34	57	57
Tonga	99	99	99	92	99	89	–	95	95	95	95	95	95	95	–	–	–	–	–	–	–
Trinidad and Tobago	94	98	93	92	92	92	100	–	97	92	91	85	92	92	–	74 x	34 x	–	–	–	–
Tunisia	96	100	89	90	97	75	100	99	99	97	97	96	97	97	96	60	57	65	–	–	–
Turkey	100	100	99	91	97	75	–	96	98	97	97	98	96	97	90	–	–	–	–	–	–
Turkmenistan	71	89	54	99	100	98	–	99	98	97	98	99	98	97	–	83 x	50 x	40 x	–	–	–
Tuvalu	98	98	97	83	86	80	–	99	99	97	97	98	97	97	–	–	–	44 x	–	–	–
Uganda	75	91	72	35	34	35	–	82	89	78	82	82	78	78	85	79	47	44	65	43	60
Ukraine	98	98	98	94	96	89	–	95	76	76	74	79	46	83	–	–	–	–	–	–	–
United Arab Emirates	100	100	100	98	98	95	–	94	94	94	94	94	94	94	–	–	–	–	–	–	–
United Kingdom	100	100	100	100	100	100	–	–	99	97	97	93	–	97	–	–	–	–	–	–	–
United Republic of Tanzania	53	79	44	12	24	7	25	99	99	92	90	97	92	92	88	71	–	44	54	72	91
United States	99	100	94	100	100	99	–	–	98	95	93	92	92	90	–	–	–	–	–	–	–
Uruguay	100	100	98	99	99	98	–	99	98	95	95	96	95	95	–	–	–	–	–	–	–
Uzbekistan	87	98	81	100	100	100	41	99	99	99	99	99	99	99	–	68 x	56 x	28 x	–	–	–
Vanuatu	91	98	88	58	65	55	–	81	78	68	67	52	59	68	75	–	–	23 x	53 x	56 x	68 x
Venezuela (Bolivarian Republic of)	–	–	–	–	–	–	100	96	90	81	73	87	81	81	50	72 x	–	38 x	–	–	–
Viet Nam	96	99	94	75	93	67	34	98	99	97	97	96	97	97	91	73	68	47	1	9	10
Yemen	55	72	47	53	93	34	15	64	89	82	89	71	82	82	66	44 x	38 x	33 x	–	–	–
Zambia	64	86	50	42	56	33	–	83	86	78	83	83	78	78	81	68 x	47 x	60 x	34	50	64
Zimbabwe	80	97	69	40	52	33	–	99	95	89	89	90	89	89	66	48	31	21	2	10	29

TABLE 3 | HEALTH

TABLE 3

Countries and areas	Use of improved drinking water sources (%) 2011			Use of improved sanitation facilities (%) 2011			Routine EPI vaccines financed by government (%) 2012	Immunization coverage (%) 2012							Newborns protected against tetanus λ (%)	Pneumonia		Diarrhoea	Malaria		
								BCG	DPT1β	DPT3β	Polio3	MCV	HepB3	Hib3		Care-seeking for children with symptoms of pneumonia (%) 2008–2012*	Antibiotic treatment for children with symptoms of pneumonia (%) 2008–2012*	Treament with oral rehydration salts (ORS) (%) 2008–2012*	Antimalarial treatment for children with fever (%) 2008–2012*	Children sleeping under ITNs (%) 2008–2012*	Households with at least one ITN (%) 2008–2012*
	total	urban	rural	total	urban	rural	2012	2012							2012						
SUMMARY INDICATORS#																					
Sub-Saharan Africa	63	84	51	30	42	24	25	81	80	71	76	72	70	64	74	46	39	31	37	36	52
Eastern and Southern Africa	63	87	52	34	53	26	34	86	88	78	80	82	76	76	76	52	26	38	33	45	58
West and Central Africa	63	82	49	27	35	22	17	76	71	63	71	62	63	51	71	41	45	26	38	28	48
Middle East and North Africa	87	93	77	83	93	69	83	93	94	89	90	88	90	55	86	70	63	35	–	–	–
South Asia	90	95	88	39	61	29	90	88	89	76	74	77	74	24	85	65	20	33	7	–	–
East Asia and Pacific	91	97	84	67	76	58	–	95	97	92	93	94	89	11	85 **	69 **	45 **	44 **	1 **	–	–
Latin America and Caribbean	94	97	82	81	86	63	97	96	96	93	93	95	92	91	85	55	–	48	–	–	–
CEE/CIS	94	98	88	83	84	82	–	96	95	94	95	95	91	71	–	–	–	–	–	–	–
Least developed countries	65	83	58	36	48	31	24	86	90	80	82	80	76	75	78	49	41	41	30	40	55
World	89	96	81	64	80	47	77**	89	91	83	84	84	79	45	81 **	59 **	34 **	35 **	19 **	–	–

For a complete list of countries and areas in the regions, subregions and country categories, see page 26.

DEFINITIONS OF THE INDICATORS

Population using improved drinking water sources – Percentage of the population using any of the following as their main drinking water source: drinking water supply piped into dwelling, plot, yard or neighbor's yard; public tap or standpipe; tube well or borehole; protected dug well; protected spring; rainwater; bottled water plus one of the previous sources as their secondary source.

Population using improved sanitation facilities – Percentage of the population using any of the following sanitation facilities, not shared with other households: flush or pour-flush latrine connected to a piped sewerage system, septic tank or pit latrine; ventilated improved pit latrine; pit latrine with a slab; covered pit; composting toilet.

Routine EPI vaccines financed by government – Percentage of vaccines that are routinely administered in a country to protect children and are financed by the national government (including loans).

EPI – Expanded programme on immunization: The immunizations in this programme include those against tuberculosis (TB); diphtheria, pertussis (whooping cough) and tetanus (DPT); polio; and measles, as well as vaccination of pregnant women to protect babies against neonatal tetanus. Other vaccines, e.g., against hepatitis B (HepB), Haemophilus influenzae type b (Hib) or yellow fever, may be included in the programme in some countries.

BCG – Percentage of live births who received bacille Calmette-Guérin (vaccine against tuberculosis).

DPT1 – Percentage of surviving infants who received their first dose of diphtheria, pertussis and tetanus vaccine.

DPT3 – Percentage of surviving infants who received three doses of diphtheria, pertussis and tetanus vaccine.

Polio3 – Percentage of surviving infants who received three doses of the polio vaccine.

MCV – Percentage of surviving infants who received the first dose of the measles-containing vaccine.

HepB3 – Percentage of surviving infants who received three doses of hepatitis B vaccine.

Hib3 – Percentage of surviving infants who received three doses of Haemophilus influenzae type b vaccine.

Newborns protected against tetanus – Percentage of newborns protected at birth against tetanus.

Care-seeking for children with symptoms of pneumonia – Percentage of children under age 5 with symptoms of pneumonia (cough and fast or difficult breathing due to a problem in the chest) in the two weeks preceding the survey for whom advice or treatment was sought from a health facility or provider.

Antibiotic treatment for children with symptoms of pneumonia – Percentage of children under age 5 with symptoms of pneumonia (cough and fast or difficult breathing due to a problem in the chest) in the two weeks preceding the survey who received antibiotics. NB: This indicator refers to antibiotic treatment among children whose caretakers report symptoms that are consistent with pneumonia. These children have not been medically diagnosed and thus this indicator should be interpreted with caution.

Diarrhoea treatment with oral rehydration salts (ORS) – Percentage of children under age 5 who had diarrhoea in the two weeks preceding the survey and who received oral rehydration salts (ORS packets or pre-packaged ORS fluids).

Antimalarial treatment for children with fever – Percentage of children under age 5 who were ill with fever in the two weeks preceding the survey and received any antimalarial medicine. NB: This indicator refers to antimalarial treatment among all febrile children, rather than among confirmed malaria cases, and thus should be interpreted with caution. For more information, please refer to <www.childinfo.org/malaria_maltreatment.php>.

Children sleeping under ITNs – Percentage of children under age 5 who slept under an insecticide-treated mosquito net the night prior to the survey.

Households with at least one ITN – Percentage of households with at least one insecticide-treated mosquito net.

MAIN DATA SOURCES

Use of improved drinking water sources and improved sanitation facilities – UNICEF and World Health Organization (WHO), Joint Monitoring Programme.

Routine EPI vaccines financed by government – As reported by governments on UNICEF and WHO Joint Reporting Form.

Immunization – UNICEF and WHO.

Care-seeking and treatment for symptoms of pneumonia – Demographic and Health Surveys (DHS), Multiple Indicator Cluster Surveys (MICS) and other national household surveys.

Diarrhoea treatment – DHS, MICS and other national household surveys.

Malaria prevention and treatment – DHS, MICS, Malaria Indicator Surveys (MIS) and other national household surveys.

NOTES

– Data not available.

x Data refer to years or periods other than those specified in the column heading. Such data are not included in the calculation of regional and global averages, with the exception of 2005–2006 data from India and 2007 data from Brazil. Estimates from data years prior to 2000 are not displayed.

β Coverage for DPT1 should be at least as high as DPT3. Discrepancies where DPT1 coverage is less than DPT3 reflect deficiencies in the data collection and reporting process. UNICEF and WHO are working with national and territorial systems to eliminate these discrepancies.

λ WHO and UNICEF have employed a model to calculate the percentage of births that can be considered as protected against tetanus because pregnant women were given two doses or more of tetanus toxoid (TT) vaccine. The model aims to improve the accuracy of this indicator by capturing or including other potential scenarios where women might be protected (e.g., women who receive doses of TT in supplemental immunization activities). A fuller explanation of the methodology can be found at <www.childinfo.org>.

* Data refer to the most recent year available during the period specified in the column heading.

** Excludes China.

TABLE 4 | HIV/AIDS >>

Countries and areas	Adult HIV prevalence (%) 2012 estimate	People of all ages living with HIV (thousands) 2012 estimate	low	high	Women living with HIV (thousands) 2012 estimate	Children living with HIV (thousands) 2012 estimate	HIV prevalence among young people (%) 2012 total	male	female	Comprehensive knowledge of HIV (%) 2008–2012* male	female	Condom use among young people with multiple partners (%) 2008–2012* male	female	Children orphaned by AIDS (thousands) 2012 estimate	Children orphaned due to all causes (thousands) 2012 estimate	Orphan school attendance ratio (%) 2008–2012*
Iraq	–	–	–	–	–	–	–	–	–	–	4	–	–	–	–	94
Ireland	–	–	6	10	–	–	–	–	–	–	–	–	–	–	–	–
Israel	–	–	7	11	–	–	–	–	–	–	–	–	–	–	–	–
Italy	–	–	110	140	–	–	–	–	–	–	–	–	–	–	–	–
Jamaica	1.7	28	23	34	9	–	0.7	0.9	0.5	36 y	51 y	76	49	–	–	–
Japan	–	–	7	11	–	–	–	–	–	–	–	–	–	–	–	–
Jordan	–	–	–	–	–	–	–	–	–	–	13 x,y	–	–	–	–	–
Kazakhstan	–	–	–	–	–	–	–	–	–	34	36	76	74	–	–	–
Kenya	6.1	1,600	1,600	1,700	820	200	2.7	1.8	3.6	55	47	67	37	1,000	2,600	–
Kiribati	–	–	–	–	–	–	–	–	–	49	44	30	2 p	–	–	–
Kuwait	–	–	–	–	–	–	–	–	–	–	–	–	–	–	–	–
Kyrgyzstan	0.3	9	6	13	2	–	0.1	0.2	<0.1	–	20 x	76	–	–	–	–
Lao People's Democratic Republic	0.3	12	10	13	5	–	0.2	0.2	0.2	28	24	–	–	–	–	80
Latvia	–	–	6	12	–	–	–	–	–	–	–	–	–	–	–	–
Lebanon	–	–	–	–	–	–	–	–	–	–	–	–	–	–	–	–
Lesotho	23.1	360	340	380	190	38	8.2	5.8	10.7	29	39	60	45	150	220	98
Liberia	0.9	22	19	26	11	4	<0.1	<0.1	0.1	27 x	21 x	28 x	16 x	23	190	85 x
Libya	–	–	–	–	–	–	–	–	–	–	–	–	–	–	–	–
Liechtenstein	–	–	–	–	–	–	–	–	–	–	–	–	–	–	–	–
Lithuania	–	–	<1	2	–	–	–	–	–	–	–	–	–	–	–	–
Luxembourg	–	–	<1	1	–	–	–	–	–	–	–	–	–	–	–	–
Madagascar	0.5	59	49	69	23	–	0.3	0.3	0.3	26	23	9	7	–	–	74
Malawi	10.8	1,100	1,100	1,200	560	180	3.6	2.7	4.5	45	42	41	31	770	1,300	97
Malaysia	0.4	82	60	110	12	–	0.1	0.1	<0.1	–	–	–	–	–	–	–
Maldives	<0.1	<0.1	<0.1	<0.1	<0.1	–	<0.1	<0.1	<0.1	–	35 y	–	–	–	–	–
Mali	0.9	100	79	120	50	–	0.2	0.2	0.3	–	15	38	8 p	–	–	92
Malta	–	–	<0.5	<0.5	–	–	–	–	–	–	–	–	–	–	–	–
Marshall Islands	–	–	–	–	–	–	–	–	–	39 x	27 x	23 x,p	9 x,p	–	–	–
Mauritania	0.4	10	8	15	5	–	0.2	0.1	0.2	–	6	–	–	–	–	100 p
Mauritius	1.2	11	10	12	3	–	0.3	0.3	0.3	–	–	–	–	–	–	–
Mexico	0.2	170	150	210	38	–	0.1	0.1	<0.1	–	–	–	–	–	–	–
Micronesia (Federated States of)	–	–	–	–	–	–	–	–	–	–	–	–	–	–	–	–
Monaco	–	–	–	–	–	–	–	–	–	–	–	–	–	–	–	–
Mongolia	<0.1	1	1	1	<1	–	<0.1	<0.1	<0.1	29	32	69	–	–	–	102
Montenegro	–	–	–	–	–	–	–	–	–	–	–	–	–	–	–	–
Morocco	0.1	30	22	40	11	–	0.1	0.1	<0.1	–	–	–	–	–	–	–
Mozambique	11.1	1,600	1,400	1,800	810	180	4.7	2.8	6.6	52	30	41	38	740	2,000	91
Myanmar	0.6	200	170	220	63	–	0.1	<0.1	0.1	–	32	–	–	–	–	–
Namibia	13.3	220	190	250	120	18	3.2	2.2	4.1	62 x	65 x	82 x	74 x	76	130	100 x
Nauru	–	–	–	–	–	–	–	–	–	10 x	13 x	17 x,p	8 x,p	–	–	–

TABLE 4 | HIV/AIDS >>

TABLE 4

Countries and areas	Adult HIV prevalence (%) 2012	People of all ages living with HIV (thousands) 2012			Mother-to-child transmission Women living with HIV (thousands) 2012	Paediatric infections Children living with HIV (thousands) 2012	Prevention among young people (aged 15–24)							Orphans		
							HIV prevalence among young people (%) 2012			Comprehensive knowledge of HIV (%) 2008–2012*		Condom use among young people with multiple partners (%) 2008–2012*		Children orphaned by AIDS (thousands) 2012	Children orphaned due to all causes (thousands) 2012	Orphan school attendance ratio (%) 2008–2012*
	estimate	estimate	low	high	estimate	estimate	total	male	female	male	female	male	female	estimate	estimate	2008–2012*
Nepal	0.3	49	39	65	14	–	<0.1	<0.1	<0.1	34	26	45	–	–	–	72 p
Netherlands	–	–	20	34	–	–	–	–	–	–	–	–	–	–	–	–
New Zealand	–	–	2	4	–	–	–	–	–	–	–	–	–	–	–	–
Nicaragua	0.3	10	7	15	3	–	0.2	0.3	0.2	–	–	–	–	–	–	–
Niger	0.5	46	39	56	20	–	0.1	<0.1	0.1	16 x	13 x	–	–	–	–	67 x
Nigeria	3.1	3,400	3,100	3,800	1,700	430	1.0	0.7	1.3	–	23	–	47	2,200	11,500	100
Niue	–	–	–	–	–	–	–	–	–	–	–	–	–	–	–	–
Norway	–	–	4	6	–	–	–	–	–	–	–	–	–	–	–	–
Oman	–	–	3	6	–	–	–	–	–	–	–	–	–	–	–	–
Pakistan	<0.1	87	50	160	24	–	<0.1	<0.1	<0.1	–	3 x	–	–	–	–	–
Palau	–	–	–	–	–	–	–	–	–	–	–	–	–	–	–	–
Panama	0.7	17	12	22	5	–	0.3	0.4	0.3	–	–	–	–	–	–	–
Papua New Guinea	0.5	25	20	31	12	3	<0.1	<0.1	0.1	–	–	–	–	13	320	–
Paraguay	0.3	13	7	24	6	–	0.2	0.2	0.3	–	–	–	51	–	–	–
Peru	0.4	76	36	230	23	–	0.2	0.2	0.2	–	19 x	–	38 x,p	–	–	–
Philippines	<0.1	15	11	23	2	–	<0.1	<0.1	<0.1	–	21	–	–	–	–	–
Poland	–	–	25	46	–	–	–	–	–	–	–	–	–	–	–	–
Portugal	–	–	38	62	–	–	–	–	–	–	–	–	–	–	–	–
Qatar	–	–	–	–	–	–	–	–	–	–	–	–	–	–	–	–
Republic of Korea	–	–	12	20	–	–	–	–	–	–	–	–	–	–	–	–
Republic of Moldova	0.7	19	15	23	7	–	0.2	0.2	0.2	39 y	42 y	–	–	–	–	–
Romania	–	–	14	21	–	–	–	–	–	–	–	–	–	–	–	–
Russian Federation	–	–	–	–	–	–	–	–	–	–	–	–	–	–	–	–
Rwanda	2.9	210	190	230	100	27	1.1	1.0	1.3	47	53	–	–	120	590	91
Saint Kitts and Nevis	–	–	–	–	–	–	–	–	–	50	53	–	–	–	–	–
Saint Lucia	–	–	–	–	–	–	–	–	–	–	–	–	–	–	–	–
Saint Vincent and the Grenadines	–	–	–	–	–	–	–	–	–	–	–	–	–	–	–	–
Samoa	–	–	–	–	–	–	–	–	–	6	3	–	–	–	–	–
San Marino	–	–	–	–	–	–	–	–	–	–	–	–	–	–	–	–
Sao Tome and Principe	1.0	1	1	2	<1	–	0.3	0.3	0.4	43	43	50	–	–	–	–
Saudi Arabia	–	–	–	–	–	–	–	–	–	–	–	–	–	–	–	–
Senegal	0.5	43	35	52	24	–	0.2	0.1	0.3	31	29	–	–	–	–	97
Serbia	–	–	2	6	–	–	–	–	–	48	54	63	65	–	–	–
Seychelles	–	–	–	–	–	–	–	–	–	–	–	–	–	–	–	–
Sierra Leone	1.5	58	42	82	31	6	0.6	0.3	1.0	–	23	–	12	26	370	88
Singapore	–	–	3	5	–	–	–	–	–	–	–	–	–	–	–	–
Slovakia	–	–	<0.5	<1	–	–	–	–	–	–	–	–	–	–	–	–
Slovenia	–	–	<0.5	<1	–	–	–	–	–	–	–	–	–	–	–	–
Solomon Islands	–	–	–	–	–	–	–	–	–	35 x	29 x	39 x	18 x	–	–	–
Somalia	0.5	31	21	47	13	–	0.2	0.2	0.2	–	4 x	–	–	–	–	78 x
South Africa	17.9	6,100	5,800	6,400	3,400	410	8.9	3.9	13.9	–	–	–	–	2,500	4,000	101

TABLE 4 | HIV/AIDS >>

Countries and areas	Adult HIV prevalence (%) 2012 estimate	People of all ages living with HIV (thousands) 2012			Mother-to-child transmission Women living with HIV (thousands) 2012 estimate	Paediatric infections Children living with HIV (thousands) 2012 estimate	Prevention among young people (aged 15–24) HIV prevalence among young people (%) 2012			Comprehensive knowledge of HIV (%) 2008–2012*		Condom use among young people with multiple partners (%) 2008–2012*		Orphans Children orphaned by AIDS (thousands) 2012 estimate	Children orphaned due to all causes (thousands) 2012 estimate	Orphan school attendance ratio (%) 2008–2012*
		estimate	low	high			total	male	female	male	female	male	female			
South Sudan	2.7	150	100	230	78	19	0.9	0.6	1.2	–	10	–	7	110	470	78
Spain	–	–	140	170	–	–	–	–	–	–	–	–	–	–	–	–
Sri Lanka	<0.1	3	2	5	<1	–	<0.1	<0.1	<0.1	–	–	–	–	–	–	–
State of Palestine	–	–	–	–	–	–	–	–	–	–	7	–	–	–	–	–
Sudan	–	–	–	–	–	–	–	–	–	–	5	–	–	–	–	–
Suriname	1.1	4	4	4	2	–	0.5	0.4	0.7	–	42	–	39	–	–	–
Swaziland	26.5	210	200	230	110	22	15.1	10.3	20.0	54	58	85	69	78	120	100
Sweden	–	–	7	13	–	–	–	–	–	–	–	–	–	–	–	–
Switzerland	–	–	16	27	–	–	–	–	–	–	–	–	–	–	–	–
Syrian Arab Republic	–	–	–	–	–	–	–	–	–	–	7 x	–	–	–	–	–
Tajikistan	0.3	12	7	24	4	–	0.1	0.1	0.1	13	14	–	–	–	–	–
Thailand	1.1	440	400	480	200	–	0.3	0.3	0.3	–	46 x	–	–	–	–	93 x
The former Yugoslav Republic of Macedonia	–	–	–	–	–	–	–	–	–	–	27 x	–	–	–	–	–
Timor-Leste	–	–	–	–	–	–	–	–	–	20	12	–	–	–	–	75
Togo	2.9	130	110	150	65	17	0.7	0.5	0.9	42	33	54	39	90	360	86
Tonga	–	–	–	–	–	–	–	–	–	–	–	–	–	–	–	–
Trinidad and Tobago	–	–	13	15	–	–	–	–	–	–	54 x	–	67 x	–	–	–
Tunisia	<0.1	2	1	4	<1	–	<0.1	<0.1	<0.1	–	20	–	–	–	–	–
Turkey	–	–	4	8	–	–	–	–	–	–	–	–	–	–	–	–
Turkmenistan	–	–	–	–	–	–	–	–	–	–	5 x	–	–	–	–	–
Tuvalu	–	–	–	–	–	–	–	–	–	61 x	39 x	–	–	–	–	–
Uganda	7.2	1,500	1,400	1,800	780	190	3.1	2.3	4.0	40	38	47	–	1,000	2,700	87
Ukraine	0.9	230	190	270	95	–	0.4	0.4	0.5	43 x	45 x	64 x	63 x	–	–	–
United Arab Emirates	–	–	–	–	–	–	–	–	–	–	–	–	–	–	–	–
United Kingdom	–	–	76	120	–	–	–	–	–	–	–	–	–	–	–	–
United Republic of Tanzania	5.1	1,500	1,300	1,600	730	230	2.7	1.8	3.6	43	48	41	34	1,200	3,100	95
United States	–	–	920	1,800	–	–	–	–	–	–	–	–	–	–	–	–
Uruguay	0.7	13	10	19	3	–	0.3	0.5	0.2	–	–	–	–	–	–	–
Uzbekistan	0.1	30	23	40	7	–	<0.1	<0.1	<0.1	–	31 x	–	–	–	–	–
Vanuatu	–	–	–	–	–	–	–	–	–	–	15 x	–	–	–	–	–
Venezuela (Bolivarian Republic of)	0.6	110	74	160	38	–	0.3	0.3	0.3	–	–	–	–	–	–	–
Viet Nam	0.4	260	70	490	71	–	0.2	0.2	0.1	–	51	–	–	–	–	–
Yemen	0.1	19	9	47	8	–	0.1	0.1	0.1	–	2 x,y	–	–	–	–	–
Zambia	12.7	1,100	1,000	1,200	490	160	4.1	3.5	4.6	41	38	43 x	42 x,p	670	1,400	92
Zimbabwe	14.7	1,400	1,300	1,500	700	180	5.1	3.9	6.3	47	52	51	39 p	890	1,200	95

TABLE 4

TABLE 4 | HIV/AIDS

Countries and areas	Adult HIV prevalence (%) 2012 estimate	People of all ages living with HIV (thousands) 2012			Mother-to-child transmission Women living with HIV (thousands) 2012 estimate	Paediatric infections Children living with HIV (thousands) 2012 estimate	Prevention among young people (aged 15–24)							Orphans		
		estimate	low	high			HIV prevalence among young people (%) 2012			Comprehensive knowledge of HIV (%) 2008–2012*		Condom use among young people with multiple partners (%) 2008–2012*		Children orphaned by AIDS (thousands) 2012 estimate	Children orphaned due to all causes (thousands) 2012 estimate	Orphan school attendance ratio (%) 2008–2012*
							total	male	female	male	female	male	female			
SUMMARY INDICATORS#																
Sub-Saharan Africa	4.5	25,100	23,500	26,700	12,900	3,000	1.9	1.2	2.4	39	28	–	35	15,100	56,000	91
Eastern and Southern Africa	6.9	18,600	17,600	19,600	9,600	2,100	3.2	2.0	4.0	41	35	46	–	10,600	27,900	90
West and Central Africa	2.3	6,500	5,800	7,100	3,300	860	0.7	0.5	1.0	–	22	–	38	4,400	28,100	92
Middle East and North Africa	0.1	230	170	340	89	14	<0.1	<0.1	<0.1	–	10	–	–	100	5,500	–
South Asia	<0.1	2,200	1,800	2,800	790	150	0.3	0.3	<0.1	34	19	33	17	610	40,800	72
East Asia and Pacific	0.2	2,600	1,700	3,600	880	63	0.1	0.1	0.1	–	23 **	–	–	780	26,900	–
Latin America and Caribbean	0.5	1,700	1,400	2,200	550	56	0.2	0.2	0.2	–	–	–	–	830	7,800	–
CEE/CIS	0.5	1,300	1,100	1,700	440	19	0.2	0.2	0.2	–	–	–	–	260	6,200	–
Least developed countries	1.7	11,000	10,200	12,000	5,400	1,500	0.9	0.6	0.9	31	24	–	–	7,600	42,900	88
World	0.8	35,300	32,200	38,800	16,100	3,300	0.4	0.3	0.5	–	22 **	–	–	17,800	150,000	–

For a complete list of countries and areas in the regions, subregions and country categories, see page 26.

DEFINITIONS OF THE INDICATORS

Adult HIV prevalence – Estimated percentage of adults (aged 15–49) living with HIV as of 2012.

People living with HIV – Estimated number of people (all ages) living with HIV as of 2012.

Women living with HIV – Estimated number of women (aged 15+) living with HIV as of 2012.

Children living with HIV – Estimated number of children (aged 0–14) living with HIV as of 2012.

HIV prevalence among young people – Estimated percentage of young men and women (aged 15–24) living with HIV as of 2012.

Comprehensive knowledge of HIV – Percentage of young men and women (aged 15–24) who correctly identify the two major ways of preventing the sexual transmission of HIV (using condoms and limiting sex to one faithful, uninfected partner), who reject the two most common local misconceptions about HIV transmission and who know that a healthy-looking person can be HIV-positive.

Condom use among young people with multiple partners – The percentage of young people aged 15–24 who reported both having had more than one sexual partner in the past 12 months and using a condom the last time they had sex with a partner.

Children orphaned by AIDS – Estimated number of children (aged 0–17) who have lost one or both parents to AIDS as of 2012.

Children orphaned due to all causes – Estimated number of children (aged 0–17) who have lost one or both parents due to any cause as of 2012.

Orphan school attendance ratio – Percentage of children (aged 10–14) who have lost both biological parents and who are currently attending school as a percentage of non-orphaned children of the same age who live with at least one parent and who are attending school.

MAIN DATA SOURCES

Estimated adult HIV prevalence – UNAIDS, *Report on the Global AIDS Epidemic*, 2013.

Estimated number of people living with HIV – UNAIDS, *Report on the Global AIDS Epidemic*, 2013.

Estimated number of women living with HIV – UNAIDS, *Report on the Global AIDS Epidemic*, 2013.

Estimated number of children living with HIV – UNAIDS, *Report on the Global AIDS Epidemic*, 2013.

HIV prevalence among young people – UNAIDS, *Report on the Global AIDS Epidemic*, 2013.

Comprehensive knowledge of HIV – AIDS Indicator Surveys (AIS), Demographic and Health Surveys (DHS), Multiple Indicator Cluster Surveys (MICS) and other national household surveys; HIV/AIDS Survey Indicators Database, <www.measuredhs.com/hivdata>.

Condom use among young people with multiple partners – AIS, DHS, MICS and other national household surveys; HIV/AIDS Survey Indicators Database, <www.measuredhs.com/hivdata>.

Children orphaned by AIDS – UNAIDS, *Report on the Global AIDS Epidemic*, 2013.

Children orphaned due to all causes – UNAIDS, *Report on the Global AIDS Epidemic*, 2013.

Orphan school attendance ratio – AIS, DHS, MICS and other national household surveys; HIV/AIDS Survey Indicators Database, <www.measuredhs.com/hivdata>.

NOTES

– Data not available.

x Data refer to years or periods other than those specified in the column heading. Such data are not included in the calculation of regional and global averages, with the exception of 2005–2006 data from India. Estimates from data years prior to 2000 are not displayed.

y Data differ from the standard definition or refer to only part of a country. If they fall within the noted reference period, such data are included in the calculation of regional and global averages.

p Based on small denominators (typically 25–49 unweighted cases).

* Data refer to the most recent year available during the period specified in the column heading.

** Excludes China.

TABLE 5 | EDUCATION

Countries and areas	Youth (15–24 years) literacy rate (%) 2008–2012*		Number per 100 population 2012		Pre-primary school participation Gross enrolment ratio (%) 2008–2012*		Primary school participation Gross enrolment ratio (%) 2008–2012*		Net enrolment ratio (%) 2008–2011*		Net attendance ratio (%) 2008–2012*		Survival rate to last primary grade (%) 2008–2011* / 2008–2012*		Secondary school participation Net enrolment ratio (%) 2008–2011*		Net attendance ratio (%) 2008–2012*	
	male	female	mobile phones	Internet users	male	female	male	female	male	female	male	female	admin. data	survey data	male	female	male	female
Afghanistan	–	–	54	5	–	–	114	81	–	–	63	46	–	84	–	–	43	21
Albania	99	99	108	55	58	57	–	–	–	–	90	91	98	100	–	–	84	82
Algeria	94 x	89 x	103	15	74	75	112	106	98	97	97 x	96 x	95	93 x	–	–	57 x	65 x
Andorra	–	–	74	86	103	99	–	–	–	–	–	–	–	–	72	74	–	–
Angola	80	66	49	17	103	105	137	112	93	78	77	75	32	83 x	15	12	21	17
Antigua and Barbuda	–	–	199	84	77	84	102	95	87	85	–	–	–	–	85	85	–	–
Argentina	99	99	143	56	74	76	119	117	–	–	99	99	95	–	80	88	87 y	91 y
Armenia	100	100	107	39	41	47	101	104	–	–	97	97	96	100 x	85	88	67	76
Australia	–	–	106	82	79	78	105	105	97	98	–	–	–	–	85	86	–	–
Austria	–	–	161	81	100	100	99	98	–	–	–	–	99	–	–	–	–	–
Azerbaijan	100	100	107	54	27	26	96	95	88	86	74 x	72 x	97	100 x	87	85	83 x	82 x
Bahamas	–	–	72	72	–	–	113	115	–	–	–	–	89	–	82	88	–	–
Bahrain	99	98	156	88	–	–	–	–	–	–	86 x	87 x	98	99 x	–	–	77 x	85 x
Bangladesh	77	80	64	6	27	26	–	–	–	–	77	81	66	94 x	43	51	43	47
Barbados	–	–	126	73	105	103	126	125	–	–	–	–	93	–	83	95	–	–
Belarus	100	100	112	47	104	101	98	98	–	–	93	90	98	100	–	–	87	92
Belgium	–	–	119	82	120	119	104	104	99	99	–	–	97	–	–	–	–	–
Belize	–	–	51	25	47	47	126	116	–	–	94	95	91	97	–	–	50	61
Benin	55 x	31 x	90	4	20	20	137	120	–	–	72 y	68 y	56	89 x	–	–	49 y	40 y
Bhutan	80 x	68 x	75	25	5	5	111	112	88	91	91	93	95	94	50	57	54	56
Bolivia (Plurinational State of)	100	99	93	34	45	46	101	99	91	91	97	97	85	96	70	70	78	75
Bosnia and Herzegovina	100	100	90	65	18	17	90	91	89	91	98	98	81	100	–	–	90	93
Botswana	93	97	150	12	19	19	112	108	87	88	86 x	88 x	93	–	57	66	36 x	44 x
Brazil	97	98	125	50	–	–	–	–	–	–	95 x	95 x	–	88 x	–	–	74 x	80 x
Brunei Darussalam	100	100	114	60	87	89	104	106	–	–	–	–	97	–	98	100	–	–
Bulgaria	98	98	146	55	80	79	103	102	99	100	–	–	97	–	84	82	–	–
Burkina Faso	47 x	33 x	57	4	3	3	82	76	65	61	54	50	69	89 x	19	16	21	17
Burundi	90	88	26	1	7	7	164	165	–	–	73	74	51	82 x	20	17	12	11
Cabo Verde	98	99	84	35	75	74	114	105	95	92	–	–	89	–	–	–	–	–
Cambodia	88	86	132	5	13	14	129	122	–	–	85 y	83 y	61	92 x	39	36	46	45
Cameroon	85	76	64	6	30	30	128	111	100	87	87	82	57	87 x	44	39	53	49
Canada	–	–	76	87	73	72	100	100	–	–	–	–	–	–	–	–	–	–
Central African Republic	72	59	23	3	6	6	109	79	78	60	78	68	46	81	18	10	23	15
Chad	54	42	35	2	2	2	115	86	–	–	55	48	49	89	–	–	22	12
Chile	99	99	138	61	114	110	103	100	93	93	–	–	98	–	83	87	–	–
China	100	100	81	42	61	62	111	115	100 z	100 z	–	–	99 z	–	–	–	–	–
Colombia	98	99	103	49	49	49	114	110	90	90	90	92	87	95	73	79	73	79
Comoros	86	86	32	6	22	21	106	90	–	–	31 x	31 x	–	19 x	–	–	10 x	11 x
Congo	–	–	101	6	13	13	119	113	95	90	86 x	87 x	–	93 x	–	–	39 x	40 x
Cook Islands	–	–	–	–	180	181	110	113	–	–	–	–	–	–	72	84	–	–

TABLE 5 | EDUCATION >>

TABLE 5

Countries and areas	Youth (15–24 years) literacy rate (%) 2008–2012* male	female	Number per 100 population 2012 mobile phones	Internet users	Pre-primary school participation Gross enrolment ratio (%) 2008–2012* male	female	Primary school participation Gross enrolment ratio (%) 2008–2012* male	female	Net enrolment ratio (%) 2008–2011* male	female	Net attendance ratio (%) 2008–2012* male	female	Survival rate to last primary grade (%) 2008–2011* admin. data	2008–2012* survey data	Secondary school participation Net enrolment ratio (%) 2008–2011* male	female	Net attendance ratio (%) 2008–2012* male	female
Costa Rica	98	99	128	48	73	73	108	107	–	–	96	96	91	–	–	–	59 x	65 x
Côte d'Ivoire	72	63	96	2	4	4	96	80	67	56	72 y	64 y	61	90 x	–	–	33 y	25 y
Croatia	100	100	113	63	62	61	93	93	95	97	–	–	99	–	88	94	–	–
Cuba	100	100	15	26	104	104	102	100	98	98	–	–	95	–	87	87	–	–
Cyprus	100	100	98	61	79	79	102	102	99	99	–	–	–	–	88	90	–	–
Czech Republic	–	–	123	75	112	109	105	105	–	–	–	–	99	–	–	–	–	–
Democratic People's Republic of Korea	100	100	7	–	–	–	–	–	–	–	99	99	–	–	–	–	98	98
Democratic Republic of the Congo	79 x	53 x	28	2	4	4	103	89	–	–	78	72	54	75	–	–	35	28
Denmark	–	–	118	93	101	98	99	99	95	97	–	–	99	–	88	91	–	–
Djibouti	–	–	23	8	4	4	62	56	55	49	67 x	66 x	64	92 x	28	20	45 x	37 x
Dominica	–	–	162	55	105	116	119	118	–	–	–	–	91	–	80	89	–	–
Dominican Republic	96	98	89	45	37	38	112	102	93	91	96 y	97 y	75	78 x	58	67	51 y	65 y
Ecuador	99	99	111	35	149	152	121	120	–	–	96 y	96 y	92	–	73	75	78 y	80 y
Egypt	92	86	115	44	27	25	105	99	–	–	89 y	87 y	99	99	–	–	70	70
El Salvador	96	96	138	26	63	64	117	112	96	96	–	–	84	–	59	61	–	–
Equatorial Guinea	98	98	68	14	74	74	88	86	59	59	61 x	60 x	55	–	–	–	23 x	22 x
Eritrea	93	88	5	1	15	15	51	42	40	34	69 x	64 x	69	–	32	25	23 x	21 x
Estonia	100	100	155	79	88	87	99	98	98	97	–	–	98	–	91	93	–	–
Ethiopia	63 x	47 x	24	1	6	5	111	101	90	84	64	65	41	84 x	–	–	16	16
Fiji	–	–	98	34	17	19	105	105	–	–	–	–	91	–	81	88	–	–
Finland	–	–	173	91	69	69	99	99	98	98	–	–	100	–	93	94	–	–
France	–	–	98	83	109	108	110	109	–	–	–	–	–	–	98	100	–	–
Gabon	99	97	187	9	41	43	184	179	–	–	87 y	87 y	–	–	–	–	50 y	58 y
Gambia	73	64	84	12	30	31	79	82	68	71	61	64	63	95	–	–	34	34
Georgia	100	100	109	46	–	–	105	108	–	–	95	96	96	98 x	–	–	85	88
Germany	–	–	131	84	114	113	103	102	–	–	–	–	96	–	–	–	–	–
Ghana	88	83	100	17	112	116	107	107	84	85	72	74	72	100	48	44	40	44
Greece	99	99	117	56	74	75	101	101	99	99	–	–	–	–	98	98	–	–
Grenada	–	–	122	42	95	102	105	102	96	99	–	–	–	–	–	–	–	–
Guatemala	89	86	137	16	66	67	118	114	99	97	–	–	68	–	48	44	–	–
Guinea	38	22	46	1	17	17	105	91	89	78	55 x	48 x	59	96 x	40	26	27 x	17 x
Guinea-Bissau	79	67	69	3	7	7	127	119	77	73	69	65	–	79	–	–	27	20
Guyana	92	94	72	34	84	88	85	89	81	85	94	96	83	100	71	81	70	79
Haiti	74 x	70 x	59	11	–	–	–	–	–	–	77 y	78 y	–	85 x	–	–	22 y	29 y
Holy See	–	–	–	–	–	–	–	–	–	–	–	–	–	–	–	–	–	–
Honduras	95	97	93	18	44	45	114	114	97	98	93 y	93 y	75	–	–	–	43 y	52 y
Hungary	99	99	116	72	88	87	101	101	97	98	–	–	98	–	92	92	–	–
Iceland	–	–	105	96	98	96	99	99	99	99	–	–	98	–	88	89	–	–
India	88 x	74 x	69	13	54	56	112	112	99	99	85 x	81 x	–	95 x	–	–	59 x	49 x

TABLE 5 | EDUCATION >>

Countries and areas	Youth (15–24 years) literacy rate (%) 2008–2012*		Number per 100 population 2012		Pre-primary school participation Gross enrolment ratio (%) 2008–2012*		Primary school participation Gross enrolment ratio (%) 2008–2012*		Net enrolment ratio (%) 2008–2011*		Net attendance ratio (%) 2008–2012*		Survival rate to last primary grade (%) 2008–2011* / 2008–2012*		Secondary school participation Net enrolment ratio (%) 2008–2011*		Net attendance ratio (%) 2008–2012*	
	male	female	mobile phones	Internet users	male	female	male	female	male	female	male	female	admin. data	survey data	male	female	male	female
Indonesia	99	99	115	15	45	46	117	119	98	100	92 y	90 y	88	–	74	74	57 x,y	59 x,y
Iran (Islamic Republic of)	99	99	77	26	41	45	108	107	–	–	96	97	98	97	82	80	–	–
Iraq	84	81	79	7	–	–	–	–	–	–	93	87	–	96	–	–	53	45
Ireland	–	–	107	79	68	66	108	107	–	–	–	–	–	–	98	100	–	–
Israel	–	–	120	73	98	97	104	105	97	98	–	–	99	–	97	100	–	–
Italy	100	100	159	58	100	96	102	101	100	99	–	–	100	–	94	94	–	–
Jamaica	93	98	97	47	113	113	91	87	83	81	97 x	98 x	95	99 x	80	87	89 x	93 x
Japan	–	–	109	79	–	–	103	103	–	–	–	–	100	–	99	100	–	–
Jordan	99	99	139	41	33	31	92	92	91	91	99 x	99 x	–	–	83	88	85 x	89 x
Kazakhstan	100	100	175	53	48	47	111	111	99	100	99	99	100	100	90	89	96	96
Kenya	83 x	82 x	72	32	52	52	115	112	84	85	72	75	–	96	52	48	40	42
Kiribati	–	–	16	11	–	–	111	115	–	–	83 y	85 y	–	–	–	–	55 y	63 y
Kuwait	99	99	191	79	81	83	104	107	97	100	–	–	96	–	86	93	–	–
Kyrgyzstan	100	100	125	22	21	21	102	100	96	96	91 x	93 x	95	99 x	81	80	88 x	91 x
Lao People's Democratic Republic	89 x	79 x	102	11	23	24	130	122	98	96	85	85	68	95	43	39	45	45
Latvia	100	100	103	74	87	84	100	100	95	96	–	–	93	–	83	83	–	–
Lebanon	98 x	99 x	93	61	83	82	109	106	97	97	98	98	90	93 x	72	80	77	85
Lesotho	74	92	59	5	–	–	105	101	74	76	87	91	66	84 x	–	–	26	40
Liberia	63 x	37 x	56	4	–	–	108	98	42	40	32 x	28 x	68	–	–	–	14 x	14 x
Libya	100	100	148	20	–	–	–	–	–	–	–	–	–	–	–	–	–	–
Liechtenstein	–	–	104	89	97	93	105	105	–	–	–	–	79	–	99	86	–	–
Lithuania	100	100	152	68	74	72	95	93	94	93	–	–	96	–	91	91	–	–
Luxembourg	–	–	145	92	90	89	96	98	94	96	–	–	–	–	85	88	–	–
Madagascar	66	64	39	2	9	9	150	147	–	–	78	80	40	89	23	24	27	28
Malawi	74	70	28	4	–	–	139	144	–	–	84	86	51	81 x	30	29	10	10
Malaysia	98	98	141	66	66	71	–	–	–	–	–	–	99	–	66	71	–	–
Maldives	99 x	99 x	173	39	113	117	105	103	94	95	82	84	–	99	–	–	52	63
Mali	56	39	90	2	3	3	87	76	72	63	60	55	75	90	36	25	36	23
Malta	97 x	99 x	129	70	119	115	101	101	93	94	–	–	80	–	82	80	–	–
Marshall Islands	–	–	–	10	45	47	102	101	–	–	–	–	83	–	–	–	–	–
Mauritania	72	66	111	5	–	–	98	104	73	77	60	62	81	78	–	–	26	22
Mauritius	96	98	113	41	102	102	–	–	–	–	–	–	97	–	–	–	–	–
Mexico	98	99	87	38	102	104	113	112	99	100	97 x	97 x	95	–	71	74	–	–
Micronesia (Federated States of)	–	–	25	26	–	–	–	–	–	–	–	–	–	–	–	–	–	–
Monaco	–	–	94	87	–	–	–	–	–	–	–	–	–	–	–	–	–	–
Mongolia	94	97	118	16	80	84	121	118	99	98	95	97	93	99	74	79	91	95
Montenegro	99	99	178	57	54	53	95	95	92	92	97 x	98 x	80	97 x	–	–	90 x	92 x
Morocco	89	74	120	55	73	53	117	110	97	96	91 x	88 x	88	–	–	–	39 x	36 x
Mozambique	80	57	33	5	–	–	116	105	92	88	77 y	77 y	31	60	18	17	25 y	22 y

TABLE 5 | EDUCATION >>

Countries and areas	Youth (15–24 years) literacy rate (%) 2008–2012*		Number per 100 population 2012		Pre-primary school participation Gross enrolment ratio (%) 2008–2012*		Primary school participation Gross enrolment ratio (%) 2008–2012*		Net enrolment ratio (%) 2008–2011*		Net attendance ratio (%) 2008–2012*		Survival rate to last primary grade (%)		Secondary school participation Net enrolment ratio (%) 2008–2011*		Net attendance ratio (%) 2008–2012*	
	male	female	mobile phones	Internet users	male	female	male	female	male	female	male	female	admin. data 2008–2011*	survey data 2008–2012*	male	female	male	female
Myanmar	96	96	11	1	10	10	126	126	–	–	90	91	75	93	49	52	58	59
Namibia	83 x	91 x	103	13	–	–	108	106	84	88	91 x	93 x	84	89 x	–	–	47 x	62 x
Nauru	–	–	66	–	96	93	90	96	–	–	83 x,y	94 x,y	–	–	–	–	52 x,y	69 x,y
Nepal	89	77	53	11	–	–	–	–	–	–	96	91	–	95 x	–	–	74	66
Netherlands	–	–	118	93	93	93	108	107	–	–	–	–	–	–	87	88	–	–
New Zealand	–	–	110	90	91	95	101	101	99	100	–	–	–	–	94	95	–	–
Nicaragua	85 x	89 x	90	14	55	56	119	116	93	95	71 y	70 y	–	56 x	43	49	35 x	47 x
Niger	52 x	23 x	32	1	6	6	77	64	70	57	44 x	31 x	69	88 x	14	10	13 x	8 x
Nigeria	76	58	68	33	14	14	87	79	60	55	72	68	80	97	–	–	54	54
Niue	–	–	–	82	–	–	–	–	–	–	–	–	–	–	–	–	–	–
Norway	–	–	116	95	100	98	99	99	99	99	–	–	–	99	94	94	–	–
Oman	97	98	182	60	54	53	105	103	98	97	–	–	–	–	94	94	–	–
Pakistan	79	61	67	10	–	–	101	83	79	65	70 x	62 x	52	–	40	29	35 x	29 x
Palau	–	–	83	–	–	–	–	–	–	–	–	–	–	–	–	–	–	–
Panama	98	97	187	45	66	67	109	106	98	97	–	–	94	–	65	71	–	–
Papua New Guinea	67	75	38	2	101	99	63	57	–	–	–	–	–	–	–	–	–	–
Paraguay	99	99	102	27	35	36	100	96	84	84	87	89	83	–	59	63	81 x	80 x
Peru	98 x	97 x	99	38	78	78	106	105	97	97	96	96	82	95	77	78	81 y	82 y
Philippines	97	98	107	36	51	52	107	105	88	90	88 x	89 x	76	90 x	56	67	55 x	70 x
Poland	100	100	133	65	71	72	99	98	97	97	–	–	99	–	90	92	–	–
Portugal	100	100	115	64	83	83	113	110	99	100	–	–	–	–	–	–	–	–
Qatar	96	98	134	88	56	58	106	104	95	95	–	–	–	–	87	96	–	–
Republic of Korea	–	–	110	84	118	119	106	105	99	98	–	–	99	–	96	95	–	–
Republic of Moldova	100	100	116	43	77	77	94	93	91	90	84 x	85 x	95	100 x	77	78	82 x	85 x
Romania	97	97	106	50	79	79	96	95	88	87	–	–	97	–	82	83	–	–
Russian Federation	100	100	184	53	91	89	99	99	95	96	–	–	96	–	–	–	–	–
Rwanda	77	78	50	8	11	12	140	143	–	–	86	89	37	76 x	–	–	15	16
Saint Kitts and Nevis	–	–	156	79	88	103	89	91	86	89	–	–	74	–	84	88	–	–
Saint Lucia	–	–	128	49	60	59	94	92	88	88	–	–	92	–	85	85	–	–
Saint Vincent and the Grenadines	–	–	124	48	79	80	109	101	–	–	–	–	–	–	84	86	–	–
Samoa	99	100	–	13	41	46	103	107	91	96	88 y	89 y	77	–	71	82	51 y	70 y
San Marino	–	–	113	51	104	113	92	91	91	93	–	–	94	–	–	–	–	–
Sao Tome and Principe	83	77	71	22	60	63	136	132	–	–	86	85	66	84	–	–	30	31
Saudi Arabia	99	97	185	54	–	–	106	106	97	97	–	–	–	–	–	–	–	–
Senegal	74	56	88	19	13	15	83	89	77	81	60	63	59	93 x	–	–	35	32
Serbia	99	99	93	48	53	53	95	95	95	94	98	99	98	99	90	91	88	90
Seychelles	99	99	159	47	103	94	113	113	–	–	–	–	94	–	–	–	–	–
Sierra Leone	70	52	36	1	7	7	129	120	–	–	73	76	–	93	–	–	40	33
Singapore	100	100	153	74	–	–	–	–	–	–	–	–	99	–	–	–	–	–
Slovakia	–	–	111	80	92	89	101	100	–	–	–	–	98	–	–	–	–	–

TABLE 5 | EDUCATION >>

Countries and areas	Youth (15–24 years) literacy rate (%) 2008–2012*		Number per 100 population 2012		Pre-primary school participation Gross enrolment ratio (%) 2008–2012*		Primary school participation								Secondary school participation			
							Gross enrolment ratio (%) 2008–2012*		Net enrolment ratio (%) 2008–2011*		Net attendance ratio (%) 2008–2012*		Survival rate to last primary grade (%)		Net enrolment ratio (%) 2008–2011*		Net attendance ratio (%) 2008–2012*	
	male	female	mobile phones	Internet users	male	female	male	female	male	female	male	female	admin. data 2008–2011*	survey data 2008–2012*	male	female	male	female
Slovenia	100	100	110	70	95	91	99	99	98	98	–	–	99	–	92	93	–	–
Solomon Islands	–	–	53	7	49	50	146	144	88	87	63 x,y	69 x,y	–	–	44	42	29 x,y	30 x,y
Somalia	–	–	7	1	–	–	–	–	–	–	18 x	15 x	–	85 x	–	–	12 x	8 x
South Africa	98	99	135	41	65	65	104	100	90	91	–	–	–	–	–	–	–	–
South Sudan	–	–	19	–	–	–	–	–	–	–	32	25	–	65	–	–	8	4
Spain	100	100	108	72	127	127	105	104	100	100	–	–	98	–	94	96	–	–
Sri Lanka	98	99	96	18	84	85	98	97	93	93	98 x	98 x	97	–	86	91	–	–
State of Palestine	99	99	71	–	41	41	92	92	90	90	91 x	92 x	96	–	77	85	–	–
Sudan	–	–	60	21	–	–	–	–	–	–	78	72	–	82	–	–	33	30
Suriname	98	99	183	35	89	89	118	112	92	93	95	96	90	96	52	63	53	66
Swaziland	92	95	66	21	26	26	121	109	–	–	96	97	67	93	32	38	42	52
Sweden	–	–	123	94	95	95	101	100	100	99	–	–	96	–	93	93	–	–
Switzerland	–	–	135	85	100	101	104	103	99	100	–	–	–	–	83	81	–	–
Syrian Arab Republic	96	94	61	24	11	11	122	121	99	100	87 x	86 x	96	100 x	68	68	63 x	63 x
Tajikistan	100	100	92	15	10	8	102	98	100	96	99 x,y	96 x,y	99	100 x	91	81	82 x,y	70 x,y
Thailand	98 x	98 x	120	27	101	100	91	90	90	89	98 x	98 x	–	99 x	70	78	77 x	83 x
The former Yugoslav Republic of Macedonia	99	99	108	63	25	26	89	91	97	99	99	98	–	99	–	–	84	81
Timor-Leste	80	79	52	1	–	–	126	122	91	91	71	73	84	91	37	41	43	48
Togo	87	73	56	4	11	11	146	133	–	–	91	87	52	90	–	–	51	40
Tonga	99 x	100 x	53	35	–	–	–	–	–	–	–	–	–	–	–	–	–	–
Trinidad and Tobago	100	100	139	60	–	–	107	103	98	97	98 x	98 x	89	98 x	–	–	84 x	90 x
Tunisia	98	96	120	41	–	–	112	108	–	–	98	98	95	97	–	–	69	77
Turkey	99	98	91	45	27	26	105	104	100	98	94 y	92 y	99	95 x	81	76	52 x	43 x
Turkmenistan	100	100	76	7	–	–	–	–	–	–	99 x	99 x	–	100 x	–	–	84 x	84 x
Tuvalu	–	–	28	35	–	–	–	–	–	–	97 x,y	99 x,y	–	–	–	–	35 x,y	47 x,y
Uganda	90	85	46	15	14	14	112	114	93	95	81	81	25	72 x	–	–	16	19
Ukraine	100	100	132	34	100	97	99	100	92	93	70 x	76 x	98	100 x	85	85	85 x	85 x
United Arab Emirates	94 x	97 x	170	85	–	–	–	–	–	–	–	–	84	–	–	–	–	–
United Kingdom	–	–	131	87	82	85	107	107	100	100	–	–	–	–	97	100	–	–
United Republic of Tanzania	76	73	57	13	35	34	92	95	98	98	79	82	81	91 x	–	–	26	24
United States	–	–	98	81	68	70	102	101	95	96	–	–	–	–	89	90	–	–
Uruguay	98	99	147	55	89	89	114	110	–	–	–	–	95	–	68	76	–	–
Uzbekistan	100	100	72	37	26	26	96	93	94	91	96 x	96 x	98	100 x	–	–	91 x	90 x
Vanuatu	94	95	54	11	58	59	120	114	–	–	80 x	82 x	71	88 x	46	49	38 x	36 x
Venezuela (Bolivarian Republic of)	98	99	102	44	72	77	104	101	95	95	91 x	93 x	95	82 x	69	77	30 x	43 x
Viet Nam	97	97	149	39	77	69	109	103	–	–	98	98	94	99	–	–	78	84
Yemen	96	76	54	17	1	1	100	81	83	70	75 x	64 x	76	73 x	48	31	49 x	27 x
Zambia	70 x	58 x	76	13	–	–	118	117	96	98	81 x	82 x	53	87 x	–	–	38 x	36 x
Zimbabwe	–	–	97	17	–	–	–	–	–	–	87	89	–	82	–	–	48	49

TABLE 5

TABLE 5 | EDUCATION

Countries and areas	Youth (15–24 years) literacy rate (%) 2008–2012*		Number per 100 population 2012		Pre-primary school participation — Gross enrolment ratio (%) 2008–2012*		Primary school participation								Secondary school participation			
							Gross enrolment ratio (%) 2008–2012*		Net enrolment ratio (%) 2008–2011*		Net attendance ratio (%) 2008–2012*		Survival rate to last primary grade (%)		Net enrolment ratio (%) 2008–2011*		Net attendance ratio (%) 2008–2012*	
	male	female	mobile phones	Internet users	male	female	male	female	male	female	male	female	admin. data 2008–2011*	survey data 2008–2012*	male	female	male	female
SUMMARY INDICATORS#																		
Sub-Saharan Africa	76	64	59	15	18	18	104	96	79	75	73	71	57	87	–	–	34	32
Eastern and Southern Africa	78	71	55	14	22	22	113	108	89	86	74	75	49	–	32	29	23	23
West and Central Africa	73	56	63	16	14	14	97	87	70	66	72	68	66	90	–	–	43	40
Middle East and North Africa	95	89	101	33	26	24	104	96	92	88	89	86	88	94	69	64	–	–
South Asia	86	74	68	12	49	50	111	109	94	91	84	80	63	94	54	46	57	48
East Asia and Pacific	99	99	90	38	60	61	111	113	97	97	92 **	91 **	89	–	71	73	64 **	66 **
Latin America and Caribbean	97	97	110	43	73	73	114	111	95	96	93	94	84	–	74	78	73	78
CEE/CIS	100	99	134	46	59	58	100	100	96	95	91	91	98	–	85	83	–	–
Least developed countries	76	67	48	7	15	15	109	103	83	79	75	73	57	–	36	30	34	32
World	92	87	89	35	50	50	108	106	92	90	83 **	81 **	75	–	64	61	55 **	51 **

For a complete list of countries and areas in the regions, subregions and country categories, see page 26.

DEFINITIONS OF THE INDICATORS

Youth literacy rate – Percentage of population aged 15–24 years, who can both read and write with understanding a short simple statement on his/her everyday life.

Mobile phones – The number of active subscriptions to a public mobile telephone service, including the number of prepaid SIM cards active during the past three months.

Internet users – The estimated number of Internet users including those using the Internet from any device (including mobile phones) during the past 12 months.

Pre-primary school gross enrolment ratio – Number of children enrolled in pre-primary school, regardless of age, expressed as a percentage of the total number of children of official pre-primary school age.

Primary school gross enrolment ratio – Number of children enrolled in primary school, regardless of age, expressed as a percentage of the total number of children of official primary school age.

Primary school net enrolment ratio – Number of children enrolled in primary or secondary school who are of official primary school age, expressed as a percentage of the total number of children of official primary school age. Because of the inclusion of primary-school-aged children enrolled in secondary school, this indicator can also be referred to as a primary adjusted net enrolment ratio.

Primary school net attendance ratio – Number of children attending primary or secondary school who are of official primary school age, expressed as a percentage of the total number of children of official primary school age. Because of the inclusion of primary-school-aged children attending secondary school, this indicator can also be referred to as a primary adjusted net attendance ratio.

Survival rate to last primary grade – Percentage of children entering the first grade of primary school who eventually reach the last grade of primary school.

Secondary school net enrolment ratio – Number of children enrolled in secondary school who are of official secondary school age, expressed as a percentage of the total number of children of official secondary school age. Secondary net enrolment ratio does not include secondary-school-aged children enrolled in tertiary education owing to challenges in age reporting and recording at that level.

Secondary school net attendance ratio – Number of children attending secondary or tertiary school who are of official secondary school age, expressed as a percentage of the total number of children of official secondary school age. Because of the inclusion of secondary-school-aged children attending tertiary school, this indicator can also be referred to as a secondary adjusted net attendance ratio.

All data refer to official International Standard Classifications of Education (ISCED) for the primary and secondary education levels and thus may not directly correspond to a country-specific school system.

MAIN DATA SOURCES

Youth literacy – UNESCO Institute for Statistics (UIS).

Mobile phone and Internet use – International Telecommunications Union, Geneva.

Pre-primary, primary and secondary enrolment – UIS. Estimates based on administrative data from international Education Management Information Systems (EMIS) with UN population estimates.

Primary and secondary school attendance – Demographic and Health Surveys (DHS), Multiple Indicator Cluster Surveys (MICS) and other national household surveys.

Survival rate to last primary grade – Administrative data: UIS; survey data: DHS, MICS and other national household surveys.

NOTES

– Data not available.

x Data refer to years or periods other than those specified in the column heading. Such data are not included in the calculation of regional and global averages, with the exception of 2005–2006 data from India and 2007 data from Brazil, Indonesia, Tajikistan and Ukraine. Estimates from data years prior to 2000 are not displayed.

y Data differ from the standard definition or refer to only part of a country. If they fall within the noted reference period, such data are included in the calculation of regional and global averages.

z Data provided by Chinese Ministry of Education. The UIS dataset does not currently include net enrolment rates or primary school survival for China.

* Data refer to the most recent year available during the period specified in the column heading.

** Excludes China.

TABLE 6 | DEMOGRAPHIC INDICATORS

Countries and areas	Population (thousands) 2012			Population annual growth rate (%)		Crude death rate			Crude birth rate			Life expectancy			Total fertility rate	Urbanized population (%)	Average annual growth rate of urban population (%)	
	total	under 18	under 5	1990–2012	2012–2030α	1970	1990	2012	1970	1990	2012	1970	1990	2012	2012	2012	1990–2012	2012–2030α
Afghanistan	29,825	16,317	4,964	4.2	2.1	28	16	8	53	50	35	37	49	61	5.1	24	5.5	3.6
Albania	3,162	857	198	-0.4	0.3	8	6	7	34	25	13	67	72	77	1.8	55	1.4	1.6
Algeria	38,482	12,608	4,468	1.7	1.3	17	6	6	47	32	25	50	67	71	2.8	74	3.3	2.0
Andorra	78	14	4	1.6	0.7	–	–	–	–	–	–	–	–	–	–	87	1.2	0.3
Angola	20,821	11,299	3,966	3.2	2.9	27	23	14	52	53	45	37	41	51	6.0	60	5.4	3.7
Antigua and Barbuda	89	27	7	1.7	0.9	7	7	6	30	19	17	66	71	76	2.1	30	0.9	1.6
Argentina	41,087	12,089	3,436	1.0	0.7	9	8	8	23	22	17	66	72	76	2.2	93	1.3	0.8
Armenia	2,969	732	215	-0.8	0.0	6	8	9	23	22	14	70	68	74	1.7	64	-1.0	0.3
Australia	23,050	5,280	1,539	1.4	1.1	9	7	7	20	15	13	71	77	82	1.9	89	1.6	1.3
Austria	8,464	1,517	402	0.4	0.3	13	11	9	15	12	9	70	75	81	1.5	68	0.6	0.7
Azerbaijan	9,309	2,556	768	1.2	0.7	9	8	7	29	27	18	65	65	71	1.9	54	1.2	1.2
Bahamas	372	100	29	1.7	1.0	6	5	6	26	24	15	66	71	75	1.9	84	1.9	1.2
Bahrain	1,318	318	98	4.4	1.2	7	3	2	38	29	16	63	72	76	2.1	89	4.5	1.3
Bangladesh	154,695	56,867	15,074	1.7	1.0	19	10	6	47	35	20	48	60	70	2.2	29	3.4	2.7
Barbados	283	65	18	0.4	0.4	10	10	9	22	16	13	65	71	75	1.8	45	1.8	1.4
Belarus	9,405	1,725	526	-0.4	-0.6	9	11	16	16	14	11	71	71	70	1.5	75	0.2	-0.2
Belgium	11,060	2,245	657	0.5	0.3	12	11	10	14	12	12	71	76	80	1.9	98	0.5	0.3
Belize	324	132	38	2.5	2.0	8	5	5	42	36	24	66	71	74	2.7	45	2.2	2.1
Benin	10,051	4,989	1,631	3.2	2.4	24	14	10	47	46	37	42	54	59	4.9	46	4.4	3.6
Bhutan	742	257	71	1.5	1.1	26	13	7	49	38	20	37	52	68	2.3	36	5.1	2.6
Bolivia (Plurinational State of)	10,496	4,374	1,264	2.0	1.5	20	10	7	46	37	26	46	59	67	3.3	67	2.8	2.0
Bosnia and Herzegovina	3,834	790	158	-0.8	-0.2	7	10	10	23	15	9	66	67	76	1.3	49	0.2	0.8
Botswana	2,004	810	232	1.7	0.9	13	7	17	46	35	24	55	63	47	2.7	62	3.5	1.6
Brazil	198,656	58,867	14,563	1.3	0.6	10	7	6	35	24	15	59	66	74	1.8	85	1.9	0.9
Brunei Darussalam	412	127	33	2.1	1.1	6	4	3	36	32	16	67	74	78	2.0	76	2.8	1.4
Bulgaria	7,278	1,188	345	-0.9	-0.9	9	13	16	16	12	10	71	71	73	1.5	74	-0.4	-0.4
Burkina Faso	16,460	8,642	2,932	2.8	2.7	25	17	11	47	47	41	39	49	56	5.7	27	5.9	5.0
Burundi	9,850	5,002	1,838	2.6	2.8	21	18	13	47	50	45	44	47	54	6.1	11	5.2	5.3
Cabo Verde	494	183	49	1.5	0.9	15	8	5	41	39	20	52	66	75	2.3	63	3.2	1.7
Cambodia	14,865	5,557	1,669	2.3	1.4	20	12	6	43	42	26	42	55	72	2.9	20	3.4	2.8
Cameroon	21,700	10,808	3,572	2.7	2.3	19	14	12	45	45	38	46	54	55	4.9	53	4.0	3.3
Canada	34,838	6,990	1,967	1.0	0.9	7	7	8	17	14	11	72	77	81	1.7	81	1.3	1.0
Central African Republic	4,525	2,117	662	2.0	1.9	23	19	15	43	41	34	42	46	50	4.5	39	2.3	2.8
Chad	12,448	6,905	2,406	3.4	2.9	23	19	15	47	51	46	41	46	51	6.4	22	3.6	3.9
Chile	17,465	4,577	1,225	1.3	0.7	10	6	6	29	23	14	62	74	80	1.8	89	1.6	0.8
China	1,377,065	302,230	88,934	0.8	0.3	8	7	7	35	23	13	63	69	75	1.7	52	3.8	1.9
Colombia	47,704	16,018	4,521	1.6	1.0	9	6	6	38	27	19	61	68	74	2.3	76	2.1	1.3
Comoros	718	346	115	2.5	2.2	18	12	9	45	38	36	48	56	61	4.8	28	2.6	2.9
Congo	4,337	2,112	722	2.7	2.5	14	12	10	43	38	38	53	55	58	5.0	64	3.5	3.0

TABLE 6 | DEMOGRAPHIC INDICATORS >>

TABLE 6

Countries and areas	Population (thousands) 2012			Population annual growth rate (%)		Crude death rate			Crude birth rate			Life expectancy			Total fertility rate	Urbanized population (%)	Average annual growth rate of urban population (%)	
	total	under 18	under 5	1990–2012	2012–2030α	1970	1990	2012	1970	1990	2012	1970	1990	2012	2012	2012	1990–2012	2012–2030α
Cook Islands	21	7	2	0.7	0.4	–	–	–	–	–	–	–	–	–	–	74	1.8	0.8
Costa Rica	4,805	1,403	361	2.0	1.0	7	4	4	33	27	15	67	76	80	1.8	65	3.2	1.6
Côte d'Ivoire	19,840	9,557	3,088	2.2	2.2	21	14	14	53	41	37	44	52	50	4.9	52	3.5	3.2
Croatia	4,307	799	223	-0.5	-0.4	10	11	12	15	12	10	68	72	77	1.5	58	-0.2	0.2
Cuba	11,271	2,298	532	0.3	-0.2	7	7	8	29	17	10	70	75	79	1.5	75	0.4	-0.1
Cyprus	1,129	242	65	1.8	0.8	7	7	7	19	19	12	73	77	80	1.5	71	2.0	1.1
Czech Republic	10,660	1,863	600	0.1	0.2	12	12	11	16	12	11	70	72	78	1.5	73	0.0	0.3
Democratic People's Republic of Korea	24,763	6,632	1,690	0.9	0.4	10	6	9	37	21	14	60	70	70	2.0	60	1.1	0.8
Democratic Republic of the Congo	65,705	34,110	11,691	2.9	2.5	20	18	16	47	48	43	44	47	50	6.0	35	3.9	4.0
Denmark	5,598	1,204	326	0.4	0.4	10	12	10	15	12	11	73	75	79	1.9	87	0.5	0.5
Djibouti	860	344	108	1.7	1.2	15	11	9	45	40	28	49	57	61	3.5	77	1.8	1.4
Dominica	72	22	6	0.0	0.4	–	–	–	–	–	–	–	–	–	–	67	0.0	0.7
Dominican Republic	10,277	3,725	1,063	1.6	1.0	11	6	6	42	30	21	58	68	73	2.5	70	2.7	1.5
Ecuador	15,492	5,568	1,594	1.9	1.3	12	6	5	41	30	21	58	69	76	2.6	68	2.9	1.9
Egypt	80,722	29,801	9,237	1.6	1.3	16	8	7	41	31	24	52	65	71	2.8	44	1.7	2.0
El Salvador	6,297	2,378	639	0.7	0.5	13	7	7	43	32	20	56	66	72	2.2	65	2.0	1.1
Equatorial Guinea	736	333	113	3.1	2.4	25	20	14	39	47	36	40	47	53	4.9	40	3.7	3.2
Eritrea	6,131	3,021	1,034	2.9	2.6	22	15	7	47	45	37	41	48	62	4.8	22	4.3	4.6
Estonia	1,291	242	73	-0.9	-0.3	11	13	13	15	14	11	70	69	74	1.6	70	-1.0	-0.1
Ethiopia	91,729	46,355	14,095	2.9	2.3	21	18	8	48	47	34	43	47	63	4.6	17	4.4	4.1
Fiji	875	300	91	0.8	0.4	8	6	7	34	29	21	60	66	70	2.6	53	1.9	1.1
Finland	5,408	1,080	306	0.4	0.2	10	10	10	14	13	11	70	75	80	1.9	84	0.6	0.4
France	63,937	14,011	3,924	0.5	0.4	11	9	9	17	13	12	72	77	82	2.0	86	1.2	0.8
Gabon	1,633	731	238	2.5	2.1	20	11	9	37	37	32	47	61	63	4.1	87	3.5	2.3
Gambia	1,791	941	328	3.0	3.0	26	14	10	50	47	43	38	52	59	5.8	58	4.9	3.7
Georgia	4,358	930	306	-1.0	-0.5	10	9	11	19	17	14	67	70	74	1.8	53	-1.2	-0.1
Germany	82,800	13,395	3,451	0.1	-0.2	12	11	11	14	10	8	71	75	81	1.4	74	0.2	0.0
Ghana	25,366	11,424	3,640	2.5	1.8	16	11	9	47	39	31	49	57	61	3.9	53	4.2	2.8
Greece	11,125	1,951	576	0.4	-0.1	10	9	10	17	10	10	71	77	81	1.5	62	0.6	0.4
Grenada	105	35	10	0.4	0.1	9	9	7	28	28	19	64	69	73	2.2	39	1.2	1.0
Guatemala	15,083	7,174	2,215	2.4	2.2	15	9	5	44	39	31	52	62	72	3.8	50	3.3	3.1
Guinea	11,451	5,627	1,856	2.9	2.3	27	17	12	45	46	37	37	50	56	5.0	36	4.0	3.7
Guinea-Bissau	1,664	801	265	2.2	2.2	20	17	13	44	45	38	44	49	54	5.0	45	4.3	3.3
Guyana	795	340	89	0.4	0.4	10	9	7	34	23	21	59	62	66	2.6	28	0.2	1.2
Haiti	10,174	4,262	1,250	1.6	1.2	18	13	9	39	37	26	47	54	63	3.2	55	4.6	2.5
Holy See	1	0	0	0.2	0.0	–	–	–	–	–	–	–	–	–	–	100	0.2	0.0
Honduras	7,936	3,370	989	2.2	1.7	15	7	5	47	38	26	53	67	74	3.1	53	3.4	2.6
Hungary	9,976	1,780	491	-0.2	-0.3	11	14	13	15	12	10	70	69	74	1.4	70	0.1	0.3
Iceland	326	81	24	1.1	0.9	7	7	6	21	17	15	74	78	82	2.1	94	1.3	1.0

TABLE 6 | DEMOGRAPHIC INDICATORS >>

Countries and areas	Population (thousands) 2012			Population annual growth rate (%)		Crude death rate			Crude birth rate			Life expectancy			Total fertility rate	Urbanized population (%)	Average annual growth rate of urban population (%)	
	total	under 18	under 5	1990–2012	2012–2030ᵅ	1970	1990	2012	1970	1990	2012	1970	1990	2012	2012	2012	1990–2012	2012–2030ᵅ
India	1,236,687	434,782	120,581	1.6	1.0	16	11	8	38	31	21	49	59	66	2.5	32	2.6	2.3
Indonesia	246,864	85,411	24,622	1.5	1.0	14	8	6	40	26	19	52	63	71	2.4	51	3.8	2.1
Iran (Islamic Republic of)	76,424	21,774	7,003	1.4	1.0	16	7	5	42	33	19	51	63	74	1.9	69	2.3	1.3
Iraq	32,778	15,421	4,824	2.8	2.5	12	6	5	46	38	31	58	68	69	4.1	66	2.6	2.6
Ireland	4,576	1,160	364	1.2	0.9	11	9	6	22	14	16	71	75	81	2.0	62	1.6	1.4
Israel	7,644	2,467	772	2.4	1.3	7	6	5	26	22	21	72	76	82	2.9	92	2.5	1.3
Italy	60,885	10,296	2,851	0.3	0.0	10	10	10	17	10	9	71	77	82	1.5	69	0.4	0.4
Jamaica	2,769	947	254	0.7	0.4	8	7	7	36	26	18	68	71	73	2.3	52	1.0	0.8
Japan	127,250	20,310	5,389	0.2	-0.3	7	7	10	19	10	8	72	79	83	1.4	92	1.0	0.0
Jordan	7,009	2,831	937	3.3	1.6	10	5	4	51	34	28	60	70	74	3.3	83	4.0	1.8
Kazakhstan	16,271	4,887	1,665	0.0	0.7	9	9	10	25	24	21	63	67	66	2.5	53	-0.2	1.0
Kenya	43,178	21,023	6,956	2.8	2.4	15	10	8	51	42	36	52	59	61	4.5	24	4.5	4.1
Kiribati	101	39	11	1.6	1.4	15	9	6	39	36	23	51	61	69	3.0	44	2.6	2.0
Kuwait	3,250	948	314	2.1	2.2	6	3	3	49	19	21	66	72	74	2.6	98	2.1	2.2
Kyrgyzstan	5,474	1,978	659	1.0	1.3	11	8	8	31	31	27	60	66	67	3.1	35	0.7	2.0
Lao People's Democratic Republic	6,646	2,860	889	2.0	1.6	18	13	6	43	43	27	46	54	68	3.1	35	5.8	3.7
Latvia	2,060	360	109	-1.2	-0.6	11	13	16	14	14	11	70	69	72	1.6	68	-1.3	-0.4
Lebanon	4,647	1,274	281	2.5	0.6	8	7	4	32	25	13	66	70	80	1.5	87	2.7	0.7
Lesotho	2,052	905	260	1.1	0.9	17	10	15	43	35	28	49	59	49	3.1	28	4.3	3.0
Liberia	4,190	2,073	678	3.1	2.3	24	18	9	49	45	36	39	47	60	4.9	49	3.9	3.2
Libya	6,155	2,134	645	1.7	1.1	13	5	4	47	29	21	56	68	75	2.4	78	1.8	1.3
Liechtenstein	37	7	2	1.1	0.7	–	–	–	–	–	–	–	–	–	–	14	0.4	1.1
Lithuania	3,028	569	167	-0.9	-0.4	9	11	14	17	15	11	71	71	72	1.5	67	-0.9	-0.1
Luxembourg	524	111	30	1.4	1.1	12	10	8	13	12	12	70	75	80	1.7	86	1.7	1.3
Madagascar	22,294	11,065	3,529	3.0	2.7	21	15	7	48	45	35	45	51	64	4.5	33	4.5	4.3
Malawi	15,906	8,344	2,859	2.4	2.7	24	18	12	52	50	40	41	47	55	5.5	16	3.8	4.3
Malaysia	29,240	9,434	2,425	2.2	1.3	7	5	5	33	28	18	64	71	75	2.0	73	3.9	1.8
Maldives	338	120	36	2.0	1.4	21	9	3	50	41	22	44	61	78	2.3	42	4.3	3.0
Mali	14,854	7,979	2,865	2.8	3.1	32	20	13	49	48	47	32	46	55	6.9	36	4.8	4.7
Malta	428	80	21	0.6	0.1	9	7	8	16	16	9	71	75	80	1.4	95	0.8	0.2
Marshall Islands	53	19	5	0.5	0.6	–	–	–	–	–	–	–	–	–	–	72	0.9	0.9
Mauritania	3,796	1,771	575	2.9	2.2	16	11	9	46	41	34	49	58	61	4.7	42	3.1	3.2
Mauritius	1,240	307	70	0.7	0.2	7	6	8	29	21	12	63	69	73	1.5	42	0.5	0.7
Mexico	120,847	42,111	11,405	1.5	1.0	10	5	5	43	28	19	61	71	77	2.2	78	2.0	1.3
Micronesia (Federated States of)	103	45	12	0.3	0.9	9	7	6	41	34	24	62	66	69	3.3	23	-0.3	1.7
Monaco	38	7	2	1.1	0.9	–	–	–	–	–	–	–	–	–	–	100	1.1	0.9
Mongolia	2,796	907	306	1.1	1.1	15	10	7	44	32	23	55	60	67	2.4	69	2.0	1.9
Montenegro	621	145	40	0.0	-0.1	8	7	10	21	14	12	70	74	75	1.7	63	1.3	0.3
Morocco	32,521	10,888	3,234	1.3	1.0	14	7	6	43	30	23	53	65	71	2.7	57	2.0	1.7

TABLE 6

TABLE 6 | DEMOGRAPHIC INDICATORS >>

Countries and areas	Population (thousands) 2012			Population annual growth rate (%)		Crude death rate			Crude birth rate			Life expectancy			Total fertility rate	Urbanized population (%)	Average annual growth rate of urban population (%)	
	total	under 18	under 5	1990–2012	2012–2030α	1970	1990	2012	1970	1990	2012	1970	1990	2012	2012	2012	1990–2012	2012–2030α
Mozambique	25,203	13,064	4,332	2.8	2.4	25	20	14	48	43	39	39	44	50	5.3	31	4.6	3.5
Myanmar	52,797	16,200	4,434	1.0	0.6	15	10	9	40	27	17	51	59	65	2.0	33	2.4	2.2
Namibia	2,259	984	283	2.1	1.7	15	9	7	43	38	26	53	61	64	3.1	39	3.7	3.0
Nauru	10	4	1	0.4	0.5	–	–	–	–	–	–	–	–	–	–	100	0.4	0.5
Nepal	27,474	11,601	2,984	1.9	1.0	21	12	7	42	38	22	42	55	68	2.4	17	4.9	3.0
Netherlands	16,714	3,469	882	0.5	0.2	8	9	9	17	13	11	74	77	81	1.8	84	1.4	0.5
New Zealand	4,460	1,093	321	1.2	0.9	8	8	7	22	17	14	71	75	81	2.1	86	1.3	1.0
Nicaragua	5,992	2,399	690	1.7	1.2	13	7	5	46	37	23	54	64	75	2.5	58	2.1	1.8
Niger	17,157	9,679	3,557	3.6	3.9	28	23	11	56	55	50	36	44	58	7.6	18	4.3	5.7
Nigeria	168,834	85,406	29,697	2.6	2.7	23	18	13	46	44	42	41	46	52	6.0	50	4.2	3.7
Niue	1	1	0	-2.4	-1.4	–	–	–	–	–	–	–	–	–	–	38	-1.4	-0.4
Norway	4,994	1,131	319	0.7	0.9	10	11	8	16	14	12	74	76	81	1.9	80	1.2	1.1
Oman	3,314	992	333	2.7	2.2	16	5	3	48	38	21	50	67	76	2.9	74	3.2	2.5
Pakistan	179,160	73,845	21,996	2.2	1.4	15	10	7	43	40	26	53	61	66	3.3	37	3.0	2.5
Palau	21	7	2	1.4	1.0	–	–	–	–	–	–	–	–	–	–	85	2.4	1.4
Panama	3,802	1,294	369	1.9	1.4	8	5	5	38	26	20	66	73	77	2.5	76	3.5	1.9
Papua New Guinea	7,167	3,218	982	2.5	1.9	17	10	8	44	35	29	46	56	62	3.8	13	1.7	3.6
Paraguay	6,687	2,606	753	2.1	1.5	7	6	6	37	33	24	65	68	72	2.9	62	3.2	2.1
Peru	29,988	10,487	2,925	1.5	1.1	14	7	5	42	30	20	53	66	75	2.4	78	2.0	1.4
Philippines	96,707	39,420	11,165	2.0	1.5	9	7	6	39	33	25	61	65	69	3.1	49	2.1	2.3
Poland	38,211	7,021	2,066	0.0	-0.1	8	10	10	17	15	11	70	71	76	1.4	61	0.0	0.1
Portugal	10,604	1,904	486	0.3	-0.1	11	10	10	21	11	9	67	74	80	1.3	62	1.5	0.6
Qatar	2,051	328	99	6.6	1.7	5	2	1	36	23	11	68	75	78	2.0	99	6.9	1.7
Republic of Korea	49,003	9,555	2,349	0.6	0.4	9	6	6	32	16	10	61	72	81	1.3	83	1.2	0.6
Republic of Moldova	3,514	719	222	-1.0	-0.8	10	10	14	20	19	12	65	68	69	1.5	48	-0.8	0.4
Romania	21,755	3,954	1,113	-0.3	-0.4	10	11	12	21	14	10	68	70	74	1.4	53	-0.4	-0.1
Russian Federation	143,170	26,369	8,228	-0.2	-0.4	9	12	15	15	14	12	69	68	68	1.5	74	-0.1	-0.1
Rwanda	11,458	5,846	1,945	2.1	2.4	20	34	7	50	48	36	44	33	64	4.6	19	7.9	4.3
Saint Kitts and Nevis	54	17	5	1.2	0.9	–	–	–	–	–	–	–	–	–	–	32	0.9	1.6
Saint Lucia	181	54	14	1.2	0.6	9	6	7	39	28	16	63	71	75	1.9	17	-1.3	-1.4
Saint Vincent and the Grenadines	109	34	9	0.1	0.0	9	7	7	40	25	17	65	70	72	2.0	50	0.9	0.8
Samoa	189	84	26	0.7	0.6	11	7	5	41	33	27	55	65	73	4.2	20	0.3	0.5
San Marino	31	6	2	1.2	0.3	–	–	–	–	–	–	–	–	–	–	94	1.4	0.4
Sao Tome and Principe	188	90	31	2.1	2.2	13	10	7	41	37	35	56	62	66	4.1	63	3.8	2.9
Saudi Arabia	28,288	9,698	2,954	2.5	1.3	15	5	3	46	36	20	53	69	75	2.7	83	2.9	1.5
Senegal	13,726	6,882	2,313	2.7	2.6	25	11	8	50	44	38	39	57	63	5.0	43	3.2	3.5
Serbia	9,553	1,929	481	-0.1	-0.6	9	10	12	18	15	10	68	72	74	1.4	57	0.5	0.0
Seychelles	92	25	7	1.3	0.4	9	7	8	35	23	17	66	71	73	2.2	54	1.7	1.0
Sierra Leone	5,979	2,886	928	1.8	1.7	30	26	17	49	44	37	35	37	45	4.8	40	2.6	2.8
Singapore	5,303	1,094	269	2.6	1.2	5	4	5	23	18	10	68	76	82	1.3	100	2.6	1.2

TABLE 6 | DEMOGRAPHIC INDICATORS >>

Countries and areas	Population (thousands) 2012			Population annual growth rate (%)		Crude death rate			Crude birth rate			Life expectancy			Total fertility rate	Urbanized population (%)	Average annual growth rate of urban population (%)	
	total	under 18	under 5	1990–2012	2012–2030α	1970	1990	2012	1970	1990	2012	1970	1990	2012	2012	2012	1990–2012	2012–2030α
Slovakia	5,446	1,006	292	0.1	-0.1	9	10	10	18	15	11	70	71	75	1.4	55	0.0	0.2
Slovenia	2,068	353	108	0.1	0.0	10	10	10	17	11	10	69	73	79	1.5	50	0.1	0.4
Solomon Islands	550	258	82	2.6	1.8	13	11	6	45	40	31	54	57	67	4.1	21	4.5	3.6
Somalia	10,195	5,531	1,923	2.2	2.8	23	20	13	46	48	44	41	45	55	6.7	38	3.3	4.1
South Africa	52,386	18,347	5,525	1.6	0.6	14	8	13	38	29	21	53	62	56	2.4	62	2.4	1.2
South Sudan	10,838	5,329	1,726	2.9	2.6	28	21	12	51	47	37	36	44	55	5.0	18	4.3	4.1
Spain	46,755	8,383	2,545	0.8	0.2	9	9	9	20	10	11	72	77	82	1.5	78	1.0	0.4
Sri Lanka	21,098	6,262	1,874	0.9	0.5	8	6	7	31	21	18	64	70	74	2.3	15	0.3	2.1
State of Palestine	4,219	2,031	605	3.2	2.3	13	5	3	50	45	31	56	68	73	4.1	75	3.6	2.6
Sudan	37,195	17,880	5,671	2.8	2.2	15	12	8	47	42	34	52	56	62	4.5	33	3.5	3.1
Suriname	535	177	46	1.2	0.7	9	7	7	37	23	18	63	67	71	2.3	70	1.9	1.1
Swaziland	1,231	560	169	1.6	1.2	18	10	14	49	43	30	48	59	49	3.4	21	1.3	1.7
Sweden	9,511	1,920	565	0.5	0.6	10	11	10	14	14	12	74	78	82	1.9	85	0.6	0.8
Switzerland	7,997	1,457	400	0.8	0.9	9	9	8	16	12	10	73	78	82	1.5	74	0.9	1.1
Syrian Arab Republic	21,890	9,124	2,624	2.6	1.7	11	5	4	46	36	24	59	70	75	3.0	56	3.2	2.4
Tajikistan	8,009	3,395	1,150	1.9	2.0	12	10	7	41	40	33	60	63	67	3.8	27	1.1	2.8
Thailand	66,785	15,107	3,706	0.8	0.1	10	6	8	38	19	10	60	70	74	1.4	34	1.5	1.4
The former Yugoslav Republic of Macedonia	2,106	440	112	0.2	-0.1	8	8	10	24	18	11	66	71	75	1.4	59	0.3	0.4
Timor-Leste	1,114	611	190	1.8	1.9	23	16	6	42	43	36	40	48	67	6.0	29	3.2	3.1
Togo	6,643	3,216	1,069	2.6	2.3	19	12	11	48	43	37	47	56	56	4.7	38	3.9	3.5
Tonga	105	46	14	0.4	0.8	7	6	6	36	31	26	65	70	73	3.8	24	0.6	1.6
Trinidad and Tobago	1,337	330	97	0.4	-0.1	7	8	9	27	21	15	65	68	70	1.8	14	2.7	1.5
Tunisia	10,875	3,048	918	1.3	0.8	14	6	6	41	27	17	51	69	76	2.0	67	1.9	1.2
Turkey	73,997	23,098	6,362	1.4	0.9	15	8	6	40	26	17	52	64	75	2.1	72	2.4	1.6
Turkmenistan	5,173	1,777	503	1.6	1.0	12	9	8	37	35	22	58	63	65	2.4	49	1.9	1.8
Tuvalu	10	4	1	0.4	0.5	–	–	–	–	–	–	–	–	–	–	51	1.4	1.2
Uganda	36,346	20,159	6,939	3.3	3.1	17	17	10	49	50	44	49	48	59	6.0	16	5.0	5.5
Ukraine	45,530	7,916	2,589	-0.6	-0.7	9	13	17	15	13	11	71	70	68	1.5	69	-0.4	-0.4
United Arab Emirates	9,206	1,625	647	7.4	1.6	7	3	1	37	26	15	62	71	77	1.8	85	7.7	1.9
United Kingdom	62,783	13,304	4,028	0.4	0.5	12	11	9	15	14	12	72	76	80	1.9	80	0.5	0.7
United Republic of Tanzania	47,783	24,516	8,487	2.9	2.8	18	15	9	48	44	40	47	50	61	5.3	27	4.5	4.5
United States	317,505	75,321	20,623	1.0	0.7	10	9	8	17	16	13	71	75	79	2.0	83	1.4	1.0
Uruguay	3,395	907	245	0.4	0.3	10	10	9	21	18	15	69	73	77	2.1	93	0.6	0.4
Uzbekistan	28,541	10,046	2,989	1.5	1.0	10	7	7	39	34	22	63	67	68	2.3	36	1.0	1.7
Vanuatu	247	108	35	2.4	2.0	14	8	5	42	36	27	52	63	71	3.4	25	3.7	3.2
Venezuela (Bolivarian Republic of)	29,955	10,289	2,951	1.9	1.2	7	5	5	37	29	20	65	71	74	2.4	94	2.4	1.3
Viet Nam	90,796	25,343	7,184	1.3	0.6	11	6	6	37	29	16	60	71	76	1.8	32	3.3	2.4
Yemen	23,852	11,485	3,397	3.2	2.0	24	12	7	52	52	31	41	58	63	4.2	33	5.3	3.6

TABLE 6

TABLE 6 | DEMOGRAPHIC INDICATORS

Countries and areas	Population (thousands) 2012			Population annual growth rate (%)		Crude death rate			Crude birth rate			Life expectancy			Total fertility rate	Urbanized population (%)	Average annual growth rate of urban population (%)	
	total	under 18	under 5	1990–2012	2012–2030ᵅ	1970	1990	2012	1970	1990	2012	1970	1990	2012	2012	2012	1990–2012	2012–2030ᵅ
Zambia	14,075	7,523	2,566	2.7	3.2	17	19	11	49	44	43	49	44	57	5.7	40	2.7	4.3
Zimbabwe	13,724	6,483	2,010	1.2	2.2	13	9	10	48	37	32	55	59	58	3.6	39	2.6	3.4

SUMMARY INDICATORS#

	total	under 18	under 5	1990–2012	2012–2030ᵅ	1970	1990	2012	1970	1990	2012	1970	1990	2012	2012	2012	1990–2012	2012–2030ᵅ
Sub-Saharan Africa	913,135	454,335	151,551	2.7	2.5	21	16	11	47	44	38	44	50	56	5.2	37	3.9	3.6
Eastern and Southern Africa	441,512	216,847	70,865	2.6	2.4	19	16	10	47	43	36	46	51	59	4.7	30	3.8	3.5
West and Central Africa	433,568	219,264	74,908	2.7	2.6	22	17	13	47	45	41	42	49	54	5.7	44	4.0	3.7
Middle East and North Africa	425,055	154,551	48,396	2.1	1.5	15	7	6	44	34	24	53	65	71	2.9	60	2.7	1.9
South Asia	1,650,019	600,051	167,580	1.7	1.1	17	10	8	40	32	21	49	59	67	2.6	31	2.7	2.4
East Asia and Pacific	2,074,608	524,629	151,130	1.0	0.5	9	7	7	36	24	15	61	68	74	1.8	51	3.4	1.9
Latin America and Caribbean	604,436	198,478	53,612	1.4	0.9	10	7	6	37	27	18	60	68	75	2.2	79	2.0	1.2
CEE/CIS	408,336	96,228	28,853	0.2	0.1	10	11	12	21	18	14	66	68	70	1.8	65	0.3	0.5
Least developed countries	878,097	412,086	130,370	2.5	2.1	21	15	9	47	42	33	44	52	61	4.4	29	3.9	3.6
World	7,040,823	2,213,677	652,093	1.3	1.0	12	9	8	32	26	20	60	66	71	2.5	52	2.2	1.7

For a complete list of countries and areas in the regions, subregions and country categories, see page 26.

DEFINITIONS OF THE INDICATORS

Crude death rate – Annual number of deaths per 1,000 population.
Crude birth rate – Annual number of births per 1,000 population.
Life expectancy – Number of years newborn children would live if subject to the mortality risks prevailing for the cross section of population at the time of their birth.
Total fertility rate – Number of children who would be born per woman if she lived to the end of her childbearing years and bore children at each age in accordance with prevailing age-specific fertility rates.
Urbanized population – Percentage of population living in urban areas as defined according to the national definition used in the most recent population census.

MAIN DATA SOURCES

Population – United Nations Population Division. Growth rates calculated by UNICEF based on data from United Nations Population Division.
Crude death and birth rates – United Nations Population Division.
Life expectancy – United Nations Population Division.
Total fertility rate – United Nations Population Division.

NOTES

– Data not available.
ɑ Based on medium-fertility variant projections.

TABLE 7 | ECONOMIC INDICATORS

Countries and areas	GNI per capita 2012 US$	GNI per capita 2012 PPP US$	GDP per capita average annual growth rate (%) 1970–1990	GDP per capita average annual growth rate (%) 1990–2012	Average annual rate of inflation (%) 1990–2012	Population below international poverty line of US$1.25 per day (%) 2007–2011*	Public spending as a % of GDP (2007–2011*) allocated to: health	Public spending as a % of GDP (2007–2011*) allocated to: education	Public spending as a % of GDP (2007–2011*) allocated to: military	ODA inflow in millions US$ 2011	ODA inflow as a % of recipient GNI 2011	Debt service as a % of exports of goods and services 2011	Share of household income (%, 2007–2011*) poorest 40%	Share of household income (%, 2007–2011*) richest 20%
Afghanistan	570 x	1,400 e,x	–	–	–	–	1	–	5	6,711	37	–	23	37
Albania	4,090	9,390	-0.9 x	5.7	13	1	3	3	2	349	3	7	20	43
Algeria	4,110 x	7,550 e,x	1.8	1.5	11	–	3	4	3	197	0	1	–	–
Andorra	d	–	-1.3	2.5 x	3 x	–	5	3	–	–	–	–	–	–
Angola	4,580	5,490	–	4.1	187	43	2	3	4	200	0	4	15	49
Antigua and Barbuda	12,640	19,260 e	7.9 x	1.4	3	–	4	–	–	15	1	–	–	–
Argentina	c		-0.8	1.3 x	6 x	1	5	6	1	84	0	15	13	49
Armenia	3,720	6,990	–	6.3	43	3	2	3	4	378	4	19	22	40
Australia	59,570	43,170	1.6	2.1	3	–	6	5	2	–	–	–	–	–
Austria	48,160	43,220	2.5	1.8	2	–	9	6	1	–	–	–	22 x	38 x
Azerbaijan	6,050	9,410	–	6.2	46	0	1	3	3	292	1	5	20	42
Bahamas	21,280 x	29,740 e,x	1.9	0.3	3	–	4	–	–	–	–	–	–	–
Bahrain	16,050 x	21,420 x	-1.0 x	0.7 x	3 x	–	3	3	3	–	–	–	–	–
Bangladesh	840	2,070	0.5	3.7	5	43	1	2	1	1,498	1	3	21	41
Barbados	d	–	1.7	0.9 x	3 x	–	4	8	–	–	–	–	–	–
Belarus	6,530	15,210	–	4.9	106	0	4	5	1	126	0	4	23	36
Belgium	44,990	39,260	2.2	1.5	2	–	8	7	1	–	–	–	22 x	41 x
Belize	4,180 x	6,880 e,x	3.1	2.2 x	1 x	–	4	7	1	28	2	13	–	–
Benin	750	1,570	0.4	1.1	5	47 x	2	4	1	672	9	–	18 x	46 x
Bhutan	2,420	6,310	7.0 x	5.4	6	10	3	5	–	144	8	11	18	45
Bolivia (Plurinational State of)	2,220	4,960	-1.2	1.7	7	16	4	8	2	729	3	4	9	59
Bosnia and Herzegovina	4,650	9,380	–	7.9 x	5 x	0	7	–	1	624	3	10	18	43
Botswana	7,720	16,520	8.0	3.7	8	–	3	8	3	121	1	1	–	–
Brazil	11,630	11,720	2.3	1.7	45	6	4	6	2	826	0	19	10	59
Brunei Darussalam	d	–	-2.2 x	-0.4	5	–	2	4	3	–	–	–	–	–
Bulgaria	6,870	15,390	3.4 x	3.4	34	0	4	5	2	–	–	12	23	37
Burkina Faso	670	1,510	1.4	2.8	3	45	4	4	1	996	10	–	18	47
Burundi	240	560	1.2	-1.7	14	81 x	3	5	3	579	25	2	21 x	43 x
Cabo Verde	3,810	4,340	3.7 x	5.1	2	21 x	4	6	0	251	14	4	13 x	56 x
Cambodia	880	2,360	–	6.0 x	4 x	19	1	3	2	792	7	1	19	44
Cameroon	1,170	2,320	3.4	0.5	3	10	2	3	1	611	2	–	17	46
Canada	50,970	42,690	2.0	1.7	2	–	8	5	1	–	–	–	20 x	40 x
Central African Republic	490	860	-1.3	-0.7	3	63	2	1	3	272	13	–	10	61
Chad	740	1,320	-0.9	2.8	6	62 x	1	3	2	468	5	–	16 x	47 x
Chile	14,280	21,590	1.5	3.4	6	1	3	4	3	161	0	15	12	58
China	5,740	9,210	6.6	9.3	5	12	3	–	2	-661	0	2	15	47
Colombia	6,990	10,110	1.9	1.7	13	8	5	4	3	1,024	0	14	10	60
Comoros	840	1,230	0.0 x	-0.7	4	46 x	3	8	–	52	8	–	8 x	68 x
Congo	2,550	3,510	3.3	0.4	8	54 x	1	6	1	260	2	–	13 x	53 x

TABLE 7 | ECONOMIC INDICATORS >>

TABLE 7

Countries and areas	GNI per capita 2012		GDP per capita average annual growth rate (%)		Average annual rate of inflation (%)	Population below international poverty line of US$1.25 per day (%)	Public spending as a % of GDP (2007–2011*) allocated to:			ODA inflow in millions US$	ODA inflow as a % of recipient GNI	Debt service as a % of exports of goods and services	Share of household income (%, 2007–2011*)	
	US$	PPP US$	1970–1990	1990–2012	1990–2012	2007–2011*	health	education	military	2011	2011	2011	poorest 40%	richest 20%
Cook Islands	–	–	–	–	–	–	–	–	–	–	–	–	–	–
Costa Rica	8,740	12,590 e	0.7	2.7	12	3	6	5	–	38	0	12	12	56
Côte d'Ivoire	1,220	1,960	-1.7	-0.5	5	24	1	5	2	1,436	6	–	16	48
Croatia	13,290	19,760	–	3.1 x	4 x	0	7	4	2	–	–	–	20	42
Cuba	c	–	3.9	3.0 x	4 x	–	11	13	3	83	–	–	–	–
Cyprus	26,000	29,400	5.9 x	1.7	3	–	3	8	2	–	–	–	–	–
Czech Republic	18,130	24,550	–	2.7	5	–	7	4	1	–	–	–	–	–
Democratic People's Republic of Korea	a	–	–	–	–	–	–	–	–	118	–	–	–	–
Democratic Republic of the Congo	220	370	-2.1	-2.1	191	88 x	2	3	1	5,532	38	–	14 x	51 x
Denmark	59,770	42,620	2.0	1.3	2	–	10	9	1	–	–	–	–	–
Djibouti	b	–	–	0.0	3	19 x	5	8	4	142	–	8	17 x	46 x
Dominica	6,460	12,190 e	5.2 x	2.0	3	–	4	3	–	24	5	7	–	–
Dominican Republic	5,470	9,820 e	2.1	3.9	10	2	2	2	1	224	0	7	14	53
Ecuador	5,190	9,590	1.7	1.2	4	5	3	5	4	163	0	9	12	54
Egypt	3,000	6,640	4.4	2.9	8	2	2	4	2	412	0	5	22	40
El Salvador	3,580	6,790 e	-1.9	2.3	4	9	4	3	1	281	1	13	13	53
Equatorial Guinea	13,560	18,880	–	16.2	11	–	3	–	–	24	0	–	–	–
Eritrea	450	560 e	–	-1.0 x	14 x	–	1	–	–	135	5	–	–	–
Estonia	15,830	21,990	–	5.3 x	6 x	1 x	5	6	2	–	–	–	19 x	43 x
Ethiopia	410	1,140	–	3.2	8	31	3	5	1	3,532	11	6	20	42
Fiji	4,200	4,880	0.6	1.2	4	6	3	4	2	75	2	–	16	50
Finland	46,940	38,210	2.9	2.4	2	–	7	7	2	–	–	–	24 x	37 x
France	41,750	36,460	2.1	1.2	2	–	9	6	3	–	–	–	–	–
Gabon	10,070	14,290	0.7	-0.8	7	5 x	2	–	1	69	0	–	16 x	48 x
Gambia	510	1,860	0.7	0.4	6	34 x	2	4	–	135	16	6	14 x	53 x
Georgia	3,280	5,860	3.1	2.9	61	18	2	3	3	590	4	21	15	48
Germany	44,010	41,370	2.3	1.3	1	–	9	5	1	–	–	–	23 x	37 x
Ghana	1,550	1,940	-0.9	2.7	25	29 x	3	8	0	1,800	5	2	15 x	49 x
Greece	23,260	24,790	1.3	2.0	5	–	7	–	3	–	–	–	19 x	41 x
Grenada	7,110	10,300 e	4.2 x	2.6	4	–	3	–	–	12	2	11	–	–
Guatemala	3,120	4,960 e	0.2	1.3	7	14 x	2	3	0	392	1	12	10 x	60 x
Guinea	460	980	–	0.7	10	43	2	3	–	201	4	10	16	46
Guinea-Bissau	550	1,190	0.9	-1.2	16	49 x	2	–	–	119	12	–	19 x	43 x
Guyana	3,410	3,400 e	-1.3	2.1	11	–	5	4	1	159	6	–	–	–
Haiti	760	1,240 e	–	-0.9 x	14 x	62 x	3	–	–	1,712	23	0	8 x	63 x
Holy See	–	–	–	–	–	–	–	–	–	–	–	–	–	–
Honduras	2,070	3,890 e	0.8	1.6	12	18	4	–	1	624	4	11	8	60
Hungary	12,390	20,200	3.0	2.4	10	0	5	5	1	–	–	–	21	40

TABLE 7 | ECONOMIC INDICATORS >>

Countries and areas	GNI per capita 2012 US$	GNI per capita 2012 PPP US$	GDP per capita average annual growth rate (%) 1970–1990	GDP per capita average annual growth rate (%) 1990–2012	Average annual rate of inflation (%) 1990–2012	Population below international poverty line of US$1.25 per day (%) 2007–2011*	Public spending as a % of GDP (2007–2011*) allocated to: health	Public spending as a % of GDP (2007–2011*) allocated to: education	Public spending as a % of GDP (2007–2011*) allocated to: military	ODA inflow in millions US$ 2011	ODA inflow as a % of recipient GNI 2011	Debt service as a % of exports of goods and services 2011	Share of household income (%, 2007–2011*) poorest 40%	Share of household income (%, 2007–2011*) richest 20%
Iceland	38,710	33,550	3.2	2.0	5	–	8	8	0	–	–	–	–	–
India	1,530	3,840	2.0	5.0	6	33	1	3	3	3,221	0	6	21	43
Indonesia	3,420	4,810	4.5	2.7	14	16	1	3	1	415	0	14	19	44
Iran (Islamic Republic of)	c	–	-2.5	2.8 x	22 x	2 x	2	5	2	102	–	–	17 x	45 x
Iraq	5,870	4,300	–	-1.7 x	18 x	3	7	–	5	1,904	1	–	22	40
Ireland	38,970	35,110	–	0.7 x	1 x	–	7	6	1	–	–	–	19 x	42 x
Israel	28,930 x	28,070 x	1.9	1.8 x	5 x	–	5	6	7	–	–	–	16 x	45 x
Italy	33,840	32,280	2.8	0.7	3	–	7	5	2	–	–	–	19 x	42 x
Jamaica	5,140	–	-1.3	0.4 x	15 x	0 x	3	6	1	44	0	25	14 x	52 x
Japan	47,870	36,320	3.4	0.7	-1	–	7	4	1	–	–	–	–	–
Jordan	4,720	6,130	2.5 x	2.6	4	0	6	–	5	978	3	5	20	44
Kazakhstan	9,730	11,950	–	4.2	51	0	3	3	1	213	0	34	22	38
Kenya	840	1,760	1.2	0.4	9	43 x	2	7	2	2,484	7	3	14 x	53 x
Kiribati	2,260	3,380 e	-5.8	0.7	3	–	8	–	–	64	27	–	–	–
Kuwait	44,730 x	49,230 x	-6.7 x	0.6 x	6 x	–	2	–	3	–	–	–	–	–
Kyrgyzstan	990	2,260	–	0.8	33	5	4	6	4	523	9	7	20	41
Lao People's Democratic Republic	1,260	2,730	–	4.7	20	34	1	3	0	397	5	11	19	45
Latvia	14,180	21,020	3.4	4.5	16	0	4	5	1	–	–	46	19	42
Lebanon	9,190	14,400	–	1.7	7	–	2	2	4	472	1	16	–	–
Lesotho	1,380	2,210	3.0	2.6	8	43 x	6	13	2	259	9	2	10 x	56 x
Liberia	370	600	-4.1	5.5	29	84	4	3	0	765	54	0	17	45
Libya	c	–	–	–	–	–	1	–	1	642	–	–	–	–
Liechtenstein	d	–	2.2	2.9 x	1 x	–	–	2	–	–	–	–	–	–
Lithuania	13,850	22,760	–	3.7	19	0	5	6	1	–	–	19	18	44
Luxembourg	76,960	63,000	2.6	2.5	3	–	6	–	1	–	–	–	21 x	39 x
Madagascar	430	950	-2.4	-0.3	13	81	3	3	1	441	5	–	14	50
Malawi	320	880	-0.1	1.2	25	62	6	5	–	804	15	1	16	50
Malaysia	9,800	16,530	4.0	3.1	4	0	2	5	2	31	0	4	14	51
Maldives	5,750	7,690	–	5.3 x	5 x	2 x	4	7	–	46	3	4	18 x	44 x
Mali	660	1,160	0.3	2.3	5	50	3	5	2	1,270	12	–	20	41
Malta	19,760	26,990	6.0	2.3	3	–	5	5	1	–	–	–	–	–
Marshall Islands	4,140	–	–	0.7	2	–	14	–	–	82	38	–	–	–
Mauritania	1,110	2,520	-1.1	1.2	8	23	2	4	3	381	9	–	16	47
Mauritius	8,570	15,820	3.2 x	3.6	6	–	3	4	0	183	2	2	–	–
Mexico	9,740	16,630	1.7	1.2	12	1	3	5	1	958	0	10	14	53
Micronesia (Federated States of)	3,310	4,090 e	–	0.8	2	31 x	12	–	–	134	41	–	7 x	64 x
Monaco	d	–	1.5	1.7 x	2 x	–	4	–	–	–	–	–	–	–
Mongolia	3,160	5,100	–	3.6	24	–	3	5	1	340	4	2	18	44

TABLE 7 | ECONOMIC INDICATORS >>

TABLE 7

Countries and areas	GNI per capita 2012 US$	GNI per capita 2012 PPP US$	GDP per capita average annual growth rate (%) 1970–1990	GDP per capita average annual growth rate (%) 1990–2012	Average annual rate of inflation (%) 1990–2012	Population below international poverty line of US$1.25 per day (%) 2007–2011*	Public spending as a % of GDP (2007–2011*) allocated to: health	education	military	ODA inflow in millions US$ 2011	ODA inflow as a % of recipient GNI 2011	Debt service as a % of exports of goods and services 2011	Share of household income (%, 2007–2011*) poorest 40%	richest 20%
Montenegro	6,940	13,930	–	3.1 x	6 x	0	6	–	2	124	3	9	22	37
Morocco	2,940	5,040	2.1	2.6	3	3	2	5	3	1,427	1	8	17	48
Mozambique	510	1,020	-1.1 x	4.2	16	60	3	–	1	2,071	17	1	14	51
Myanmar	a	–	1.4	7.3 x	24 x	–	0	1	–	376	–	0	–	–
Namibia	5,670	7,470	-2.1 x	2.2	9	32 x	3	8	4	274	2	–	8 x	69 x
Nauru	–	–	–	–	–	–	–	–	–	–	–	–	–	–
Nepal	700	1,500	1.2	2.3	7	25	2	5	2	892	5	3	20	41
Netherlands	48,250	43,360	1.6	1.8	2	–	10	6	2	–	–	–	–	–
New Zealand	30,620 x	29,960 x	1.3 x	1.7	2 x	–	8	7	1	–	–	–	–	–
Nicaragua	1,650	3,960 e	-3.7	2.0	17	12 x	6	5	1	695	7	12	16 x	47 x
Niger	370	650	-1.9	-0.7	5	44	2	4	1	646	11	–	20	43
Nigeria	1,430	2,420	-1.3	2.1	19	54	2	–	1	1,777	1	0	16	46
Niue	–	–	–	–	–	–	–	–	–	–	–	–	–	–
Norway	98,860	64,030	3.2	1.8	4	–	8	7	2	–	–	–	24 x	37 x
Oman	19,120 x	25,580 x	3.2	2.4 x	5 x	–	2	4	10	–	–	–	–	–
Pakistan	1,260	3,030	2.6	2.0	10	21	1	2	3	3,509	2	6	23	40
Palau	9,860	17,150 e	–	-0.1 x	5 x	–	8	–	–	28	15	–	–	–
Panama	9,910	17,830 e	0.2	3.5	3	7	6	4	–	110	0	4	11	56
Papua New Guinea	1,790	2,780 e	-1.0	0.3	8	–	3	–	0	611	5	–	–	–
Paraguay	3,290	5,610	3.7	0.4	10	7	3	4	1	94	0	3	11	56
Peru	5,880	10,240	-0.6	3.3	9	5	3	3	1	599	0	6	12	53
Philippines	2,470	4,400	0.6	2.0	7	18	1	3	1	-192	0	14	15	50
Poland	12,670	20,920	–	4.3	9	0	5	5	2	–	–	–	20	41
Portugal	20,580	24,670	2.5	1.4	3	–	7	6	2	–	–	–	–	–
Qatar	78,720 x	84,670 x	–	0.9 x	11 x	–	2	2	2	–	–	–	–	52
Republic of Korea	22,670	30,890	6.2	4.1	4	–	4	5	3	–	–	–	–	–
Republic of Moldova	2,070	3,690	1.8 x	0.2	36	0	5	9	0	469	6	10	20	41
Romania	8,420	16,310	0.9 x	2.8	41	0	4	4	1	–	–	25	23	36
Russian Federation	12,700	22,760	–	2.4	49	0	3	4	4	–	–	10	16	47
Rwanda	560 x	1,250 x	1.1	2.7	9	63	6	5	1	1,262	20	2	13	57
Saint Kitts and Nevis	13,330	17,280 e	6.5 x	2.0	5	–	2	4	–	16	2	–	–	–
Saint Lucia	6,530	11,020 e	5.1 x	1.2	3	–	3	4	–	35	3	7	–	–
Saint Vincent and the Grenadines	6,380	10,810 e	3.3	3.2	3	–	4	5	–	18	3	14	–	–
Samoa	3,220	4,270 e	–	2.6	5	–	5	6	–	100	16	3	–	–
San Marino	d	–	1.7	3.3 x	3 x	–	6	–	–	–	–	–	–	–
Sao Tome and Principe	1,320	1,850	–	1.8 x	16 x	28 x	3	–	–	75	30	4	14 x	56 x
Saudi Arabia	18,030 x	25,010 x	-1.4	0.2 x	5 x	–	2	6	8	–	–	–	–	–
Senegal	1,040	1,920	-0.6	1.1	4	30	3	6	2	1,049	7	–	16	47
Serbia	5,280	11,180	–	1.5	21 x	0	6	5	2	1,378	3	26	21	38

TABLE 7 | ECONOMIC INDICATORS >>

Countries and areas	GNI per capita 2012 US$	GNI per capita 2012 PPP US$	GDP per capita average annual growth rate (%) 1970–1990	GDP per capita average annual growth rate (%) 1990–2012	Average annual rate of inflation (%) 1990–2012	Population below international poverty line of US$1.25 per day (%) 2007–2011*	Public spending as a % of GDP (2007–2011*) allocated to: health	education	military	ODA inflow in millions US$ 2011	ODA inflow as a % of recipient GNI 2011	Debt service as a % of exports of goods and services 2011	Share of household income (%, 2007–2011*) poorest 40%	richest 20%
Seychelles	11,640	25,760 e	3.5	2.0	6	0	3	–	1	21	2	2	10	70
Sierra Leone	580	1,360	-0.7	0.9	19	52	3	4	1	424	15	2	20	44
Singapore	47,210	61,100	5.9	3.4	1	–	1	3	4	–	–	–	–	–
Slovakia	17,170	24,370	–	3.7	6	0	6	4	2	–	–	–	24	36
Slovenia	22,710	26,470	–	3.0	11	0 x	7	6	2	–	–	–	21 x	39 x
Solomon Islands	1,130	2,170 e	–	-0.5	7	–	7	7	–	334	50	3	–	–
Somalia	a	–	–	–	–	–	–	–	–	1,096	–	–	–	–
South Africa	7,610	11,190	0.1	1.4	8	14	4	6	1	1,398	0	5	8	68
South Sudan	650	–	–	–	–	–	1	–	3	1,087	7	–	–	–
Spain	30,110	31,780	1.9	1.8	3	–	7	5	1	–	–	–	19 x	42 x
Sri Lanka	2,920	6,120	3.0	4.2	10	4	2	2	3	611	1	6	19	45
State of Palestine	b	–	–	–	4 x	0	–	–	–	2,417	–	–	19	43
Sudan	1,450	2,030	-0.1	3.1	25	20	2	–	–	1,123	2	5	19	42
Suriname	8,480	8,500 e	-2.3 x	1.9	41	–	3	–	–	95	2	–	–	–
Swaziland	2,860	4,840	3.1	1.0	9	41	6	8	3	125	3	–	11	57
Sweden	56,210	43,160	1.8	2.1	2	–	8	7	1	–	–	–	23 x	37 x
Switzerland	82,730	54,870	1.7 x	0.9	1	–	7	5	1	–	–	–	20 x	41 x
Syrian Arab Republic	2,610 x	5,200	2.1	1.7 x	7 x	2 x	2	5	4	335	–	–	19 x	44 x
Tajikistan	860	2,220	–	0.2	67	7	2	4	–	355	6	14	21	39
Thailand	5,210	9,430	4.8	2.9	3	0	3	4	2	-153	0	4	18	47
The former Yugoslav Republic of Macedonia	4,690	11,570	–	1.4	20	1	4	–	1	193	2	16	14	49
Timor-Leste	3,670	6,410 e	–	2.7 x	7 x	–	4	10	3	284	7	–	–	–
Togo	500	920	-0.5	0.0	4	28	4	5	2	557	17	–	16	46
Tonga	4,240	5,140 e	–	1.5	6	–	4	–	–	94	21	–	–	–
Trinidad and Tobago	14,400	22,400 e	0.4	4.7	5	–	3	–	–	–	–	–	–	–
Tunisia	4,150	9,360	2.5	3.3	4	1	3	6	1	918	2	11	19	43
Turkey	10,830	17,500	1.9	2.5	41	1	5	–	2	3,193	0	27	17	46
Turkmenistan	5,550	9,640 e	–	2.7	86	–	2	–	–	38	0	–	–	–
Tuvalu	6,070	–	–	1.5	4	–	17	–	–	43	77	–	–	–
Uganda	440	1,140	–	3.5	8	38	2	3	2	1,582	10	1	16	51
Ukraine	3,500	7,290	–	0.8	62	0	4	5	3	811	1	29	24	36
United Arab Emirates	36,040 x	42,380 e,x	-4.3 x	-2.5 x	5 x	–	3	–	5	–	–	–	–	–
United Kingdom	38,250	35,800	2.0	2.1	2	–	8	6	3	–	–	–	–	–
United Republic of Tanzania	570	1,590	–	2.6	13	68	3	6	1	2,436	10	2	18	45
United States	50,120	50,610	2.1	1.6	2	–	8	5	5	–	–	–	16 x	46 x
Uruguay	13,510	15,570	0.9	2.3	15	0	5	–	2	15	0	11	14	51
Uzbekistan	1,720	3,750 e	–	2.7	73	–	3	–	–	215	0	–	19 x	44 x
Vanuatu	3,080	4,500 e	1.1 x	0.6	3	–	5	7	–	91	12	1	–	–

TABLE 7 | ECONOMIC INDICATORS

TABLE 7

Countries and areas	GNI per capita 2012 US$	GNI per capita 2012 PPP US$	GDP per capita average annual growth rate (%) 1970–1990	GDP per capita average annual growth rate (%) 1990–2012	Average annual rate of inflation (%) 1990–2012	Population below international poverty line of US$1.25 per day (%) 2007–2011*	Public spending as a % of GDP (2007–2011*) allocated to: health	education	military	ODA inflow in millions US$ 2011	ODA inflow as a % of recipient GNI 2011	Debt service as a % of exports of goods and services 2011	Share of household income (%, 2007–2011*) poorest 40%	richest 20%
Venezuela (Bolivarian Republic of)	12,470	13,120	-1.6	0.5	32	7 x	3	4	1	44	0	6	14 x	49 x
Viet Nam	1,400	3,440	–	5.9	10	17	3	7	3	3,595	3	3	19	43
Yemen	1,110 x	2,310 x	–	1.2	15	18 x	2	5	4	502	2	2	18 x	45 x
Zambia	1,350	1,620	-2.2	0.9	27	75	4	1	2	1,046	6	2	10	62
Zimbabwe	680	–	-0.4	-3.1	2	–	–	3	1	716	8	–	–	–
SUMMARY INDICATORS#														
Sub-Saharan Africa	1,397	2,349	0.0	2.1	29	44	3	5	2	42,959	3	3	16	48
Eastern and Southern Africa	1,729	2,971	0.3	2.0	34	45	3	5	2	21,904	3	4	15	51
West and Central Africa	1,071	1,810	-0.4	2.1	20	46	–	–	–	19,790	4	1	17	46
Middle East and North Africa	–	5,455	0.0	–	–	–	2	5	5	11,569	1	6	–	–
South Asia	1,440	3,573	2.0	4.6	7	32	1	3	3	16,631	1	5	21	42
East Asia and Pacific	5,592	8,847	5.6	7.5	5	12	3 **	4 **	2**	6,996	0	4	16	47
Latin America and Caribbean	9,212	12,123	1.4	1.7	29	5	4	5	1	9,303	0	12	12	56
CEE/CIS	8,727	15,463	–	2.6	48	1	4	4	3	9,870	1	17	19	43
Least developed countries	779	1,557	-0.2	3.2	47	44	2	4	2	45,373	7	3	19	45
World	10,132	12,047	2.4	2.7	8	20	7 **	5 **	3**	96,063	0	8	17	46

\# For a complete list of countries and areas in the regions, subregions and country categories, see page 26

DEFINITIONS OF THE INDICATORS

GNI per capita – Gross national income (GNI) is the sum of value added by all resident producers plus any product taxes (less subsidies) not included in the valuation of output plus net receipts of primary income (compensation of employees and property income) from abroad. GNI per capita is gross national income divided by midyear population. GNI per capita in US dollars is converted using the World Bank Atlas method.

GNI per capita (PPP US$) – GNI per capita converted to international dollars taking into account differences in price levels (purchasing power) between countries. Based on data from the International Comparison Programme.

GDP per capita – Gross domestic product (GDP) is the sum of value added by all resident producers plus any product taxes (less subsidies) not included in the valuation of output. GDP per capita is gross domestic product divided by midyear population. Growth is calculated from constant price GDP data in local currency.

Population below international poverty line of US$1.25 per day – Percentage of the population living on less than US$1.25 per day at 2005 prices, adjusted for purchasing power parity. The new poverty threshold reflects revisions to purchasing power parity exchange rates based on the results of the 2005 International Comparison Programme. The revisions reveal that the cost of living is higher across the developing world than previously estimated. As a result of these revisions, poverty rates for individual countries cannot be compared with poverty rates reported in previous editions. More detailed information on the definition, methodology and sources of the data presented is available at <www.worldbank.org>.

ODA – Net official development assistance.

Debt service – Sum of interest payments and repayments of principal on external public and publicly guaranteed long-term debts.

Share of household income – Percentage of income received by the 20 per cent of households with the highest income and by the 40 per cent of households with the lowest income.

MAIN DATA SOURCES

GNI per capita – The World Bank.
GDP per capita – The World Bank.
Rate of inflation – The World Bank.
Population below international poverty line of US$1.25 per day – The World Bank.
Public spending on health, education and military – The World Bank.
ODA – Organisation for Economic Co-operation and Development.
Debt service – The World Bank.
Share of household income – The World Bank.

NOTES

a low-income country (GNI per capita is $1,035 or less).
b lower-middle-income country (GNI per capita is $1,036 to $4,085).
c upper-middle-income country (GNI per capita is $4,086 to $12,615).
d high-income country (GNI per capita is $12,616 or more).
– Data not available.
x Data refer to years or periods other than those specified in the column heading. Such data are not included in the calculation of regional and global averages.
e Estimate is based on regression; other PPP figures are extrapolated from the 2005 International Comparison Programme benchmark estimates.
* Data refer to the most recent year available during the period specified in the column heading.
** Excludes China.

TABLE 8 | WOMEN

Countries and areas	Life expectancy: females as a % of males 2012	Adult literacy rate: females as a % of males 2008–2012*	Enrolment ratios: females as a % of males 2008–2012* primary GER	Enrolment ratios: females as a % of males 2008–2012* secondary GER	Survival rate to the last grade of primary: females as a % of males 2008–2011*	Contraceptive prevalence (%) 2008–2012*	Antenatal care (%) 2008–2012* at least one visit	Antenatal care (%) 2008–2012* at least four visits	Delivery care (%) 2008–2012* skilled attendant at birth	Delivery care (%) 2008–2012* institutional delivery	Delivery care (%) 2008–2012* C-section	Maternal mortality ratio† 2008–2012 reported	Maternal mortality ratio† 2010 adjusted	Maternal mortality ratio† 2010 lifetime risk of maternal death (1 in:)
Afghanistan	104	–	71	55	–	21	48	15	39	33	4	330	460	32
Albania	108	98	–	–	100	69	97	67	99	97	19	21	27	2,200
Algeria	105	79 x	94	104	101	61 x	89 x	–	95 x	95 x	–	–	97	430
Andorra	–	–	–	103	–	–	–	–	–	–	–	–	–	–
Angola	106	71	81	69	73	–	80 x	–	47 x	46 x	–	–	450	39
Antigua and Barbuda	107	101	93	98	–	–	100	–	100	–	–	0 x	–	–
Argentina	110	100	98	111	101	78 x	99 x	89 x	97	99	–	40	77	560
Armenia	109	100	102	102	100	55	99	93	100	99	13	14	30	1,700
Australia	106	–	99	95	–	72 x	98	92	–	99	31	–	7	8,100
Austria	107	–	99	96	101	–	–	–	–	–	24 x	–	4	18,200
Azerbaijan	109	100	98	98	97	51 x	77 x	45 x	99	78 x	5 x	24	43	1,000
Bahamas	108	–	102	105	96	45 x	98 x	–	99 x	–	–	0 x	47	1,100
Bahrain	102	95	–	–	101	–	100 x	–	100	–	–	–	20	1,800
Bangladesh	102	86	–	117	114	61	55	26	32	29	17	220	240	170
Barbados	107	–	98	112	–	–	100 x	–	100 x	–	–	0 x	51	1,300
Belarus	118	100	100	97	103	63	100	100	100	100	25	1	4	16,300
Belgium	107	–	100	97	103	75 x	–	–	–	–	18 x	–	8	7,500
Belize	109	–	92	–	95	55	96	83	96	94	28	55	53	610
Benin	105	45 x	87	60	91	13	86	61 x	84	87	4 x	400 x	350	53
Bhutan	101	59 x	101	104	108	66	97	77	65	63	12	150	180	210
Bolivia (Plurinational State of)	107	91	99	98	99	61	86	72	71	68	19	310	190	140
Bosnia and Herzegovina	107	97	101	103	99	46	87	84	100	100	14	3	8	11,400
Botswana	97	101	96	106	104	53 x	94 x	73 x	95 x	99	–	160	160	220
Brazil	110	101	–	–	–	81 x	98	91	97 x	98	50	75 x	56	910
Brunei Darussalam	105	97	101	102	–	–	99	–	100	100	–	–	24	1,900
Bulgaria	110	99	100	95	99	–	–	–	100	93	31	3	11	5,900
Burkina Faso	102	59 x	93	78	111	16	94	34	66	66	2	340	300	55
Burundi	107	95	100	74	115	22	99	33	60	60	4	500	800	31
Cabo Verde	111	89	92	117	99	61 x	98 x	72 x	78 x	76	11 x	54	79	480
Cambodia	108	80	95	85	102	51	89	59	71	61	3	210	250	150
Cameroon	104	83	87	84	101	23	85	62	64	61	4	780	690	31
Canada	105	–	100	98	–	74 x	100 x	99 x	100 x	99 x	26 x	–	12	5,200
Central African Republic	108	63	73	55	90	15	68	38	54	53	5	540 x	890	26
Chad	103	56	75	44	92	5	53	23	23	16	2	1,100 x	1,100	15
Chile	107	100	97	103	99	58 x	–	–	100	100	–	18	25	2,200
China	103	95	104	105	–	85 x	94	–	100	99	36	26	37	1,700
Colombia	110	100	96	109	99	79	97	89	99	99	44	73	92	430
Comoros	105	88	85	–	–	19	92	–	82	76	–	380 x	280	67
Congo	105	–	95	–	–	45	93	75 x	94	92	3 x	780 x	560	39
Cook Islands	–	–	103	120	–	29 x	100	–	100	100	–	0	–	–
Costa Rica	106	100	99	105	103	82	90	86	99	99	21	23	40	1,300

TABLE 8 | WOMEN >>

TABLE 8

Countries and areas	Life expectancy: females as a % of males 2012	Adult literacy rate: females as a % of males 2008–2012*	Enrolment ratios: females as a % of males 2008–2012* primary GER	secondary GER	Survival rate to the last grade of primary: females as a % of males 2008–2011*	Contraceptive prevalence (%) 2008–2012*	Antenatal care (%) 2008–2012* at least one visit	at least four visits	Delivery care (%) 2008–2012* skilled attendant at birth	institutional delivery	C-section	Maternal mortality ratio† 2008–2012 reported	2010 adjusted	2010 lifetime risk of maternal death (1 in:)
Côte d'Ivoire	103	72	83	–	96	18	91	44	59	57	3	610	400	53
Croatia	109	99	100	107	101	–	–	–	100	–	18	10	17	4,100
Cuba	105	100	98	99	102	74	100	100	100	100	–	33	73	1,000
Cyprus	105	99	100	101	–	–	99 x	–	–	100 x	–	–	10	6,300
Czech Republic	108	–	100	100	100	–	–	–	100	–	20 x	2	5	12,100
Democratic People's Republic of Korea	111	100	–	–	–	69 x	100	94	100	95	13	77	81	670
Democratic Republic of the Congo	107	60 x	87	59	81	17	89	45	80	75	7	550 x	540	30
Denmark	106	–	100	101	101	–	–	–	–	–	21 x	–	12	4,500
Djibouti	105	–	90	80	101	23	92 x	7 x	93 x	87 x	12	550 x	200	140
Dominica	–	–	99	107	113	–	100	–	100	–	–	0 x	–	–
Dominican Republic	109	100	91	113	–	73 x	99 x	95 x	98 x	98 x	42 x	160 x	150	240
Ecuador	108	97	100	102	102	73 x	84 x	58 x	98 x	85 x	26 x	69	110	350
Egypt	107	81	94	96	100	60	74	66	79	72	28	55	66	490
El Salvador	114	94	95	100	105	73	94	78	96	85	25	51	81	490
Equatorial Guinea	106	94	98	–	111	10 x	86 x	–	65 x	–	–	–	240	88
Eritrea	108	74	83	78	94	8 x	70 x	41 x	28 x	26 x	3 x	–	240	86
Estonia	115	100	99	100	100	–	–	–	100 x	–	–	7 x	2	25,100
Ethiopia	105	59 x	91	87	105	29	43	19	10	10	2	680	350	67
Fiji	109	–	100	108	95	32	100	–	100	–	–	23	26	1,400
Finland	108	–	99	105	100	–	100 x	–	–	100	16 x	–	5	12,200
France	109	–	99	101	–	71 x	100 x	–	–	–	21 x	–	8	6,200
Gabon	103	93	97	–	–	31	95	78	89	90	10	320	230	130
Gambia	105	69	103	95	110	13	98	72	57	56	3	730 x	360	56
Georgia	110	100	103	–	105	53	98	90	100	98	35	28	67	960
Germany	106	–	100	95	101	–	100 x	–	–	–	29 x	–	7	10,600
Ghana	103	83	100	91	91	34	96	87	68	67	11	450 x	350	68
Greece	106	98	100	96	–	76 x	–	–	–	–	–	–	3	25,500
Grenada	107	–	97	103	–	54 x	100 x	–	99 x	–	–	0 x	24	1,700
Guatemala	110	88	96	92	100	54	93	–	52	51	16	140 x	120	190
Guinea	103	33	87	64	80	6	85	50 x	45	40	2 x	980 x	610	30
Guinea-Bissau	106	61	94	–	–	14	93	68	43	41	2	410 x	790	25
Guyana	108	106	104	110	96	43	92	79	92	89	13	86	280	150
Haiti	106	84 x	–	–	–	35	90	67	37	36	6	630 x	350	83
Holy See	–	–	–	–	–	–	–	–	–	–	–	–	–	–
Honduras	107	100	100	122	110	73	97	89	83	83	19	–	100	270
Hungary	112	100	99	98	100	–	–	–	99	–	31 x	19	21	3,300
Iceland	104	–	100	102	101	–	–	–	–	–	17 x	–	5	8,900
India	105	68 x	100	92	–	55	74 x	37 x	52	47	9 x	210	200	170
Indonesia	106	94	102	100	–	62	96	88	83	63	12	360	220	210
Iran (Islamic Republic of)	105	90	99	96	100	77	97	94 x	96	95	46	25 x	21	2,400

TABLE 8 | WOMEN >>

Countries and areas	Life expectancy: females as a % of males 2012	Adult literacy rate: females as a % of males 2008–2012*	Enrolment ratios: females as a % of males 2008–2012* primary GER	Enrolment ratios: females as a % of males 2008–2012* secondary GER	Survival rate to the last grade of primary: females as a % of males 2008–2011*	Contraceptive prevalence (%) 2008–2012*	Antenatal care (%) 2008–2012* at least one visit	Antenatal care (%) 2008–2012* at least four visits	Delivery care (%) 2008–2012* skilled attendant at birth	Delivery care (%) 2008–2012* institutional delivery	Delivery care (%) 2008–2012* C-section	Maternal mortality ratio† 2008–2012 reported	Maternal mortality ratio† 2010 adjusted	Maternal mortality ratio† 2010 lifetime risk of maternal death (1 in:)
Iraq	111	83	–	–	–	53	78	50	91	77	22	84 x	63	310
Ireland	106	–	100	103	–	65 x	100 x	–	100 x	100 x	25 x	–	6	8,100
Israel	105	–	100	102	–	–	–	–	–	–	–	–	7	5,100
Italy	107	100	99	99	100	–	99 x	68 x	–	99 x	40 x	–	4	20,300
Jamaica	107	112	95	103	102	72	99	87	98	97	15	95 x	110	370
Japan	109	–	100	100	100	54 x	–	–	–	100 x	–	–	5	13,100
Jordan	105	96	100	106	–	61	99	94 x	100	99	19 x	19	63	470
Kazakhstan	119	100	100	97	100	51	99	87	100	100	16	17	51	770
Kenya	106	86 x	98	90	–	46	92	47	44	43	6	490	360	55
Kiribati	109	–	104	111	–	22	88	71	80	66	10	0	–	–
Kuwait	103	97	103	107	100	–	100 x	–	100 x	–	–	–	14	2,900
Kyrgyzstan	113	99	99	100	101	36	97	–	99	99	–	64	71	480
Lao People's Democratic Republic	104	77 x	94	85	103	50	54	37	42	38	4	360	470	74
Latvia	116	100	99	96	99	–	92 x	–	100 x	–	–	32	34	2,000
Lebanon	105	92 x	97	111	107	54	96 x	–	98 x	–	–	–	25	2,100
Lesotho	101	130	97	140	131	47	92	70	62	59	7	1,200	620	53
Liberia	103	44 x	91	81	85	11 x	79 x	66 x	46 x	37 x	4 x	990 x	770	24
Libya	105	87	–	–	–	–	93 x	–	100	–	–	–	58	620
Liechtenstein	–	–	101	83	96	–	–	–	–	–	–	–	–	–
Lithuania	119	100	98	97	101	–	100 x	–	100 x	–	–	9	8	9,400
Luxembourg	107	–	101	103	–	–	–	–	100 x	100 x	29 x	–	20	3,200
Madagascar	105	91	98	94	103	40	86	49	44	35	2	500	240	81
Malawi	100	71	104	91	103	46	95	46	71	73	5	680	460	36
Malaysia	106	95	–	107	101	49 x	97	–	99	99	–	26	29	1,300
Maldives	103	100 x	98	–	–	35	99	85	95	95	32	140 x	60	870
Mali	99	57	88	71	95	10	75	35	56	56	4	460 x	540	28
Malta	106	103 x	101	89	91	–	100 x	–	–	100	–	–	8	8,900
Marshall Islands	–	–	99	103	91	45 x	81 x	77 x	99	85 x	9 x	140	–	–
Mauritania	105	80	106	84	102	9 x	84	48	65	65	10	630	510	44
Mauritius	110	95	–	–	101	76 x	–	–	98 x	98 x	–	22 x	60	1,000
Mexico	106	97	99	107	102	73	96	86	96	80 x	46	43	50	790
Micronesia (Federated States of)	103	–	–	–	–	55	80	–	100	–	–	0	100	290
Monaco	–	–	–	–	–	–	–	–	–	–	–	–	–	–
Mongolia	113	101	98	106	102	55	99	81	99	99	21	47	63	600
Montenegro	106	98	100	100	102	39 x	97 x	–	100	100	–	13 x	8	7,400
Morocco	105	76	94	86	99	67	77	31 x	74	73	16	130	100	400
Mozambique	104	54	91	87	93	12	91	51	54	55	4	410	490	43
Myanmar	107	95	100	106	107	46	83	73 x	71	36	–	320 x	200	250
Namibia	109	105 x	99	–	106	55 x	95 x	70 x	81 x	81 x	13 x	450 x	200	160
Nauru	–	–	106	120	–	36 x	95 x	40 x	97 x	99 x	8 x	0	–	–

TABLE 8 | WOMEN >>

Countries and areas	Life expectancy: females as a % of males 2012	Adult literacy rate: females as a % of males 2008–2012*	Enrolment ratios: females as a % of males 2008–2012*		Survival rate to the last grade of primary: females as a % of males 2008–2011*	Contraceptive prevalence (%) 2008–2012*	Antenatal care (%) 2008–2012*		Delivery care (%) 2008–2012*			Maternal mortality ratio†		
			primary GER	secondary GER			at least one visit	at least four visits	skilled attendant at birth	institutional delivery	C-section	2008–2012 reported	2010 adjusted	2010 lifetime risk of maternal death (1 in:)
Nepal	103	66	–	–	–	50	58	50	36	35	5	280 x	170	190
Netherlands	105	–	99	99	–	69	–	–	–	100 x	14 x	–	6	10,500
New Zealand	105	–	100	105	–	–	–	–	–	–	23 x	–	15	3,300
Nicaragua	109	100 x	98	110	–	72 x	90 x	78 x	74 x	86	20 x	63	95	350
Niger	101	35 x	84	65	94	14	83	15 x	29	30	1 x	650 x	590	23
Nigeria	101	68	91	88	107	18	66	57	49	45	5	550	630	29
Niue	–	–	–	–	–	23 x	100	–	100	–	–	0	–	–
Norway	105	–	100	98	100	88 x	–	–	–	–	16 x	–	7	7,900
Oman	106	91	98	98	–	24	99	96	99	99 x	14 x	16	32	1,200
Pakistan	103	59	82	73	96	27	61 x	28 x	43	41	7 x	250 x	260	110
Palau	–	–	–	–	–	22	90	81	100	100	–	0	–	–
Panama	108	99	97	108	104	52	96	–	89	88	–	60 x	92	410
Papua New Guinea	107	91	89	–	–	32 x	79 x	55 x	53 x	52 x	–	730 x	230	110
Paraguay	106	98	96	105	103	79	96	91	82	85	33	100	99	310
Peru	108	89 x	99	99	98	76	96	94	87	87	25	93	67	570
Philippines	111	101	98	108	111	49	91	78	62	44	10	160 x	99	300
Poland	112	100	99	99	100	–	–	–	100 x	–	21 x	2	5	14,400
Portugal	108	97	97	102	–	67 x	100 x	–	100 x	–	31 x	–	8	9,200
Qatar	102	99	98	109	–	–	100	–	100	–	–	13	7	5,400
Republic of Korea	109	–	99	99	100	80	–	–	–	–	32 x	–	16	4,800
Republic of Moldova	112	99	99	102	100	68 x	98 x	89 x	99	99	9 x	30	41	1,500
Romania	110	99	99	99	100	70 x	94 x	76 x	99	98 x	19 x	21	27	2,600
Russian Federation	120	100	100	98	–	80 x	–	–	100	–	–	17	34	2,000
Rwanda	105	87	103	105	111	52	98	35	69	69	7	480	340	54
Saint Kitts and Nevis	–	–	102	104	90	54	100 x	–	100	–	–	0 x	–	–
Saint Lucia	107	–	98	97	104	–	99 x	–	100 x	–	–	0 x	35	1,400
Saint Vincent and the Grenadines	106	–	93	102	–	48 x	100	–	99	–	–	0 x	48	940
Samoa	109	100	104	115	106	29	93	58	81	81	13	29 x	100	260
San Marino	–	–	99	101	–	–	–	–	–	–	–	–	–	–
Sao Tome and Principe	106	75	97	115	–	38	98	72	82	79	5	160	70	330
Saudi Arabia	105	91	100	88	–	24 x	97	–	97	–	–	–	24	1,400
Senegal	105	63	107	92	101	13	93	50	65	73	6	390	370	54
Serbia	108	98	100	102	101	61	99	94	100	100	25	9	12	4,900
Seychelles	113	101	100	112	99	–	–	–	–	–	–	57 x	–	–
Sierra Leone	101	60	93	–	–	11	93	75	63	50	5	860	890	23
Singapore	106	96	–	–	100	–	–	–	–	100 x	–	–	3	25,300
Slovakia	111	–	99	101	101	–	97 x	–	99	–	24 x	10	6	12,200
Slovenia	109	100	100	99	99	–	100 x	–	100	–	–	10	12	5,900
Solomon Islands	104	–	99	88	–	35 x	74 x	65 x	86 x	85 x	6 x	150	93	240
Somalia	106	–	–	–	–	15 x	26 x	6 x	33 x	9 x	–	1,000 x	1,000	16
South Africa	107	98	96	105	–	60 x	97	87	91 x	89 x	21 x	400 x	300	140

TABLE 8 | WOMEN >>

Countries and areas	Life expectancy: females as a % of males 2012	Adult literacy rate: females as a % of males 2008–2012*	Enrolment ratios: females as a % of males 2008–2012*		Survival rate to the last grade of primary: females as a % of males 2008–2011*	Contraceptive prevalence (%) 2008–2012*	Antenatal care (%) 2008–2012*		Delivery care (%) 2008–2012*			Maternal mortality ratio†		
			primary GER	secondary GER			at least one visit	at least four visits	skilled attendant at birth	institutional delivery	C-section	2008–2012 reported	2010 adjusted	2010 lifetime risk of maternal death (1 in:)
South Sudan	104	–	–	–	–	4	40	17	19	12	1	2,100 x	–	–
Spain	108	98	99	101	99	66 x	–	–	–	–	26 x	–	6	12,000
Sri Lanka	109	97	99	104	95	68 x	99 x	93 x	99 x	98 x	24 x	39 x	35	1,200
State of Palestine	105	95	99	110	–	53	98	94	99	98	17	–	64	330
Sudan	106	–	–	–	–	9	74	47	23	21	7	94 x	–	–
Suriname	109	99	96	131	122	48	91	67	91	92	19	83	130	320
Swaziland	98	99	90	97	–	65	97	77	82	80	12	590 x	320	95
Sweden	105	–	100	99	100	–	100 x	–	–	–	–	–	4	14,100
Switzerland	106	–	100	97	–	–	–	–	–	–	30 x	–	8	9,500
Syrian Arab Republic	108	86	99	100	101	54	88	64	96	78	26	65 x	70	460
Tajikistan	110	100	96	87	100	28	79	49 x	87	77	–	37	65	430
Thailand	109	96 x	99	108	–	80	99	80	100	99	24	12 x	48	1,400
The former Yugoslav Republic of Macedonia	106	97	101	99	–	40	99	94	98	98	25	4	10	6,300
Timor-Leste	105	83	96	103	104	22	84	55	29	22	2	560	300	55
Togo	103	65	91	–	86	15	72	55	59	67	9	–	300	80
Tonga	108	100 x	–	–	–	32	98	–	98	98	–	36	110	230
Trinidad and Tobago	111	99	97	107	106	43 x	96 x	–	98 x	97 x	–	–	46	1,300
Tunisia	106	81	96	103	102	63	98	85	99	99	27	–	56	860
Turkey	110	92	99	92	102	73	92	74	91	90	37	29 x	20	2,200
Turkmenistan	114	100	–	–	100	48 x	99 x	83 x	100 x	98 x	3 x	12	67	590
Tuvalu	–	–	–	–	–	31 x	97 x	67 x	98 x	93 x	7 x	0	–	–
Uganda	104	78	102	82	97	30	93	48	57	57	5	440	310	49
Ukraine	118	100	101	97	101	67 x	99 x	75 x	100	99 x	10 x	16	32	2,200
United Arab Emirates	103	102 x	–	–	100	–	100 x	–	100	100	–	0 x	12	4,000
United Kingdom	105	–	99	101	–	84	–	–	–	–	26 x	–	12	4,600
United Republic of Tanzania	104	81	103	87	113	34	88	43	49	50	5	450	460	38
United States	106	–	99	101	–	79	–	–	–	–	31 x	13 x	21	2,400
Uruguay	109	101	97	114	103	78 x	96 x	90 x	100	–	34 x	8	29	1,600
Uzbekistan	110	100	97	98	101	65 x	99 x	–	100 x	97 x	–	21	28	1,400
Vanuatu	106	96	95	102	94	38 x	84 x	–	74 x	80 x	–	86 x	110	230
Venezuela (Bolivarian Republic of)	108	100	97	109	106	–	94 x	–	95 x	95 x	–	63	92	410
Viet Nam	113	96	94	–	–	78	94	60	93	92	20	67	59	870
Yemen	104	59	82	63	83	28 x	47 x	14 x	36 x	24 x	9 x	370 x	200	90
Zambia	106	72 x	99	–	95	41 x	94 x	60 x	47 x	48 x	3 x	480	440	37
Zimbabwe	103	91	–	–	–	59	90	65	66	65	5	960	570	52

TABLE 8 | WOMEN

TABLE 8

Countries and areas	Life expectancy: females as a % of males 2012	Adult literacy rate: females as a % of males 2008–2012*	Enrolment ratios: females as a % of males 2008–2012* primary GER	secondary GER	Survival rate to the last grade of primary: females as a % of males 2008–2011*	Contraceptive prevalence (%) 2008–2012*	Antenatal care (%) 2008–2012* at least one visit	at least four visits	Delivery care (%) 2008–2012* skilled attendant at birth	institutional delivery	C-section	Maternal mortality ratio† 2008–2012 reported	2010 adjusted	lifetime risk of maternal death (1 in:)
SUMMARY INDICATORS#														
Sub-Saharan Africa	104	74	93	83	100	24	78	48	50	48	5	–	500	39
Eastern and Southern Africa	105	81	96	90	103	34	79	43	42	41	4	–	410	52
West and Central Africa	103	66	90	76	97	18	78	52	57	55	5	–	570	32
Middle East and North Africa	106	83	93	94	99	59	83	60	79	71	25	–	170	190
South Asia	105	69	98	92	106	52	71	35	49	44	9	–	220	150
East Asia and Pacific	105	95	102	103	101	64 **	93	79 **	92	86	28	–	82	680
Latin America and Caribbean	109	99	97	107	105	75	96	88	91	90	40	–	81	520
CEE/CIS	115	99	99	96	101	–	–	–	97	–	–	–	32	1,700
Least developed countries	104	75	94	86	101	35	74	37	46	43	6	–	430	52
World	106	90	97	97	102	55 **	83	53 **	68	63	17	–	210	180

For a complete list of countries and areas in the regions, subregions and country categories, see page 26.

DEFINITIONS OF THE INDICATORS

Life expectancy – Number of years newborn children would live if subject to the mortality risks prevailing for the cross section of population at the time of their birth.

Adult literacy rate – Percentage of population aged 15 years and over who can both read and write with understanding a short, simple statement on his/her everyday life.

Primary gross enrolment ratio (GER) – Total enrolment in primary school, regardless of age, expressed as a percentage of the official primary-school-aged population.

Secondary gross enrolment ratio (GER) – Total enrolment in secondary school, regardless of age, expressed as a percentage of the official secondary-school-aged population.

Survival rate to the last grade of primary – Percentage of children entering the first grade of primary school who eventually reach the last grade (administrative data).

Contraceptive prevalence – Percentage of women (aged 15–49) in union currently using any contraceptive method.

Antenatal care – Percentage of women (aged 15–49) attended at least once during pregnancy by skilled health personnel (doctor, nurse or midwife) and the percentage attended by any provider at least four times.

Skilled attendant at birth – Percentage of births attended by skilled heath personnel (doctor, nurse or midwife).

Institutional delivery – Percentage of women (aged 15–49) who gave birth in a health facility.

C-section – Percentage of births delivered by Caesarean section. (C-section rates between 5 per cent and 15 per cent expected with adequate levels of emergency obstetric care.)

Maternal mortality ratio – Number of deaths of women from pregnancy-related causes per 100,000 live births during the same time period. The 'reported' column shows country-reported figures that are not adjusted for under-reporting and misclassification. For the 'adjusted' column, see note below (†). Maternal mortality ratio values have been rounded according to the following scheme: <100, no rounding; 100–999, rounded to nearest 10, and >1,000, rounded to nearest 100.

Lifetime risk of maternal death – Lifetime risk of maternal death takes into account both the probability of becoming pregnant and the probability of dying as a result of that pregnancy, accumulated across a woman's reproductive years.

MAIN DATA SOURCES

Life expectancy – United Nations Population Division.

Adult literacy rate – UNESCO Institute for Statistics (UIS).

Primary and secondary school enrolment – UIS.

Survival rate to the last grade of primary – UIS.

Contraceptive prevalence – Multiple Indicator Cluster Surveys (MICS), Demographic and Health Surveys (DHS) and other nationally representative sources; United Nations Population Division.

Antenatal care – MICS, DHS and other nationally representative sources.

Skilled attendant at birth – MICS, DHS and other nationally representative sources.

Institutional delivery – MICS, DHS and other nationally representative sources.

C-section – MICS, DHS and other nationally representative sources.

Maternal mortality ratio (reported) – Nationally representative sources, including household surveys and vital registration.

Maternal mortality ratio (adjusted) – United Nations Maternal Mortality Estimation Inter-agency Group (WHO, UNICEF, UNFPA and the World Bank).

Lifetime risk of maternal death – United Nations Maternal Mortality Estimation Inter-agency Group (WHO, UNICEF, UNFPA and the World Bank).

NOTES

– Data not available.

x Data refer to years or periods other than those specified in the column heading. Such data are not included in the calculation of regional and global averages, with the exception of 2005–2006 data from India and 2006 data from Brazil. Estimates from data years prior to 2000 are not displayed.

* Data refer to the most recent year available during the period specified in the column heading.

** Excludes China.

† The maternal mortality data in the column headed 'reported' refer to data reported by national authorities. The data in the column headed 'adjusted' refer to the 2010 United Nations inter-agency maternal mortality estimates that were released in May 2012. Periodically, the United Nations Maternal Mortality Estimation Inter-agency Group (WHO, UNICEF, UNFPA and the World Bank) produces internationally comparable sets of maternal mortality data that account for the well-documented problems of under-reporting and misclassification of maternal deaths, including also estimates for countries with no data. Please note that owing to an evolving methodology, these values are not comparable with previously reported maternal mortality ratio 'adjusted' values. Comparable time series on maternal mortality ratios for the years 1990, 1995, 2000, 2005 and 2010 are available at <www.childinfo.org>.

TABLE 9 | CHILD PROTECTION

Countries and areas	Child labour (%)+ 2005–2012* total	male	female	Child marriage (%) 2005–2012* married by 15	married by 18	Birth registration (%)+ 2005–2012* total	Female genital mutilation/cutting (%)+ 2002–2012* prevalence women[a]	girls[b]	attitudes support for the practice[c]	Justification of wife beating (%) 2005–2012* male	female	Violent discipline (%)+ 2005–2012* total	male	female
Afghanistan	10	11	10	15	40	37	–	–	–	–	90	74	75	74
Albania	12	14	9	0	10	99	–	–	–	36	30	75	78	71
Algeria	5 y	6 y	4 y	0	2	99	–	–	–	–	68	88	89	87
Andorra	–	–	–	–	–	100 v	–	–	–	–	–	–	–	–
Angola	24 x	22 x	25 x	–	–	36 x	–	–	–	–	–	–	–	–
Antigua and Barbuda	–	–	–	–	–	–	–	–	–	–	–	–	–	–
Argentina	7 y	8 y	5 y	–	–	99 y	–	–	–	–	–	–	–	–
Armenia	4	5	3	0	7	100	–	–	–	20	9	70	72	67
Australia	–	–	–	–	–	100 v	–	–	–	–	–	–	–	–
Austria	–	–	–	–	–	100 v	–	–	–	–	–	–	–	–
Azerbaijan	7 y	8 y	5 y	1	12	94	–	–	–	58	49	75	79	71
Bahamas	–	–	–	–	–	–	–	–	–	–	–	–	–	–
Bahrain	5 x	6 x	3 x	–	–	–	–	–	–	–	–	–	–	–
Bangladesh	13	18	8	29	65	31	–	–	–	–	33 y	–	–	–
Barbados	–	–	–	–	–	–	–	–	–	–	–	–	–	–
Belarus	1	1	2	0	3	100 y	–	–	–	4	4	65 y	67 y	62 y
Belgium	–	–	–	–	–	100 v	–	–	–	–	–	–	–	–
Belize	6	7	5	3	26	95	–	–	–	–	9	71	71	70
Benin	46	47	45	8	34	80	13	2 y	1	14	47	–	–	–
Bhutan	3	3	3	6	26	100	–	–	–	–	68	–	–	–
Bolivia (Plurinational State of)	26 y	28 y	24 y	3	22	76 y	–	–	–	–	16	–	–	–
Bosnia and Herzegovina	5	7	4	0	4	100	–	–	–	6	5	55	60	50
Botswana	9 y	11 y	7 y	–	–	72	–	–	–	–	–	–	–	–
Brazil	9 y	11 y	6 y	11	36	93 y	–	–	–	–	–	–	–	–
Brunei Darussalam	–	–	–	–	–	–	–	–	–	–	–	–	–	–
Bulgaria	–	–	–	–	–	100 v	–	–	–	–	–	–	–	–
Burkina Faso	39	42	36	10	52	77	76	13	9	34	44	83	84	82
Burundi	26	26	27	3	20	75	–	–	–	44	73	–	–	–
Cabo Verde	3 x,y	4 x,y	3 x,y	3	18	91	–	–	–	16 y	17	–	–	–
Cambodia	36 y	36 y	36 y	2	18	62	–	–	–	22 y	46 y	–	–	–
Cameroon	42	43	40	13	38	61	1	1 y	7	39	47	93	93	93
Canada	–	–	–	–	–	100 v	–	–	–	–	–	–	–	–
Central African Republic	29	27	30	29	68	61	24	1	11	80 y	80	92	92	92
Chad	26	25	28	29	68	16	44	18 y	38	–	62	84	85	84
Chile	3 x	3 x	2 x	–	–	100 y	–	–	–	–	–	–	–	–
China	–	–	–	–	–	–	–	–	–	–	–	–	–	–
Colombia	13 y	17 y	9 y	6	23	97	–	–	–	–	–	–	–	–
Comoros	27 x	26 x	28 x	–	–	88 x	–	–	–	–	–	–	–	–
Congo	25	24	25	7	33	91	–	–	–	–	76	–	–	–

TABLE 9 | CHILD PROTECTION >>

TABLE 9

Countries and areas	Child labour (%)* 2005–2012*			Child marriage (%) 2005–2012*		Birth registration (%)+ 2005–2012* total	Female genital mutilation/cutting (%)+ 2002–2012*			Justification of wife beating (%) 2005–2012*		Violent discipline (%)+ 2005–2012*		
							prevalence		attitudes					
	total	male	female	married by 15	married by 18		women[a]	girls[b]	support for the practice[c]	male	female	total	male	female
Cook Islands	–	–	–	–	–	–	–	–	–	–	–	–	–	–
Costa Rica	5 x	6 x	3 x	–	–	–	–	–	–	–	–	–	–	–
Côte d'Ivoire	26	25	28	10	33	65	38	10	14	42	48	91	91	91
Croatia	–	–	–	–	–	–	–	–	–	–	–	–	–	–
Cuba	–	–	–	9	40	100 y	–	–	–	–	–	–	–	–
Cyprus	–	–	–	–	–	100 v	–	–	–	–	–	–	–	–
Czech Republic	–	–	–	–	–	100 v	–	–	–	–	–	–	–	–
Democratic People's Republic of Korea	–	–	–	–	–	100	–	–	–	–	–	–	–	–
Democratic Republic of the Congo	15	13	17	9	39	28	–	–	–	–	76	92	92	91
Denmark	–	–	–	–	–	100 v	–	–	–	–	–	–	–	–
Djibouti	8	8	8	2	5	92	93	49 y	37	–	–	72	73	71
Dominica	–	–	–	–	–	–	–	–	–	–	–	–	–	–
Dominican Republic	13	18	8	12	41	82	–	–	–	–	4	67	69	65
Ecuador	8	7	8	4 x	22 x	90	–	–	–	–	–	–	–	–
Egypt	9 y	14 y	4 y	2	17	99 y	91	17	54	–	39 y	91	92	90
El Salvador	10 y	–	–	5	25	99	–	–	–	–	–	–	–	–
Equatorial Guinea	28 x	28 x	28 x	–	–	37 x	–	–	–	–	–	–	–	–
Eritrea	–	–	–	20 x	47 x	–	89	63 y	49	–	71 x	–	–	–
Estonia	–	–	–	–	–	100 v	–	–	–	–	–	–	–	–
Ethiopia	27	31	24	16	41	7	74	24	31	45	68	–	–	–
Fiji	–	–	–	–	–	–	–	–	–	–	–	72 y	–	–
Finland	–	–	–	–	–	100 v	–	–	–	–	–	–	–	–
France	–	–	–	–	–	100 v	–	–	–	–	–	–	–	–
Gabon	13	15	12	6	22	90	–	–	–	40	50	–	–	–
Gambia	19	21	18	7	36	53	76	56	64	–	75	90	90	91
Georgia	18	20	17	1	14	99	–	–	–	–	7	67	70	63
Germany	–	–	–	–	–	100 v	–	–	–	–	–	–	–	–
Ghana	34	34	34	5	21	63	4	1	2	26 v	44	94	94	94
Greece	–	–	–	–	–	100 v	–	–	–	–	–	–	–	–
Grenada	–	–	–	–	–	–	–	–	–	–	–	–	–	–
Guatemala	26 y	35 y	16 y	7	30	97	–	–	–	–	–	–	–	–
Guinea	40 y	40 y	40 y	20	63	43	96	57 y	69	–	86	–	–	–
Guinea-Bissau	38	40	36	7	22	24	50	39 y	34	–	40 y	82	82	81
Guyana	16	17	16	6	23	88	–	–	–	19	16	76	79	74
Haiti	24	25	24	3	18	80	–	–	–	15	17	86	87	85
Holy See	–	–	–	–	–	–	–	–	–	–	–	–	–	–
Honduras	16 x	16 x	15 x	8	34	94	–	–	–	10	12	–	–	–
Hungary	–	–	–	–	–	100 v	–	–	–	–	–	–	–	–

TABLE 9 | CHILD PROTECTION >>

Countries and areas	Child labour (%)[+] 2005–2012*			Child marriage (%) 2005–2012*		Birth registration (%)[+] 2005–2012* total	Female genital mutilation/cutting (%)[+] 2002–2012*			Justification of wife beating (%) 2005–2012*		Violent discipline (%)[+] 2005–2012*		
							prevalence		attitudes					
	total	male	female	married by 15	married by 18		women[a]	girls[b]	support for the practice[c]	male	female	total	male	female
Iceland	–	–	–	–	–	100 v	–	–	–	–	–	–	–	–
India	12	12	12	18	47	41	–	–	–	51	54	–	–	–
Indonesia	7 y	8 y	6 y	3	17	67	–	–	–	17 y	35	–	–	–
Iran (Islamic Republic of)	11 y	13 y	10 y	3	17	99 y	–	–	–	–	–	–	–	–
Iraq	5	5	4	5	24	99	8	3 y	5	–	51	79	81	77
Ireland	–	–	–	–	–	100 v	–	–	–	–	–	–	–	–
Israel	–	–	–	–	–	100 v	–	–	–	–	–	–	–	–
Italy	–	–	–	–	–	100 v	–	–	–	–	–	–	–	–
Jamaica	6	7	5	1	9	98	–	–	–	22 y	3 y	89	90	87
Japan	–	–	–	–	–	100 v	–	–	–	–	–	–	–	–
Jordan	2 y	3 y	0 y	1	10	99	–	–	–	–	90 y	–	–	–
Kazakhstan	2	2	2	0	6	100	–	–	–	17	12	49	54	45
Kenya	26 x	27 x	25 x	6	26	60	27	8 y	10	44	53	–	–	–
Kiribati	–	–	–	3	20	94	–	–	–	60	76	81 y	–	–
Kuwait	–	–	–	–	–	–	–	–	–	–	–	–	–	–
Kyrgyzstan	4	4	3	1	10	96	–	–	–	–	38	54 y	58 y	49 y
Lao People's Democratic Republic	10 y	9 y	11 y	9	35	75	–	–	–	49	58	76	77	74
Latvia	–	–	–	–	–	100 v	–	–	–	–	–	–	–	–
Lebanon	2	3	1	1	6	100	–	–	–	–	10 y	82	82	82
Lesotho	23 x	25 x	21 x	2	19	45	–	–	–	48	37	–	–	–
Liberia	21	21	21	11	38	4 y	66	–	45	30	59	94	94	94
Libya	–	–	–	–	–	–	–	–	–	–	–	–	–	–
Liechtenstein	–	–	–	–	–	100 v	–	–	–	–	–	–	–	–
Lithuania	–	–	–	–	–	100 v	–	–	–	–	–	–	–	–
Luxembourg	–	–	–	–	–	100 v	–	–	–	–	–	–	–	–
Madagascar	28 y	29 y	27 y	14	48	80	–	–	–	30	32	–	–	–
Malawi	26	25	26	12	50	–	–	–	–	13	13	–	–	–
Malaysia	–	–	–	–	–	–	–	–	–	–	–	–	–	–
Maldives	–	–	–	0	4	93	–	–	–	14 y	31 y	–	–	–
Mali	21	22	21	15	55	81	89	74 y	73	–	87	–	–	–
Malta	–	–	–	–	–	100 v	–	–	–	–	–	–	–	–
Marshall Islands	–	–	–	6	26	96	–	–	–	58	56	–	–	–
Mauritania	15	14	15	14	34	59	69	54	41	–	38	87	87	87
Mauritius	–	–	–	–	–	–	–	–	–	–	–	–	–	–
Mexico	6 y	7 y	5 y	5	23	93 y	–	–	–	–	–	–	–	–
Micronesia (Federated States of)	–	–	–	–	–	–	–	–	–	–	–	–	–	–
Monaco	–	–	–	–	–	100 v	–	–	–	–	–	–	–	–
Mongolia	10	10	11	0	5	99	–	–	–	9 y	10	46	48	43

TABLE 9 | CHILD PROTECTION >>

TABLE 9

Countries and areas	Child labour (%)+ 2005–2012*			Child marriage (%) 2005–2012*		Birth registration (%)+ 2005–2012* total	Female genital mutilation/cutting (%)+ 2002–2012*			Justification of wife beating (%) 2005–2012*		Violent discipline (%)+ 2005–2012*		
							prevalence		attitudes					
	total	male	female	married by 15	married by 18		women[a]	girls[b]	support for the practice[c]	male	female	total	male	female
Montenegro	10	12	8	0	5	99	–	–	–	–	11	63	64	61
Morocco	8	9	8	3 x	16 x	94 y	–	–	–	–	64 x	91	92	90
Mozambique	22	21	24	14	48	48	–	–	–	20	23	–	–	–
Myanmar	–	–	–	–	–	72	–	–	–	–	–	–	–	–
Namibia	–	–	–	2	9	78 y	–	–	–	41	35	–	–	–
Nauru	–	–	–	2	27	83	–	–	–	–	–	–	–	–
Nepal	34 y	30 y	38 y	10	41	42	–	–	–	22	23	–	–	–
Netherlands	–	–	–	–	–	100 v	–	–	–	–	–	–	–	–
New Zealand	–	–	–	–	–	100 v	–	–	–	–	–	–	–	–
Nicaragua	15 x	18 x	11 x	10	41	85	–	–	–	–	14	–	–	–
Niger	43	43	43	36	75	32	2	1 y	3	–	70	–	–	–
Nigeria	25	24	25	20	39	42	27	14	21	–	46	91	91	90
Niue	–	–	–	–	–	–	–	–	–	–	–	–	–	–
Norway	–	–	–	–	–	100 v	–	–	–	–	–	–	–	–
Oman	–	–	–	–	–	–	–	–	–	–	–	–	–	–
Pakistan	–	–	–	7	24	27	–	–	–	–	–	–	–	–
Palau	–	–	–	–	–	–	–	–	–	–	–	–	–	–
Panama	6 y	8 y	3 y	–	–	–	–	–	–	–	–	–	–	–
Papua New Guinea	–	–	–	2	21	–	–	–	–	–	–	–	–	–
Paraguay	15 x	17 x	12 x	–	18 x	76 y	–	–	–	–	–	–	–	–
Peru	34 y	31 y	36 y	3	19	96 y	–	–	–	–	–	–	–	–
Philippines	–	–	–	2	14	90	–	–	–	–	14	–	–	–
Poland	–	–	–	–	–	100 v	–	–	–	–	–	–	–	–
Portugal	3 x,y	4 x,y	3 x,y	–	–	100 v	–	–	–	–	–	–	–	–
Qatar	–	–	–	–	–	–	–	–	–	–	–	–	–	–
Republic of Korea	–	–	–	–	–	–	–	–	–	–	–	–	–	–
Republic of Moldova	16	20	12	1	19	100	–	–	–	22 y	21	–	–	–
Romania	1 x	1 x	1 x	–	–	–	–	–	–	–	–	–	–	–
Russian Federation	–	–	–	–	–	100 v	–	–	–	–	–	–	–	–
Rwanda	29	27	30	1	8	63	–	–	–	25	56	–	–	–
Saint Kitts and Nevis	–	–	–	–	–	–	–	–	–	–	–	–	–	–
Saint Lucia	–	–	–	–	–	–	–	–	–	–	–	–	–	–
Saint Vincent and the Grenadines	–	–	–	–	–	–	–	–	–	–	–	–	–	–
Samoa	–	–	–	–	–	48	–	–	–	46	61	–	–	–
San Marino	–	–	–	–	–	100 v	–	–	–	–	–	–	–	–
Sao Tome and Principe	8	8	7	5	34	75	–	–	–	22	20	–	–	–
Saudi Arabia	–	–	–	–	–	–	–	–	–	–	–	–	–	–
Senegal	17	18	16	12	33	75	26	18	17	25	60	–	–	–
Serbia	4	5	4	1	5	99	–	–	–	7 y	3	67	70	64

TABLE 9 | CHILD PROTECTION >>

Countries and areas	Child labour (%)[+] 2005–2012*			Child marriage (%) 2005–2012*		Birth registration (%)[+] 2005–2012*	Female genital mutilation/cutting (%)[+] 2002–2012*			Justification of wife beating (%) 2005–2012*		Violent discipline (%)[+] 2005–2012*		
							prevalence		attitudes					
	total	male	female	married by 15	married by 18	total	women[a]	girls[b]	support for the practice[c]	male	female	total	male	female
Seychelles	–	–	–	–	–	–	–	–	–	–	–	–	–	–
Sierra Leone	26	27	25	18	44	78	88	13	66	–	73	82	81	82
Singapore	–	–	–	–	–	–	–	–	–	–	–	–	–	–
Slovakia	–	–	–	–	–	100 v	–	–	–	–	–	–	–	–
Slovenia	–	–	–	–	–	100 v	–	–	–	–	–	–	–	–
Solomon Islands	–	–	–	3	22	–	–	–	–	65	69	72 y	–	–
Somalia	49	45	54	8	45	3	98	46 y	65	–	76 y	–	–	–
South Africa	–	–	–	1 x	6 x	95 y	–	–	–	–	–	–	–	–
South Sudan	–	–	–	9	52	35	–	–	–	–	79	–	–	–
Spain	–	–	–	–	–	100 v	–	–	–	–	–	–	–	–
Sri Lanka	–	–	–	2	12	97	–	–	–	–	53 y	–	–	–
State of Palestine	6	7	4	2	21	99	–	–	–	–	–	93	94	92
Sudan	–	–	–	7	33	59	88	37	42	–	47	–	–	–
Suriname	4	4	4	5	19	99	–	–	–	–	13	86	87	85
Swaziland	7	8	7	1	7	50	–	–	–	23 y	28	89	90	88
Sweden	–	–	–	–	–	100 v	–	–	–	–	–	–	–	–
Switzerland	–	–	–	–	–	100 v	–	–	–	–	–	–	–	–
Syrian Arab Republic	4	5	3	3	13	96	–	–	–	–	–	89	90	88
Tajikistan	10	9	11	1	13	88	–	–	–	–	74 y	78	80	75
Thailand	8	8	8	3	20	100	–	–	–	–	–	–	–	–
The former Yugoslav Republic of Macedonia	13	12	13	1	7	100	–	–	–	–	15	69	71	67
Timor-Leste	4 x	4 x	4 x	3	19	55	–	–	–	81	86	–	–	–
Togo	28	28	29	6	25	78	4	0	2	–	43	93	94	93
Tonga	–	–	–	–	–	–	–	–	–	–	–	–	–	–
Trinidad and Tobago	1	1	1	2	8	97	–	–	–	–	8	77	78	77
Tunisia	2	3	2	0	2	99	–	–	–	–	30	93	94	92
Turkey	3 y	3 y	2 y	3	14	94	–	–	–	–	25	–	–	–
Turkmenistan	–	–	–	1	7	96	–	–	–	–	38 y	–	–	–
Tuvalu	–	–	–	0	10	50	–	–	–	73	70	–	–	–
Uganda	25 y	27 y	24 y	10	40	30	1	1	9	44	58	–	–	–
Ukraine	7	8	7	0	10	100	–	–	–	11	4	70	76	65
United Arab Emirates	–	–	–	–	–	100 y	–	–	–	–	–	–	–	–
United Kingdom	–	–	–	–	–	100 v	–	–	–	–	–	–	–	–
United Republic of Tanzania	21 y	23 y	19 y	7	37	16	15	3 y	6	38	54	–	–	–
United States	–	–	–	–	–	100 v	–	–	–	–	–	–	–	–
Uruguay	8 y	8 y	8 y	–	–	100 y	–	–	–	–	–	–	–	–
Uzbekistan	–	–	–	0	7	100	–	–	–	59 x,y	70 x	–	–	–
Vanuatu	–	–	–	9	27	43	–	–	–	–	60 y	78 y	–	–

TABLE 9

TABLE 9 | CHILD PROTECTION

Countries and areas	Child labour (%)[+] 2005–2012*			Child marriage (%) 2005–2012*		Birth registration (%)[+] 2005–2012* total	Female genital mutilation/cutting (%)[+] 2002–2012*			Justification of wife beating (%) 2005–2012*		Violent discipline (%)[+] 2005–2012*		
							prevalence		attitudes					
	total	male	female	married by 15	married by 18		women[a]	girls[b]	support for the practice[c]	male	female	total	male	female
Venezuela (Bolivarian Republic of)	8 x	9 x	6 x	–	–	81 y	–	–	–	–	–	–	–	–
Viet Nam	7	7	7	1	9	95	–	–	–	–	36	74	76	71
Yemen	23	21	24	12	32	17 y	17	15	41 x,y	–	–	95	95	95
Zambia	41 y	42 y	40 y	9	42	14	–	–	–	49	62	–	–	–
Zimbabwe	–	–	–	4	31	49	–	–	–	34	40	–	–	–

SUMMARY INDICATORS[≠]

Countries and areas	total	male	female	married by 15	married by 18	total	women[a]	girls[b]	support for the practice[c]	male	female	total	male	female
Sub-Saharan Africa	27	27	26	13	39	44	40	17	22	–	54	–	–	–
Eastern and Southern Africa	27	28	25	10	38	38	44	15	21	38	54	–	–	–
West and Central Africa	26	26	27	16	41	47	32	16	21	–	56	90	91	90
Middle East and North Africa	9	11	7	3	18	87	–	–	–	–	–	89	90	88
South Asia	12	13	12	18	46	39	–	–	–	50	52	–	–	–
East Asia and Pacific	8 **	9 **	8 **	2 **	16 **	–	–	–	–	–	31 **	–	–	–
Latin America and Caribbean	11	13	9	7	29	92	–	–	–	–	–	–	–	–
CEE/CIS	5	5	4	1	10	98	–	–	–	–	20	–	–	–
Least developed countries	23	25	22	15	45	38	–	–	–	–	52	–	–	–
World	15 **	16 **	14 **	11 **	34 **	65 **	–	–	–	–	46 **	–	–	–

[≠] For a complete list of countries and areas in the regions, subregions and country categories, see page 26.

DEFINITIONS OF THE INDICATORS

Child labour – Percentage of children 5–14 years old involved in child labour at the time of the survey. A child is considered to be involved in child labour under the following conditions: (a) children 5–11 years old who, during the reference week, did at least one hour of economic activity or at least 28 hours of household chores, or (b) children 12–14 years old who, during the reference week, did at least 14 hours of economic activity or at least 28 hours of household chores.

Child marriage – Percentage of women 20–24 years old who were first married or in union before they were 15 years old and percentage of women 20–24 years old who were first married or in union before they were 18 years old.

Birth registration – Percentage of children less than 5 years old who were registered at the time of the survey. The numerator of this indicator includes children whose birth certificate was seen by the interviewer or whose mother or caretaker says the birth has been registered.

Female genital mutilation/cutting (FGM/C) – (a) Women: percentage of women 15–49 years old who have undergone FGM/C; **(b) girls:** percentage of girls 0–14 years old who have undergone FGM/C (as reported by their mothers); **(c) support for the practice:** percentage of women 15–49 years old who have heard about FGM/C and think the practice should continue.

Justification of wife beating – Percentage of women and men 15–49 years old who consider a husband to be justified in hitting or beating his wife for at least one of the specified reasons, i.e., if his wife burns the food, argues with him, goes out without telling him, neglects the children or refuses sexual relations.

Violent discipline – Percentage of children 2–14 years old who experience any violent discipline (psychological aggression and/or physical punishment).

MAIN DATA SOURCES

Child labour – Multiple Indicator Cluster Surveys (MICS), Demographic and Health Surveys (DHS) and other national surveys.

Child marriage – MICS, DHS and other national surveys.

Birth registration – MICS, DHS, other national household surveys, censuses and vital registration systems.

Female genital mutilation/cutting – MICS, DHS and other national surveys.

Justification of wife beating – MICS, DHS and other national surveys.

Violent discipline – MICS, DHS and other national surveys.

NOTES

– Data not available.

v Estimates of 100% were assumed given that civil registration systems in these countries are complete and all vital events (including births) are registered. Source: United Nations, Department of Economic and Social Affairs, Statistics Division, *Population and Vital Statistics Report*, Series A, Vol. 65, New York, 2013.

x Data refer to years or periods other than those specified in the column heading. Such data are not included in the calculation of regional and global averages.

y Data differ from the standard definition or refer to only part of a country. If they fall within the noted reference period, such data are included in the calculation of regional and global averages.

[+] A more detailed explanation of the methodology and the changes in calculating these estimates can be found in the General Note on the Data, page 22.

* Data refer to the most recent year available during the period specified in the column heading.

** Excludes China.

TABLE 10 | THE RATE OF PROGRESS

Countries and areas	Under-5 mortality rank	Under-5 mortality rate				Annual rate of reduction (%)⊖ Under-5 mortality rate				Reduction since 1990 (%)⊖	Reduction since 2000 (%)⊖	GDP per capita average annual growth rate (%)		Total fertility rate			Average annual rate of reduction (%) Total fertility rate	
		1970	1990	2000	2012	1970–1990	1990–2000	2000–2012	1990–2012			1970–1990	1990–2012	1970	1990	2012	1970–1990	1990–2012
Afghanistan	18	307	176	134	99	2.8	2.7	2.6	2.6	44	26	–	–	7.7	7.7	5.1	0.0	1.8
Albania	109	–	43	29	17	–	4.0	4.5	4.2	61	42	-0.9 x	5.7	5.1	3.0	1.8	2.7	2.4
Algeria	95	235	50	35	20	7.8	3.6	4.6	4.1	60	42	1.8	1.5	7.6	4.8	2.8	2.4	2.4
Andorra	185	–	8	5	3	–	5.1	3.7	4.3	61	36	-1.3	2.5 x	–	–	–	–	–
Angola	2	–	213	203	164	–	0.5	1.8	1.2	23	20	–	4.1	7.3	7.2	6.0	0.1	0.8
Antigua and Barbuda	136	–	24	16	10	–	4.0	3.8	3.9	58	37	7.9 x	1.4	3.7	2.1	2.1	2.9	-0.1
Argentina	120	73	28	20	14	4.9	3.1	2.9	3.0	48	30	-0.8	1.3 x	3.1	3.0	2.2	0.1	1.4
Armenia	112	–	49	30	16	–	5.0	5.1	5.0	67	46	–	6.3	3.2	2.5	1.7	1.2	1.7
Australia	161	21	9	6	5	4.2	3.9	2.0	2.9	47	21	1.6	2.1	2.7	1.9	1.9	1.9	-0.1
Austria	170	29	10	6	4	5.6	5.5	2.7	3.9	58	27	2.5	1.8	2.3	1.5	1.5	2.3	0.0
Azerbaijan	68	–	93	72	35	–	2.5	6.0	4.4	62	51	–	6.2	4.6	3.0	1.9	2.2	1.9
Bahamas	109	31	23	17	17	1.4	3.0	0.1	1.4	27	2	1.9	0.3	3.5	2.6	1.9	1.5	1.5
Bahrain	136	75	23	13	10	5.9	6.1	2.3	4.0	59	24	-1.0 x	0.7 x	6.5	3.7	2.1	2.8	2.6
Bangladesh	60	221	144	88	41	2.1	4.9	6.4	5.7	72	53	0.5	3.7	6.9	4.6	2.2	2.1	3.3
Barbados	100	48	18	18	18	5.0	-0.1	-0.3	-0.2	-5	-4	1.7	0.9 x	3.1	1.7	1.8	2.9	-0.3
Belarus	161	–	17	14	5	–	1.4	8.5	5.3	69	64	–	4.9	2.3	1.9	1.5	1.0	1.1
Belgium	170	24	10	6	4	4.4	5.4	2.7	3.9	58	28	2.2	1.5	2.2	1.6	1.9	1.7	-0.7
Belize	100	–	43	25	18	–	5.5	2.6	3.9	58	27	3.1	2.2 x	6.3	4.5	2.7	1.7	2.3
Benin	22	265	181	147	90	1.9	2.0	4.2	3.2	50	39	0.4	1.1	6.7	6.7	4.9	0.0	1.4
Bhutan	57	271	131	80	45	3.6	4.9	4.9	4.9	66	44	7.0 x	5.4	6.7	5.6	2.3	0.8	4.1
Bolivia (Plurinational State of)	60	228	123	78	41	3.1	4.6	5.3	5.0	66	47	-1.2	1.7	6.6	4.9	3.3	1.5	1.9
Bosnia and Herzegovina	150	–	18	10	7	–	6.0	3.4	4.6	64	34	–	7.9 x	2.9	1.7	1.3	2.6	1.4
Botswana	52	120	48	85	53	4.6	-5.8	3.9	-0.5	-11	38	8.0	3.7	6.6	4.7	2.7	1.7	2.6
Brazil	120	131	62	33	14	3.8	6.2	6.9	6.6	77	56	2.3	1.7	5.0	2.8	1.8	2.9	2.0
Brunei Darussalam	147	–	12	10	8	–	2.6	1.4	2.0	35	16	-2.2 x	-0.4	5.8	3.5	2.0	2.4	2.6
Bulgaria	129	39	22	21	12	2.8	0.5	4.6	2.7	45	43	3.4 x	3.4	2.1	1.8	1.5	0.9	0.7
Burkina Faso	14	316	202	186	102	2.2	0.8	5.0	3.1	49	45	1.4	2.8	6.6	7.0	5.7	-0.3	0.9
Burundi	12	245	164	150	104	2.0	0.9	3.0	2.1	36	30	1.2	-1.7	7.3	7.5	6.1	-0.2	0.9
Cabo Verde	88	178	62	38	22	5.3	4.9	4.4	4.6	64	41	3.7 x	5.1	6.9	5.3	2.3	1.3	3.7
Cambodia	62	–	116	111	40	–	0.5	8.5	4.9	66	64	–	6.0 x	6.5	5.6	2.9	0.7	3.0
Cameroon	21	209	135	150	95	2.2	-1.1	3.8	1.6	30	37	3.4	0.5	6.2	6.4	4.9	-0.2	1.3
Canada	161	22	8	6	5	4.9	2.9	1.3	2.0	36	15	2.0	1.7	2.2	1.7	1.7	1.5	0.0
Central African Republic	6	210	171	164	129	1.0	0.4	2.0	1.3	25	22	-1.3	-0.7	6.0	5.8	4.5	0.1	1.2
Chad	3	262	209	189	150	1.1	1.0	1.9	1.5	28	21	-0.9	2.8	6.5	7.3	6.4	-0.6	0.6
Chile	141	80	19	11	9	7.2	5.6	1.5	3.4	52	17	1.5	3.4	4.0	2.6	1.8	2.1	1.6
China	120	111	54	37	14	3.6	3.8	8.1	6.1	74	62	6.6	9.3	5.5	2.5	1.7	3.9	1.9
Colombia	100	97	35	25	18	5.1	3.3	3.0	3.1	50	30	1.9	1.7	5.6	3.1	2.3	2.9	1.3
Comoros	30	223	124	99	78	2.9	2.2	2.0	2.1	37	22	0.0 x	-0.7	7.1	5.6	4.8	1.2	0.7
Congo	19	150	100	118	96	2.0	-1.7	1.7	0.2	4	19	3.3	0.4	6.3	5.3	5.0	0.8	0.3
Cook Islands	132	51	25	17	11	3.6	3.6	4.1	3.9	57	39	–	–	–	–	–	–	–

TABLE 10 | THE RATE OF PROGRESS >>

Countries and areas	Under-5 mortality rank	Under-5 mortality rate				Annual rate of reduction (%) Under-5 mortality rate				Reduction since 1990 (%)	Reduction since 2000 (%)	GDP per capita average annual growth rate (%)		Total fertility rate			Average annual rate of reduction (%) Total fertility rate	
		1970	1990	2000	2012	1970–1990	1990–2000	2000–2012	1990–2012			1970–1990	1990–2012	1970	1990	2012	1970–1990	1990–2012
Costa Rica	136	76	17	13	10	7.5	2.5	2.3	2.4	41	24	0.7	2.7	5.0	3.2	1.8	2.3	2.6
Côte d'Ivoire	11	242	152	145	108	2.3	0.4	2.5	1.6	29	26	-1.7	-0.5	7.9	6.4	4.9	1.1	1.2
Croatia	161	–	13	8	5	–	4.4	4.7	4.6	64	43	–	3.1 x	2.0	1.7	1.5	0.9	0.5
Cuba	157	43	13	8	6	5.9	4.5	3.5	4.0	58	35	3.9	3.0 x	4.0	1.8	1.5	4.2	0.9
Cyprus	185	–	11	7	3	–	5.2	6.0	5.7	71	52	5.9 x	1.7	2.6	2.4	1.5	0.4	2.3
Czech Republic	170	–	15	7	4	–	7.9	4.6	6.1	74	42	–	2.7	2.0	1.8	1.5	0.6	0.7
Democratic People's Republic of Korea	77	–	44	60	29	–	-3.2	6.1	1.9	34	52	–	–	4.3	2.3	2.0	3.2	0.6
Democratic Republic of the Congo	5	254	171	171	146	2.0	0.0	1.3	0.7	15	15	-2.1	-2.1	6.2	7.1	6.0	-0.7	0.8
Denmark	170	17	9	6	4	3.1	4.7	3.5	4.0	59	34	2.0	1.3	2.1	1.7	1.9	1.2	-0.6
Djibouti	28	–	119	108	81	–	1.0	2.4	1.8	32	25	–	0.0	6.8	6.1	3.5	0.6	2.6
Dominica	125	64	17	16	13	6.5	1.0	1.8	1.4	27	19	5.2 x	2.0	–	–	–	–	–
Dominican Republic	79	121	60	40	27	3.5	4.0	3.2	3.6	55	32	2.1	3.9	6.2	3.5	2.5	2.9	1.5
Ecuador	83	138	56	34	23	4.5	4.9	3.2	4.0	58	32	1.7	1.2	6.1	3.8	2.6	2.4	1.7
Egypt	91	237	86	45	21	5.1	6.4	6.4	6.4	75	53	4.4	2.9	5.9	4.4	2.8	1.6	2.0
El Salvador	112	154	59	32	16	4.8	6.2	5.8	6.0	73	50	-1.9	2.3	6.2	4.0	2.2	2.3	2.6
Equatorial Guinea	16	–	182	143	100	–	2.4	2.9	2.7	45	30	–	16.2	5.7	5.9	4.9	-0.2	0.8
Eritrea	55	215	150	89	52	1.8	5.2	4.5	4.8	65	42	–	-1.0 x	6.7	6.5	4.8	0.1	1.4
Estonia	170	–	20	11	4	–	6.1	9.3	7.9	82	67	–	5.3 x	2.1	1.9	1.6	0.4	0.9
Ethiopia	40	237	204	146	68	0.7	3.4	6.3	5.0	67	53	–	3.2	7.0	7.2	4.6	-0.2	2.0
Fiji	88	55	31	24	22	2.9	2.3	0.7	1.4	27	8	0.6	1.2	4.5	3.4	2.6	1.5	1.2
Finland	185	16	7	4	3	4.4	4.4	3.3	3.8	57	33	2.9	2.4	1.9	1.7	1.9	0.3	-0.3
France	170	18	9	5	4	3.5	5.1	2.3	3.6	54	24	2.1	1.2	2.5	1.8	2.0	1.8	-0.6
Gabon	42	–	92	86	62	–	0.7	2.7	1.8	33	28	0.7	-0.8	5.1	5.4	4.1	-0.3	1.2
Gambia	33	301	170	116	73	2.9	3.8	3.9	3.8	57	37	0.7	0.4	6.1	6.1	5.8	0.0	0.3
Georgia	95	–	35	34	20	–	0.2	4.5	2.5	43	42	3.1	2.9	2.6	2.2	1.8	0.9	0.8
Germany	170	26	9	5	4	5.5	4.5	2.3	3.3	52	24	2.3	1.3	2.0	1.4	1.4	2.0	-0.2
Ghana	36	200	128	103	72	2.2	2.1	3.0	2.6	44	30	-0.9	2.7	7.0	5.6	3.9	1.1	1.6
Greece	161	38	13	8	5	5.5	4.7	4.0	4.4	62	38	1.3	2.0	2.4	1.4	1.5	2.5	-0.3
Grenada	120	–	22	16	14	–	3.3	1.4	2.2	39	15	4.2 x	2.6	4.6	3.8	2.2	0.9	2.5
Guatemala	71	173	80	51	32	3.8	4.6	3.8	4.2	60	37	0.2	1.3	6.2	5.6	3.8	0.6	1.7
Guinea	15	323	241	171	101	1.5	3.4	4.4	3.9	58	41	–	0.7	6.2	6.6	5.0	-0.3	1.2
Guinea-Bissau	6	–	206	174	129	–	1.7	2.5	2.1	37	26	0.9	-1.2	6.1	6.6	5.0	-0.5	1.3
Guyana	68	74	60	46	35	1.1	2.6	2.3	2.4	41	24	-1.3	2.1	5.1	2.5	2.6	3.6	-0.2
Haiti	31	246	144	105	76	2.7	3.2	2.7	2.9	48	28	–	-0.9 x	5.8	5.4	3.2	0.3	2.4
Holy See	196	–	–	–	–	–	–	–	–	–	–	–	–	–	–	–	–	–
Honduras	83	146	59	38	23	4.5	4.4	4.2	4.3	61	40	0.8	1.6	7.3	5.1	3.1	1.7	2.4
Hungary	157	43	19	11	6	4.0	5.2	5.0	5.1	67	45	3.0	2.4	2.0	1.8	1.4	0.5	1.2
Iceland	194	16	6	4	2	4.5	4.7	4.6	4.7	64	43	3.2	2.0	3.0	2.2	2.1	1.7	0.1
India	49	211	126	92	56	2.6	3.2	4.0	3.6	55	38	2.0	5.0	5.5	3.9	2.5	1.7	2.0

TABLE 10 | THE RATE OF PROGRESS >>

Countries and areas	Under-5 mortality rank	Under-5 mortality rate				Annual rate of reduction (%)⊖ Under-5 mortality rate				Reduction since 1990 (%)⊖	Reduction since 2000 (%)⊖	GDP per capita average annual growth rate (%)		Total fertility rate			Average annual rate of reduction (%) Total fertility rate	
		1970	1990	2000	2012	1970–1990	1990–2000	2000–2012	1990–2012			1970–1990	1990–2012	1970	1990	2012	1970–1990	1990–2012
Indonesia	72	165	84	52	31	3.4	4.7	4.4	4.5	63	41	4.5	2.7	5.5	3.1	2.4	2.8	1.3
Iran (Islamic Republic of)	100	226	56	35	18	6.9	4.9	5.6	5.3	69	49	-2.5	2.8 x	6.4	4.8	1.9	1.4	4.2
Iraq	70	114	53	45	34	3.8	1.7	2.2	2.0	35	23	–	-1.7 x	7.4	5.9	4.1	1.1	1.7
Ireland	170	22	9	7	4	4.4	2.5	4.9	3.8	57	44	–	0.7 x	3.8	2.0	2.0	3.2	0.0
Israel	170	–	12	7	4	–	5.2	4.1	4.6	64	39	1.9	1.8 x	3.8	3.0	2.9	1.2	0.1
Italy	170	34	10	6	4	6.2	5.7	3.1	4.3	61	31	2.8	0.7	2.5	1.3	1.5	3.2	-0.6
Jamaica	109	57	30	23	17	3.2	2.5	2.8	2.6	44	28	-1.3	0.4 x	5.5	2.9	2.3	3.1	1.2
Japan	185	18	6	5	3	5.1	3.4	3.4	3.4	52	33	3.4	0.7	2.1	1.6	1.4	1.5	0.5
Jordan	97	89	37	28	19	4.4	2.8	3.1	3.0	48	31	2.5 x	2.6	7.9	5.5	3.3	1.8	2.3
Kazakhstan	97	–	54	44	19	–	2.0	7.2	4.8	65	58	–	4.2	3.5	2.8	2.5	1.1	0.6
Kenya	33	146	98	110	73	2.0	-1.2	3.5	1.4	26	34	1.2	0.4	8.1	6.0	4.5	1.5	1.4
Kiribati	43	138	94	71	60	1.9	2.8	1.4	2.1	36	16	-5.8	0.7	6.1	4.6	3.0	1.3	2.0
Kuwait	132	71	16	13	11	7.4	2.3	1.3	1.8	33	15	-6.7 x	0.6 x	7.2	2.4	2.6	5.6	-0.5
Kyrgyzstan	79	120	71	50	27	2.6	3.5	5.2	4.4	62	47	–	0.8	4.9	3.9	3.1	1.2	1.0
Lao People's Democratic Republic	36	–	163	120	72	–	3.1	4.3	3.7	56	40	–	4.7	6.0	6.2	3.1	-0.1	3.1
Latvia	141	–	20	17	9	–	1.8	5.6	3.9	57	49	3.4	4.5	1.9	1.9	1.6	0.0	0.9
Lebanon	141	59	33	20	9	2.9	5.0	6.3	5.7	72	53	–	1.7	4.9	3.0	1.5	2.5	3.2
Lesotho	16	175	85	114	100	3.6	-3.0	1.1	-0.7	-18	12	3.0	2.6	5.8	4.9	3.1	0.8	2.1
Liberia	32	277	248	176	75	0.6	3.4	7.1	5.4	70	58	-4.1	5.5	6.7	6.5	4.9	0.1	1.3
Libya	116	139	43	28	15	5.9	4.1	5.1	4.7	64	46	–	–	7.9	5.0	2.4	2.3	3.3
Liechtenstein	197	–	–	–	–	–	–	–	–	–	–	2.2	2.9 x	–	–	–	–	–
Lithuania	161	25	17	12	5	2.0	3.5	6.5	5.1	68	54	–	3.7	2.3	2.0	1.5	0.8	1.2
Luxembourg	194	22	9	5	2	4.7	5.9	6.5	6.2	75	54	2.6	2.5	2.0	1.6	1.7	1.1	-0.3
Madagascar	46	162	159	109	58	0.1	3.8	5.2	4.6	63	46	-2.4	-0.3	7.3	6.3	4.5	0.8	1.5
Malawi	38	339	244	174	71	1.7	3.4	7.5	5.6	71	59	-0.1	1.2	7.3	7.0	5.5	0.2	1.1
Malaysia	141	56	17	10	9	6.1	4.9	1.5	3.0	49	17	4.0	3.1	4.9	3.5	2.0	1.6	2.6
Maldives	132	258	94	45	11	5.1	7.4	12.1	10.0	89	77	–	5.3 x	7.2	6.1	2.3	0.8	4.5
Mali	8	392	253	220	128	2.2	1.4	4.5	3.1	49	42	0.3	2.3	6.9	7.1	6.9	-0.1	0.1
Malta	150	27	11	8	7	4.4	4.1	0.9	2.3	40	11	6.0	2.3	2.0	2.1	1.4	-0.2	1.9
Marshall Islands	66	86	49	41	38	2.8	1.7	0.7	1.2	23	8	–	0.7	–	–	–	–	–
Mauritania	27	194	128	111	84	2.1	1.5	2.3	1.9	34	24	-1.1	1.2	6.8	6.0	4.7	0.6	1.1
Mauritius	116	80	23	19	15	6.2	2.2	1.7	1.9	34	18	3.2 x	3.6	4.0	2.3	1.5	2.7	1.9
Mexico	112	107	46	25	16	4.2	6.0	3.7	4.8	65	36	1.7	1.2	6.7	3.4	2.2	3.4	1.9
Micronesia (Federated States of)	64	–	55	54	39	–	0.3	2.8	1.6	30	28	–	0.8	6.9	5.0	3.3	1.7	1.8
Monaco	170	–	8	5	4	–	4.1	2.6	3.3	51	27	1.5	1.7 x	–	–	–	–	–
Mongolia	78	–	107	63	28	–	5.2	6.9	6.2	74	56	–	3.6	7.6	4.1	2.4	3.1	2.3
Montenegro	157	–	17	14	6	–	2.2	7.0	4.8	65	57	–	3.1 x	2.7	1.9	1.7	1.8	0.5
Morocco	72	187	80	50	31	4.3	4.6	4.0	4.3	61	38	2.1	2.6	6.7	4.1	2.7	2.5	1.8
Mozambique	22	264	233	166	90	0.6	3.4	5.1	4.3	61	46	-1.1 x	4.2	6.6	6.2	5.3	0.3	0.8

TABLE 10 | THE RATE OF PROGRESS >>

TABLE 10

Countries and areas	Under-5 mortality rank	Under-5 mortality rate				Annual rate of reduction (%)[e] Under-5 mortality rate				Reduction since 1990 (%)[e]	Reduction since 2000 (%)[e]	GDP per capita average annual growth rate (%)		Total fertility rate			Average annual rate of reduction (%) Total fertility rate	
		1970	1990	2000	2012	1970–1990	1990–2000	2000–2012	1990–2012			1970–1990	1990–2012	1970	1990	2012	1970–1990	1990–2012
Myanmar	55	170	106	79	52	2.3	3.0	3.4	3.2	51	34	1.4	7.3 x	6.0	3.4	2.0	2.8	2.5
Namibia	64	97	73	73	39	1.4	0.0	5.3	2.9	47	47	-2.1 x	2.2	6.5	5.2	3.1	1.1	2.4
Nauru	67	–	58	42	37	–	3.2	1.1	2.0	36	12	–	–	–	–	–	–	–
Nepal	59	269	142	82	42	3.2	5.5	5.7	5.6	71	49	1.2	2.3	6.0	5.2	2.4	0.7	3.5
Netherlands	170	16	8	6	4	3.2	2.9	3.4	3.2	51	34	1.6	1.8	2.4	1.6	1.8	2.2	-0.5
New Zealand	157	21	11	7	6	3.1	4.1	2.2	3.1	49	23	1.3 x	1.7	3.1	2.1	2.1	2.0	0.0
Nicaragua	82	172	66	40	24	4.8	5.0	4.1	4.5	63	39	-3.7	2.0	6.9	4.8	2.5	1.9	2.8
Niger	10	319	326	227	114	-0.1	3.6	5.8	4.8	65	50	-1.9	-0.7	7.4	7.8	7.6	-0.2	0.1
Nigeria	9	284	213	188	124	1.4	1.2	3.5	2.5	42	34	-1.3	2.1	6.5	6.5	6.0	0.0	0.4
Niue	81	–	14	23	25	–	-5.2	-0.6	-2.7	-81	-8	–	–	–	–	–	–	–
Norway	185	16	9	5	3	3.1	5.7	4.7	5.2	68	43	3.2	1.8	2.5	1.9	1.9	1.5	-0.2
Oman	129	227	39	17	12	8.8	8.3	3.3	5.5	70	33	3.2	2.4 x	7.3	7.2	2.9	0.1	4.1
Pakistan	26	186	138	112	86	1.5	2.1	2.2	2.2	38	23	2.6	2.0	6.6	6.0	3.3	0.5	2.8
Palau	91	–	34	28	21	–	1.8	2.6	2.2	39	27	–	-0.1 x	–	–	–	–	–
Panama	97	67	32	26	19	3.7	2.1	2.8	2.4	42	28	0.2	3.5	5.2	3.1	2.5	2.6	1.0
Papua New Guinea	41	143	89	79	63	2.4	1.3	1.9	1.6	29	20	-1.0	0.3	6.2	4.8	3.8	1.2	1.0
Paraguay	88	77	46	33	22	2.6	3.3	3.3	3.3	52	33	3.7	0.4	5.7	4.5	2.9	1.2	2.0
Peru	100	161	79	40	18	3.6	6.9	6.5	6.7	77	54	-0.6	3.3	6.3	3.8	2.4	2.5	2.0
Philippines	75	83	59	40	30	1.8	3.7	2.5	3.1	49	26	0.6	2.0	6.3	4.3	3.1	1.9	1.5
Poland	161	37	17	9	5	3.7	6.3	5.2	5.7	71	46	–	4.3	2.2	2.0	1.4	0.4	1.7
Portugal	170	69	15	7	4	7.7	6.9	6.0	6.4	76	51	2.5	1.4	3.0	1.5	1.3	3.3	0.7
Qatar	150	64	21	12	7	5.6	5.1	4.3	4.7	64	40	–	0.9 x	6.9	4.0	2.0	2.7	3.1
Republic of Korea	170	52	7	6	4	9.9	1.5	3.9	2.8	46	38	6.2	4.1	4.5	1.6	1.3	5.2	1.0
Republic of Moldova	100	–	32	30	18	–	0.5	4.6	2.7	45	42	1.8 x	0.2	2.6	2.4	1.5	0.3	2.3
Romania	129	66	38	27	12	2.8	3.5	6.5	5.1	68	54	0.9 x	2.8	2.9	1.9	1.4	2.1	1.4
Russian Federation	136	44	26	23	10	2.7	1.2	6.8	4.2	61	56	–	2.4	2.0	1.9	1.5	0.3	0.9
Rwanda	50	215	151	182	55	1.8	-1.9	10.0	4.6	64	70	1.1	2.7	8.2	7.3	4.6	0.6	2.1
Saint Kitts and Nevis	141	67	29	18	9	4.2	4.8	5.5	5.2	68	48	6.5 x	2.0	–	–	–	–	–
Saint Lucia	100	74	22	18	18	6.0	2.2	0.2	1.1	22	2	5.1 x	1.2	6.1	3.4	1.9	2.9	2.6
Saint Vincent and the Grenadines	83	82	25	22	23	6.0	1.2	-0.5	0.2	5	-6	3.3	3.2	6.0	3.0	2.0	3.6	1.7
Samoa	100	–	30	22	18	–	3.4	1.6	2.4	41	17	–	2.6	7.2	5.1	4.2	1.7	0.9
San Marino	185	–	11	6	3	–	6.8	4.3	5.4	70	40	1.7	3.3 x	–	–	–	–	–
Sao Tome and Principe	52	86	104	87	53	-0.9	1.8	4.1	3.0	49	38	–	1.8 x	6.5	5.4	4.1	0.9	1.2
Saudi Arabia	141	–	47	22	9	–	7.4	7.9	7.7	82	61	-1.4	0.2 x	7.3	5.8	2.7	1.1	3.5
Senegal	43	289	142	139	60	3.6	0.2	7.1	3.9	58	57	-0.6	1.1	7.3	6.6	5.0	0.5	1.3
Serbia	150	–	28	13	7	–	8.0	5.4	6.6	77	48	–	1.5	2.4	2.1	1.4	0.6	2.0
Seychelles	125	72	17	14	13	7.3	1.8	0.4	1.1	21	5	3.5	2.0	5.8	2.7	2.2	3.7	1.0
Sierra Leone	1	329	257	234	182	1.2	0.9	2.1	1.6	29	22	-0.7	0.9	6.7	6.5	4.8	0.1	1.4
Singapore	185	27	8	4	3	6.4	6.7	2.5	4.4	62	26	5.9	3.4	3.2	1.7	1.3	3.1	1.4
Slovakia	147	–	18	12	8	–	4.1	3.8	3.9	58	36	–	3.7	2.5	2.0	1.4	1.0	1.8

TABLE 10 | THE RATE OF PROGRESS >>

Countries and areas	Under-5 mortality rank	Under-5 mortality rate 1970	1990	2000	2012	Annual rate of reduction (%) Under-5 mortality rate 1970–1990	1990–2000	2000–2012	1990–2012	Reduction since 1990 (%)	Reduction since 2000 (%)	GDP per capita average annual growth rate (%) 1970–1990	1990–2012	Total fertility rate 1970	1990	2012	Average annual rate of reduction (%) Total fertility rate 1970–1990	1990–2012
Slovenia	185	–	10	6	3	–	6.3	4.8	5.5	70	44	–	3.0	2.3	1.5	1.5	2.2	-0.1
Solomon Islands	72	106	39	35	31	5.0	1.0	0.9	1.0	19	10	–	-0.5	6.9	5.9	4.1	0.8	1.6
Somalia	4	–	177	171	147	–	0.4	1.2	0.8	17	14	–	–	7.2	7.4	6.7	-0.1	0.5
South Africa	57	–	61	74	45	–	-2.0	4.2	1.4	27	40	0.1	1.4	5.6	3.7	2.4	2.1	1.9
South Sudan	12	–	251	181	104	–	3.3	4.6	4.0	59	42	–	–	6.9	6.8	5.0	0.1	1.4
Spain	161	29	11	7	5	4.9	5.3	3.1	4.1	59	31	1.9	1.8	2.9	1.3	1.5	3.8	-0.5
Sri Lanka	136	72	21	17	10	6.0	2.2	4.9	3.6	55	44	3.0	4.2	4.3	2.5	2.3	2.8	0.3
State of Palestine	83	–	43	30	23	–	3.6	2.3	2.9	47	24	–	–	7.9	6.5	4.1	0.9	2.1
Sudan	33	152	128	106	73	0.8	1.9	3.1	2.6	43	31	-0.1	3.1	6.9	6.2	4.5	0.6	1.4
Suriname	91	–	51	33	21	–	4.3	3.8	4.0	59	37	-2.3 x	1.9	5.7	2.7	2.3	3.6	0.8
Swaziland	29	169	71	121	80	4.3	-5.4	3.5	-0.5	-12	34	3.1	1.0	6.9	5.7	3.4	0.9	2.4
Sweden	185	13	7	4	3	3.3	5.2	2.9	3.9	58	29	1.8	2.1	2.0	2.0	1.9	0.1	0.2
Switzerland	170	18	8	6	4	4.0	3.8	2.2	2.9	48	23	1.7 x	0.9	2.1	1.5	1.5	1.6	0.1
Syrian Arab Republic	116	107	38	24	15	5.2	4.7	3.7	4.1	60	36	2.1	1.7 x	7.6	5.3	3.0	1.8	2.6
Tajikistan	46	–	105	91	58	–	1.4	3.7	2.7	44	36	–	0.2	6.9	5.2	3.8	1.4	1.4
Thailand	125	99	38	23	13	4.8	5.2	4.5	4.8	65	42	4.8	2.9	5.6	2.1	1.4	4.9	1.8
The former Yugoslav Republic of Macedonia	150	–	37	16	7	–	8.3	6.4	7.3	80	54	–	1.4	3.0	2.2	1.4	1.4	2.0
Timor-Leste	48	–	171	106	57	–	4.8	5.2	5.0	67	47	–	2.7 x	5.9	5.3	6.0	0.5	-0.5
Togo	19	220	143	122	96	2.1	1.6	2.0	1.8	33	21	-0.5	0.0	7.1	6.3	4.7	0.6	1.4
Tonga	125	51	23	18	13	4.0	2.4	2.9	2.6	44	29	–	1.5	5.9	4.6	3.8	1.2	0.9
Trinidad and Tobago	91	52	33	28	21	2.3	1.8	2.5	2.1	38	26	0.4	4.7	3.6	2.5	1.8	1.9	1.4
Tunisia	112	177	51	30	16	6.2	5.4	5.1	5.3	69	46	2.5	3.3	6.4	3.5	2.0	3.0	2.5
Turkey	120	186	74	37	14	4.6	6.8	8.1	7.5	81	62	1.9	2.5	5.6	3.1	2.1	3.0	1.8
Turkmenistan	52	–	90	79	53	–	1.4	3.3	2.4	42	33	–	2.7	6.3	4.3	2.4	1.9	2.8
Tuvalu	75	–	58	42	30	–	3.1	2.9	3.0	48	30	–	1.5	–	–	–	–	–
Uganda	39	181	178	147	69	0.1	1.9	6.3	4.3	61	53	–	3.5	7.1	7.1	6.0	0.0	0.8
Ukraine	132	–	20	19	11	–	0.5	4.6	2.8	45	42	–	0.8	2.0	1.9	1.5	0.4	1.1
United Arab Emirates	147	100	17	11	8	8.9	4.1	2.4	3.2	50	25	-4.3 x	-2.5 x	6.6	4.4	1.8	2.0	4.0
United Kingdom	161	21	9	7	5	4.1	3.4	2.7	3.0	48	27	2.0	2.1	2.3	1.8	1.9	1.2	-0.2
United Republic of Tanzania	51	212	166	132	54	1.2	2.3	7.4	5.1	68	59	–	2.6	6.8	6.2	5.3	0.4	0.7
United States	150	23	11	8	7	3.7	2.9	1.4	2.1	37	15	2.1	1.6	2.3	2.0	2.0	0.6	0.0
Uruguay	150	53	23	16	7	4.2	3.5	6.8	5.3	69	56	0.9	2.3	2.9	2.5	2.1	0.7	0.9
Uzbekistan	62	–	74	61	40	–	1.8	3.7	2.8	46	36	–	2.7	6.5	4.2	2.3	2.2	2.6
Vanuatu	100	107	35	24	18	5.6	3.6	2.5	3.0	48	26	1.1 x	0.6	6.3	4.9	3.4	1.2	1.7
Venezuela (Bolivarian Republic of)	116	63	30	21	15	3.8	3.3	2.8	3.0	48	28	-1.6	0.5	5.4	3.4	2.4	2.2	1.6
Viet Nam	83	84	51	32	23	2.6	4.7	2.6	3.6	54	27	–	5.9	6.5	3.6	1.8	3.0	3.2
Yemen	43	321	125	97	60	4.7	2.5	4.0	3.3	52	38	–	1.2	7.5	8.7	4.2	-0.7	3.3

TABLE 10 | THE RATE OF PROGRESS

TABLE 10

Countries and areas	Under-5 mortality rank	Under-5 mortality rate				Annual rate of reduction (%)[Θ] Under-5 mortality rate				Reduction since 1990 (%)[Θ]	Reduction since 2000 (%)[Θ]	GDP per capita average annual growth rate (%)		Total fertility rate			Average annual rate of reduction (%) Total fertility rate	
		1970	1990	2000	2012	1970–1990	1990–2000	2000–2012	1990–2012			1970–1990	1990–2012	1970	1990	2012	1970–1990	1990–2012
Zambia	25	179	192	169	89	-0.3	1.3	5.4	3.5	54	48	-2.2	0.9	7.4	6.5	5.7	0.7	0.5
Zimbabwe	22	111	74	102	90	2.0	-3.2	1.1	-0.9	-21	12	-0.4	-3.1	7.4	5.2	3.6	1.8	1.7

SUMMARY INDICATORS#

Countries and areas	Under-5 mortality rank	1970	1990	2000	2012	1970–1990	1990–2000	2000–2012	1990–2012	Reduction since 1990	Reduction since 2000	1970–1990	1990–2012	1970	1990	2012	1970–1990	1990–2012
Sub-Saharan Africa		242	177	155	98	1.6	1.4	3.8	2.7	45	37	0.0	2.1	6.7	6.3	5.1	0.3	1.0
Eastern and Southern Africa		209	163	139	77	1.2	1.6	4.9	3.4	53	45	0.3	2.0	6.9	6.1	4.7	0.6	1.3
West and Central Africa		274	195	174	118	1.7	1.1	3.2	2.3	39	32	-0.4	2.1	6.6	6.6	5.6	0.0	0.7
Middle East and North Africa		202	71	50	30	5.3	3.5	4.3	3.9	58	40	0.0	–	6.7	5.0	2.9	1.5	2.5
South Asia		211	129	94	60	2.5	3.2	3.8	3.5	54	37	2.0	4.6	5.7	4.2	2.6	1.6	2.2
East Asia and Pacific		114	58	41	20	3.4	3.5	5.8	4.8	65	50	5.6	7.5	5.5	2.7	1.8	3.6	1.7
Latin America and Caribbean		118	54	32	19	3.9	5.1	4.4	4.7	65	41	1.4	1.7	5.3	3.2	2.2	2.5	1.8
CEE/CIS		97	47	36	19	3.6	2.7	5.3	4.2	60	47	–	2.6	2.8	2.3	1.8	0.9	1.2
Least developed countries		238	172	138	85	1.6	2.2	4.1	3.2	51	39	-0.2	3.2	6.8	6.0	4.2	0.6	1.6
World		145	90	75	48	2.4	1.7	3.8	2.9	47	37	2.4	2.7	4.7	3.3	2.5	1.8	1.3

For a complete list of countries and areas in the regions, subregions and country categories, see page 26.

DEFINITIONS OF THE INDICATORS

Under-5 mortality rate – Probability of dying between birth and exactly 5 years of age, expressed per 1,000 live births.

Reduction since 1990 – Percentage reduction in the under-five mortality rate (U5MR) from 1990 to 2012. The United Nations Millennium Declaration in 2000 established a goal of a two-thirds (67 per cent) reduction in U5MR from 1990 to 2015. This indicator provides a current assessment of progress towards this goal.

GDP per capita – Gross domestic product (GDP) is the sum of value added by all resident producers plus any product taxes (less subsidies) not included in the valuation of output. GDP per capita is gross domestic product divided by midyear population. Growth is calculated from constant price GDP data in local currency.

Total fertility rate – Number of children who would be born per woman if she lived to the end of her childbearing years and bore children at each age in accordance with prevailing age-specific fertility rates.

MAIN DATA SOURCES

Under-5 mortality rate – United Nations Inter-agency Group for Child Mortality Estimation (UNICEF, World Health Organization, United Nations Population Division and the World Bank).

GDP per capita – The World Bank.

Total fertility rate – United Nations Population Division.

NOTES

– Data not available.

Θ A negative value indicates an increase in the under-five mortality rate.

x Data refer to years or periods other than those specified in the column heading. Such data are not included in the calculation of regional and global averages.

TABLE 11 | ADOLESCENTS

Countries and areas	Adolescent population — Aged 10–19 (thousands) 2012	Adolescent population — Proportion of total population (%) 2012	Adolescents currently married/in union (%) 2005–2012* male	Adolescents currently married/in union (%) 2005–2012* female	Births by age 18 (%) 2008–2012*	Adolescent birth rate 2008–2011*	Justification of wife beating among adolescents (%) 2005–2012* male	Justification of wife beating among adolescents (%) 2005–2012* female	Use of mass media among adolescents (%) 2005–2012* male	Use of mass media among adolescents (%) 2005–2012* female	Lower secondary school gross enrolment ratio 2008–2012*	Upper secondary school gross enrolment ratio 2008–2012*	Comprehensive knowledge of HIV among adolescents (%) 2008–2012* male	Comprehensive knowledge of HIV among adolescents (%) 2008–2012* female
Afghanistan	7,753	26	–	20	26	90	–	84	–	–	60	35	–	2
Albania	572	18	1	8	3	11 x	37	24	97	99	–	89	21	36
Algeria	6,391	17	–	2	–	4 x	–	66	–	–	135	64	–	12 x
Andorra	–	–	–	–	–	5	–	–	–	–	87	88	–	–
Angola	4,879	23	–	–	–	165 x	–	–	–	–	39	22	–	–
Antigua and Barbuda	16	18	–	–	–	67 x	–	–	–	–	119	84	–	–
Argentina	6,733	16	–	–	–	68	–	–	–	–	112	68	–	–
Armenia	415	14	1	8	2	28	21	8	94	92	96	96	4	10
Australia	2,929	13	–	–	–	16	–	–	–	–	113	167	–	–
Austria	922	11	–	–	–	9	–	–	–	–	102	95	–	–
Azerbaijan	1,513	16	0	10	4 x	41	63	39	97	95	92	115	2 x	3 x
Bahamas	60	16	–	–	–	41 x	–	–	–	–	101	90	–	–
Bahrain	159	12	–	–	–	14	–	–	–	–	–	–	–	–
Bangladesh	32,280	21	2	45	40	128	–	33 y	–	57 y	68	40	–	11
Barbados	38	13	–	–	–	50 x	–	–	–	–	105	102	–	–
Belarus	971	10	–	7	3 x	21	–	3	–	–	97	121	–	–
Belgium	1,236	11	–	–	–	11	–	–	–	–	117	107	–	–
Belize	70	22	–	15	17	90 x	–	11	–	–	–	51	–	39
Benin	2,330	23	2	22	23 x	94	12	41	83	64	64	33	31 x	17 x
Bhutan	147	20	–	15	15	59	–	70	–	–	84	44	–	22
Bolivia (Plurinational State of)	2,308	22	4	13	20	89 x	–	17	100	97	93	74	24	20
Bosnia and Herzegovina	539	14	0	1	–	17	5	1	100	100	92	86	41	42
Botswana	444	22	–	–	–	51 x	–	–	–	–	91	68	–	–
Brazil	34,205	17	–	25	–	71	–	–	–	–	–	–	–	–
Brunei Darussalam	70	17	–	–	–	18	–	–	–	–	118	109	–	–
Bulgaria	664	9	–	2 y	–	41	–	–	–	–	83	94	–	–
Burkina Faso	3,907	24	2	32	28	130	40	39	61	55	31	10	31	29
Burundi	2,184	22	1	9	11	65	56	74	83	69	38	15	45	43
Cabo Verde	109	22	2	8	22 x	92 x	24	23	88	88	113	67	–	–
Cambodia	3,055	21	2	10	7	48	25 y	42 y	73	76	59	28	41	43
Cameroon	5,045	23	2	24	30	127	43	50	77	66	64	34	30	26
Canada	4,078	12	–	–	–	14	–	–	–	–	100	102	–	–
Central African Republic	1,042	23	11	55	45	229	87 y	79	–	–	24	9	26 x	16 x
Chad	3,026	24	–	48	47	203	–	59	55 x	24 x	29	19	–	10
Chile	2,724	16	–	–	–	54	–	–	–	–	98	86	–	–
China	174,700	13	–	2	–	6	–	–	–	–	90	73	–	–
Colombia	8,797	18	–	14	20	85	–	–	–	–	106	81	–	21 y
Comoros	155	22	–	–	–	95 x	–	–	–	–	53	–	–	–
Congo	947	22	2	19	29 x	147	–	76	75	63	–	–	25	16

TABLE 11 | ADOLESCENTS >>

TABLE 11

Countries and areas	Adolescent population		Adolescents currently married/in union (%) 2005–2012*		Births by age 18 (%) 2008–2012*	Adolescent birth rate 2008–2011*	Justification of wife beating among adolescents (%) 2005–2012*		Use of mass media among adolescents (%) 2005–2012*		Lower secondary school gross enrolment ratio	Upper secondary school gross enrolment ratio	Comprehensive knowledge of HIV among adolescents (%) 2008–2012*	
	Aged 10–19 (thousands) 2012	Proportion of total population (%) 2012	male	female			male	female	male	female	2008–2012*	2008–2012*	male	female
Cook Islands	–	–	–	–	–	47 x	–	–	–	–	98	62	–	–
Costa Rica	830	17	3	11	9	67	–	–	–	–	119	76	–	–
Côte d'Ivoire	4,591	23	1	21	31	128	51	51	73	62	–	–	21	15
Croatia	471	11	–	–	–	13	–	–	–	–	105	87	–	–
Cuba	1,430	13	–	20	9	51	–	–	–	–	96	84	–	54
Cyprus	151	13	–	–	–	4	–	–	–	–	97	87	–	–
Czech Republic	995	9	–	–	–	10	–	–	–	–	97	86	–	–
Democratic People's Republic of Korea	3,940	16	–	–	–	1	–	–	–	–	–	–	–	7
Democratic Republic of the Congo	15,400	23	–	25	25	135	–	72	55	43	48	32	–	13
Denmark	696	12	–	–	–	5	–	–	–	–	117	121	–	–
Djibouti	179	21	–	4	–	27 x	–	–	–	–	44	25	–	16 x
Dominica	–	–	–	–	–	48 x	–	–	–	–	108	85	–	–
Dominican Republic	1,997	19	–	17	25 x	98 x	–	7	98	98	86	71	33 x	39 x
Ecuador	2,966	19	–	16 x	–	100 x	–	–	–	–	97	78	–	–
Egypt	15,236	19	–	13	7	50 x	–	50 y	–	97 y	96	51	16	3
El Salvador	1,425	23	–	21	–	65 x	–	–	–	–	89	46	–	–
Equatorial Guinea	156	21	–	–	–	128 x	–	–	–	–	45	–	–	–
Eritrea	1,344	22	–	29 x	25 x	85 x	–	70 x	–	85 x	45	23	–	–
Estonia	129	10	–	–	–	16	–	–	–	–	104	109	–	–
Ethiopia	22,993	25	2	19	22	79	51	64	42	38	47	17	32	24
Fiji	158	18	–	–	–	31 x	–	–	–	–	102	76	–	–
Finland	620	11	–	–	–	8	–	–	–	–	100	116	–	–
France	7,753	12	–	–	–	12	–	–	–	–	110	118	–	–
Gabon	351	22	1	14	28	114	47	58	95	94	–	–	35	29
Gambia	416	23	–	24	23	118	–	74	–	–	62	45	–	33
Georgia	507	12	–	11	6	43	–	5	–	–	108	81	–	–
Germany	8,075	10	–	–	–	8	–	–	–	–	101	107	–	–
Ghana	5,576	22	1	7	16	70 x	37	53	93	87	83	39	34	35
Greece	1,061	10	–	–	–	10	–	–	–	–	109	110	–	–
Grenada	20	19	–	–	–	53 x	–	–	–	–	121	89	–	–
Guatemala	3,537	23	–	20	22	92 x	–	–	–	–	71	54	24	20
Guinea	2,633	23	3	36	44 x	146	–	79	66	55	49	31	–	–
Guinea-Bissau	376	23	–	19	33	137	–	39 y	–	–	–	–	–	12
Guyana	173	22	1	16	16	97 x	25	18	94	94	98	84	45	53
Haiti	2,243	22	2	12	13	66	22	24	85	80	–	–	25	32
Holy See	–	–	–	–	–	–	–	–	–	–	–	–	–	–
Honduras	1,793	23	5	23	22	108 x	18	15	98	94	75	72	33	29
Hungary	1,046	10	–	–	–	18	–	–	–	–	100	102	–	–

TABLE 11 | ADOLESCENTS >>

Countries and areas	Adolescent population Aged 10–19 (thousands) 2012	Proportion of total population (%) 2012	Adolescents currently married/in union (%) 2005–2012* male	female	Births by age 18 (%) 2008–2012*	Adolescent birth rate 2008–2011*	Justification of wife beating among adolescents (%) 2005–2012* male	female	Use of mass media among adolescents (%) 2005–2012* male	female	Lower secondary school gross enrolment ratio 2008–2012*	Upper secondary school gross enrolment ratio 2008–2012*	Comprehensive knowledge of HIV among adolescents (%) 2008–2012* male	female
Iceland	45	14	–	–	–	11	–	–	–	–	96	117	–	–
India	238,563	19	5	30	22 x	39	57	53	88	72	81	50	35 x	19 x
Indonesia	44,619	18	–	13	7	48	48 y	45	88 y	91	94	68	4 p,y	9
Iran (Islamic Republic of)	11,790	15	–	16	5	31 x	–	–	–	–	102	76	–	–
Iraq	7,492	23	–	21	12	68 x	–	50	–	–	–	–	–	3
Ireland	584	13	–	–	–	16	–	–	–	–	111	131	–	–
Israel	1,224	16	–	–	–	14	–	–	–	–	103	102	–	–
Italy	5,788	10	–	–	–	7	–	–	–	–	107	97	–	–
Jamaica	560	20	–	5	16	72 x	28 y	4 y	–	–	91	95	34 y	39 y
Japan	11,822	9	–	–	–	5	–	–	–	–	103	102	–	–
Jordan	1,399	20	–	7	4	32 x	–	91 y	–	97 y	94	73	–	12 x,y
Kazakhstan	2,420	15	1	5	2	31	14	9	99	99	106	87	30	30
Kenya	9,622	22	0	12	26	106 x	54	57	91	81	91	44	51	42
Kiribati	22	22	5	16	9	39 x	65	77	58	57	95	72	46	41
Kuwait	466	14	–	–	–	13	–	–	–	–	110	89	–	–
Kyrgyzstan	1,047	19	–	8	2 x	34	–	28	–	–	93	78	–	19 x
Lao People's Democratic Republic	1,554	23	9	25	18	110 x	50	56	92	93	57	31	25	23
Latvia	198	10	–	–	–	15	–	–	–	–	95	97	–	–
Lebanon	861	19	–	3	–	18 x	–	22 y	–	–	90	76	–	–
Lesotho	498	24	1	16	13	92 x	54	48	64	69	60	33	28	35
Liberia	949	23	3	19	38	177 x	37	48	73	63	50	39	21 x	18 x
Libya	1,097	18	–	–	–	4 x	–	–	–	–	–	–	–	–
Liechtenstein	–	–	–	–	–	4 x	–	–	–	–	103	124	–	–
Lithuania	343	11	–	–	–	17	–	–	–	–	96	106	–	–
Luxembourg	64	12	–	–	–	7	–	–	–	–	115	90	–	–
Madagascar	5,319	24	11	34	36	147 x	33	35	61	60	42	15	26	23
Malawi	3,796	24	2	23	35	157	21	16	82	65	42	17	45	40
Malaysia	5,558	19	5	6	–	15	–	–	–	–	90	52	–	–
Maldives	68	20	–	5	1	16	–	41 y	–	100	118	–	–	22 y
Mali	3,412	23	–	40	46 x	190 x	–	83	81	79	53	24	–	14
Malta	51	12	–	–	–	20	–	–	–	–	103	97	–	–
Marshall Islands	–	–	5	21	21 x	105 x	71	47	86	85	126	92	35 x	27 x
Mauritania	841	22	–	26	19 x	88 x	–	36	55 x	44 x	29	23	–	5
Mauritius	192	15	–	–	–	31	–	–	–	–	96	–	–	–
Mexico	23,529	19	–	15	39	87	–	–	–	–	119	63	–	–
Micronesia (Federated States of)	26	25	–	–	–	52 x	–	–	–	–	–	–	35 x	–
Monaco	–	–	–	–	–	–	–	–	–	–	–	–	–	–
Mongolia	473	17	1	5	2	20	9	14	99	98	88	101	24	28

TABLE 11 | ADOLESCENTS >>

Countries and areas	Adolescent population		Adolescents currently married/in union (%) 2005–2012*		Births by age 18 (%) 2008–2012*	Adolescent birth rate 2008–2011*	Justification of wife beating among adolescents (%) 2005–2012*		Use of mass media among adolescents (%) 2005–2012*		Lower secondary school gross enrolment ratio	Upper secondary school gross enrolment ratio	Comprehensive knowledge of HIV among adolescents (%) 2008–2012*	
	Aged 10–19 (thousands) 2012	Proportion of total population (%) 2012	male	female			male	female	male	female	2008–2012*		male	female
Montenegro	85	14	–	2	–	24	–	6	–	–	96	98	–	–
Morocco	6,063	19	1	11	8x	18x	–	64x	–	90x	82	52	–	–
Mozambique	5,835	23	8	37	40	167	20	24	73	57	35	12	49	27
Myanmar	9,299	18	–	7	13x	17x	–	–	–	–	62	38	–	31
Namibia	530	23	0	5	17x	74x	44	38	86	88	–	–	59x	62x
Nauru	–	–	9	18	22x	84x	–	–	89	86	–	–	8x	8x
Nepal	6,354	23	7	29	19	81	27	24	86	76	–	–	33	25
Netherlands	2,007	12	–	–	–	5	–	–	–	–	127	116	–	–
New Zealand	606	14	–	–	–	26	–	–	–	–	104	137	–	–
Nicaragua	1,319	22	–	24	28x	109x	–	19	–	95x	80	54	–	–
Niger	3,956	23	3	59	51x	206	–	68	66	48	20	5	14x	12x
Nigeria	37,675	22	–	20	29	113	–	41	82	64	47	41	–	22
Niue	–	–	–	–	–	16	–	–	–	–	–	–	–	–
Norway	642	13	–	–	–	10	–	–	–	–	98	124	–	–
Oman	557	17	–	–	–	12	–	–	–	–	107	101	–	–
Pakistan	39,901	22	–	16	10x	16x	–	–	–	–	46	27	–	2x
Palau	–	–	–	–	–	27x	–	–	–	–	–	–	–	–
Panama	690	18	–	–	–	86	–	–	–	–	92	54	–	–
Papua New Guinea	1,601	22	3	15	14x	70x	–	–	–	–	–	–	–	–
Paraguay	1,395	21	–	11x	–	63x	–	–	–	–	79	56	–	–
Peru	5,804	19	–	11	15	72	–	–	–	92	100	78	–	17x
Philippines	20,817	22	–	10	7	53x	–	15	–	94	88	76	–	19
Poland	4,132	11	–	–	–	16	–	–	–	–	97	97	–	–
Portugal	1,094	10	–	–	–	16	–	–	–	–	116	102	–	–
Qatar	171	8	–	–	–	16	–	–	–	–	99	86	–	–
Republic of Korea	6,350	13	–	–	–	2	–	–	–	–	100	94	–	–
Republic of Moldova	424	12	1	10	5x	26	25	24	99	98	88	87	–	–
Romania	2,230	10	–	–	–	41	–	–	–	–	96	98	–	–
Russian Federation	14,071	10	–	–	–	30	–	–	–	–	90	86	–	–
Rwanda	2,774	24	0	3	5	41	35	56	88	73	47	23	44	49
Saint Kitts and Nevis	–	–	–	–	–	67x	–	–	–	–	99	87	–	–
Saint Lucia	32	18	–	–	–	49x	–	–	–	–	94	97	–	–
Saint Vincent and the Grenadines	20	18	–	–	–	70	–	–	–	–	119	91	–	–
Samoa	42	22	1	7	5	29x	50	58	97	97	99	75	5	2
San Marino	–	–	–	–	–	1x	–	–	–	–	95	95	–	–
Sao Tome and Principe	40	21	1	20	25	110x	25	23	96	95	82	23	39	39
Saudi Arabia	4,723	17	–	–	–	7x	–	–	–	–	115	100	–	–
Senegal	3,162	23	1	24	22	96	31	61	86	81	41	17	28	26
Serbia	1,180	12	1	5	3	19	6	2	99	100	98	86	43	53

TABLE 11 | ADOLESCENTS >>

Countries and areas	Adolescent population Aged 10–19 (thousands) 2012	Proportion of total population (%) 2012	Adolescents currently married/in union (%) 2005–2012* male	female	Births by age 18 (%) 2008–2012*	Adolescent birth rate 2008–2011*	Justification of wife beating among adolescents (%) 2005–2012* male	female	Use of mass media among adolescents (%) 2005–2012* male	female	Lower secondary school gross enrolment ratio 2008–2012*	Upper secondary school gross enrolment ratio 2008–2012*	Comprehensive knowledge of HIV among adolescents (%) 2008–2012* male	female
Seychelles	14	15	–	–	–	78	–	–	–	–	131	115	–	–
Sierra Leone	1,358	23	–	23	38	122	–	63	66	51	58	–	–	23
Singapore	702	13	–	–	–	4	–	–	–	–	–	–	–	–
Slovakia	595	11	–	–	–	21	–	–	–	–	95	88	–	–
Slovenia	191	9	–	–	–	5	–	–	–	–	95	99	–	–
Solomon Islands	124	23	0	13	15 x	70 x	73	72	71	54	70	31	26 x	29 x
Somalia	2,440	24	–	25	–	123 x	–	75 y	–	–	–	–	–	3 x
South Africa	9,578	18	2 x	4 x	15 x	54 x	–	–	–	–	96	92	–	–
South Sudan	2,544	23	–	40	28	38	–	72	–	–	–	–	–	8
Spain	4,304	9	–	–	–	13 x	–	–	–	–	122	141	–	–
Sri Lanka	3,248	15	–	9	4 x	24 x	–	54 y	–	88 y	103	102	–	–
State of Palestine	1,060	25	–	12	–	60 x	–	–	–	–	87	74	–	5
Sudan	8,546	23	–	24	14	49	–	52	–	–	–	–	–	4
Suriname	97	18	–	12	–	66 x	–	19	–	99	90	79	–	40
Swaziland	299	24	0	4	22	89	34	42	94	89	69	47	52	56
Sweden	1,084	11	–	–	–	6	–	–	–	–	98	99	–	–
Switzerland	865	11	–	–	–	4	–	–	–	–	109	86	–	–
Syrian Arab Republic	4,749	22	–	10	9 x	75 x	–	–	–	–	92	40	–	6 x
Tajikistan	1,710	21	–	6	4 x	54	–	85 y	–	–	98	65	9	11
Thailand	9,059	14	–	15	8 x	47	–	–	–	–	92	67	–	46 x
The former Yugoslav Republic of Macedonia	273	13	–	4	2	20	–	14	–	–	90	78	–	23 x
Timor-Leste	312	28	0	8	9	54 x	72	81	61	62	64	51	15	11
Togo	1,498	23	0	12	17	88	–	41	–	–	70	37	36	33
Tonga	23	22	–	–	–	16 x	–	–	–	–	–	–	–	–
Trinidad and Tobago	177	13	–	6	–	33 x	–	10	–	–	89	87	–	49 x
Tunisia	1,692	16	–	1	1	6 x	–	27	–	–	117	76	–	15
Turkey	12,846	17	–	10	8 x	38 x	–	30	–	–	99	70	–	–
Turkmenistan	994	19	–	5	2 x	21 x	–	37 y	–	96 x	–	–	–	4 x
Tuvalu	–	–	2	8	3 x	28 x	83	69	89	95	–	–	57 x	31 x
Uganda	8,890	24	2	20	33	146	52	62	88	82	35	15	35	36
Ukraine	4,389	10	3	6	3 x	30 x	8	3	99	99	100	81	33 x	39 x
United Arab Emirates	812	9	–	–	–	34	–	–	–	–	–	–	–	–
United Kingdom	7,264	12	–	–	–	25	–	–	–	–	113	100	–	–
United Republic of Tanzania	10,828	23	4	18	28	128	39	52	79	70	47	10	41	46
United States	42,958	14	–	–	–	34	–	–	–	–	103	90	–	–
Uruguay	521	15	–	–	–	60 x	–	–	–	–	111	71	–	–
Uzbekistan	5,696	20	–	5	2 x	26 x	63 x	63 x	–	–	95	129	–	27 x
Vanuatu	52	21	–	13	–	–	–	–	–	–	65	41	–	14 x

TABLE 11

TABLE 11 | ADOLESCENTS

| Countries and areas | Adolescent population | | Adolescents currently married/in union (%) 2005–2012* | | Births by age 18 (%) 2008–2012* | Adolescent birth rate 2008–2011* | Justification of wife beating among adolescents (%) 2005–2012* | | Use of mass media among adolescents (%) 2005–2012* | | Lower secondary school gross enrolment ratio | Upper secondary school gross enrolment ratio | Comprehensive knowledge of HIV among adolescents (%) 2008–2012* | |
	Aged 10–19 (thousands) 2012	Proportion of total population (%) 2012	male	female			male	female	male	female	2008–2012*		male	female
Venezuela (Bolivarian Republic of)	5,537	18	–	16 x	–	101 x	–	–	–	–	90	73	–	–
Viet Nam	14,819	16	–	8	3	35	–	35	97	94	90	–	–	51
Yemen	6,010	25	–	13	–	80 x	–	–	–	–	56	36	–	2 x,y
Zambia	3,357	24	1	18	34 x	151 x	55	61	80	71	70	–	38	36
Zimbabwe	3,327	24	1	23	21	115	48	48	59	53	–	–	42	46

SUMMARY INDICATORS#

Countries and areas	Aged 10–19 (thousands) 2012	Proportion of total population (%) 2012	male	female	Births by age 18 (%)	Adolescent birth rate	male	female	male	female	Lower secondary	Upper secondary	male	female
Sub-Saharan Africa	209,363	23	3	23	27	115	43	54	72	61	49	31	36	26
Eastern and Southern Africa	101,842	23	3	21	27	107	45	54	69	61	50	30	39	34
West and Central Africa	98,796	23	–	25	28	128	–	54	75	62	48	32	–	21
Middle East and North Africa	79,451	19	–	13	7	–	–	53	–	–	91	57	–	–
South Asia	328,314	20	4	29	24	51	56	51	88	70	75	46	34	17
East Asia and Pacific	297,376	14	–	5	6 **	16	–	36 **	89 **	91 **	89	68	–	21 **
Latin America and Caribbean	111,047	18	–	19	–	76	–	–	–	–	102	77	–	–
CEE/CIS	53,017	13	–	7	–	32	–	24	–	–	95	85	–	–
Least developed countries	200,309	23	3	27	29	113	–	52	68	59	51	28	–	22
World	1,185,392	17	–	18	21 **	49	–	48 **	–	73 **	82	59	–	20 **

For a complete list of countries and areas in the regions, subregions and country categories, see page 26.

DEFINITIONS OF THE INDICATORS

Adolescents currently married/in union – Percentage of boys and girls aged 15–19 who are currently married or in union. This indicator is meant to provide a snapshot of the current marital status of boys and girls in this age group. However, it is worth noting that those not married at the time of the survey are still exposed to the risk of marrying before they exit adolescence.

Births by age 18 – Percentage of women aged 20–24 who gave birth before age 18. This standardized indicator from population-based surveys captures levels of fertility among adolescents up to the age of 18. Note that the data are based on the answers of women aged 20–24, whose risk of giving birth before the age of 18 is behind them.

Adolescent birth rate – Number of births per 1,000 adolescent girls aged 15–19.

Justification of wife beating among adolescents – The percentage of boys and girls aged 15–19 who consider a husband to be justified in hitting or beating his wife for at least one of the specified reasons: if his wife burns the food, argues with him, goes out without telling him, neglects the children or refuses sexual relations.

Use of mass media among adolescents – The percentage of boys and girls aged 15–19 who make use of at least one of the following types of information media at least once a week: newspaper, magazine, television or radio.

Lower secondary school gross enrolment ratio – Number of children enrolled in lower secondary school, regardless of age, expressed as a percentage of the total number of children of official lower secondary school age.

Upper secondary school gross enrolment ratio – Number of children enrolled in upper secondary school, regardless of age, expressed as a percentage of the total number of children of official upper secondary school age.

Comprehensive knowledge of HIV among adolescents – Percentage of young men and women aged 15–19 who correctly identify the two major ways of preventing the sexual transmission of HIV (using condoms and limiting sex to one faithful, uninfected partner), who reject the two most common local misconceptions about HIV transmission and who know that a healthy-looking person can be HIV-positive.

MAIN DATA SOURCES

Adolescent population – United Nations Population Division.

Adolescents currently married/in union – Demographic and Health Surveys (DHS), Multiple Indicator Cluster Surveys (MICS) and other national surveys.

Births by age 18 – DHS and MICS.

Adolescent birth rate – United Nations Population Division.

Justification of wife beating among adolescents – DHS, MICS and other national surveys.

Use of mass media among adolescents – AIDS Indicator Surveys (AIS), DHS, MICS and other national surveys.

Gross enrolment ratio – UNESCO Institute for Statistics (UIS).

Comprehensive knowledge of HIV among adolescents – AIS, DHS, MICS, Reproductive Health Surveys (RHS) and other national household surveys; HIV/AIDS Survey Indicators Database, <www.measuredhs.com/hivdata>.

NOTES

– Data not available.

x Data refer to years or periods other than those specified in the column heading. Such data are not included in the calculation of regional and global averages, with the exception of 2005–2006 data from India. Estimates from data years prior to 2000 are not displayed.

y Data differ from the standard definition or refer to only part of a country. If they fall within the noted reference period, such data are included in the calculation of regional and global averages.

p Based on small denominators (typically 25–49 unweighted cases).

* Data refer to the most recent year available during the period specified in the column heading.

** Excludes China.

TABLE 12 | DISPARITIES BY RESIDENCE

Countries and areas	Birth registration (%)[++] 2005–2012*			Skilled attendant at birth (%) 2008–2012*			Underweight prevalence in children under 5 (%) 2008–2012*			Diarrhoea treatment with oral rehydration salts (ORS) (%) 2008–2012*			Primary school net attendance ratio 2008–2012*			Comprehensive knowledge of HIV (%) Females 15–24 2008–2012*			Use of improved sanitation facilities (%) 2011		
	urban	rural	ratio of urban to rural	urban	rural	ratio of urban to rural	urban	rural	ratio of rural to urban	urban	rural	ratio of urban to rural	urban	rural	ratio of urban to rural	urban	rural	ratio of urban to rural	urban	rural	ratio of urban to rural
Afghanistan	60	33	1.8	74	31	2.4	–	–	–	48	54	0.9	78	50	1.5	5	1	4.9	46	23	2.0
Albania	99	98	1.0	100	99	1.0	5	6	1.2	33 x	36 x	0.9 x	90	91	1.0	51	26	2.0	95	93	1.0
Algeria	100	99	1.0	98 x	92 x	1.1 x	3 x	4 x	1.3 x	18 x	19 x	1.0 x	98 x	95 x	1.0 x	16 x	10 x	1.7 x	98	88	1.1
Andorra	–	–	–	–	–	–	–	–	–	–	–	–	–	–	–	–	–	–	100	100	1.0
Angola	40 x	26 x	1.5 x	71 x	26 x	2.8 x	–	–	–	–	–	–	85	67	1.3	–	–	–	86	19	4.4
Antigua and Barbuda	–	–	–	–	–	–	–	–	–	–	–	–	–	–	–	–	–	–	91	91	1.0
Argentina	–	–	–	–	–	–	–	–	–	–	–	–	–	–	–	–	–	–	96	98	1.0
Armenia	99	100	1.0	100	99	1.0	3	7	2.6	22 x	28 x	0.8 x	97	98	1.0	16	16	1.0	96	81	1.2
Australia	–	–	–	–	–	–	–	–	–	–	–	–	–	–	–	–	–	–	100	100	1.0
Austria	–	–	–	–	–	–	–	–	–	–	–	–	–	–	–	–	–	–	100	100	1.0
Azerbaijan	96	92	1.0	97 x	80 x	1.2 x	4 x	12 x	3.0 x	19 x	5 x	3.6 x	74 x	72 x	1.0 x	7 x	2 x	3.3 x	86	78	1.1
Bahamas	–	–	–	–	–	–	–	–	–	–	–	–	–	–	–	–	–	–	–	–	–
Bahrain	–	–	–	–	–	–	–	–	–	–	–	–	–	–	–	–	–	–	99	99	1.0
Bangladesh	35	29	1.2	54	25	2.1	28	39	1.4	84	76	1.1	77	80	1.0	–	–	–	55	55	1.0
Barbados	–	–	–	–	–	–	–	–	–	–	–	–	–	–	–	–	–	–	–	–	–
Belarus	–	–	–	100	100	1.0	1 x	2 x	2.0 x	38 x	33 x	1.1 x	91	93	1.0	–	–	–	92	97	0.9
Belgium	–	–	–	–	–	–	–	–	–	–	–	–	–	–	–	–	–	–	100	100	1.0
Belize	95	96	1.0	98	95	1.0	5	7	1.2	–	–	–	98	92	1.1	55	33	1.7	93	87	1.1
Benin	87	76	1.1	92	79	1.2	19	23	1.2	54	47	1.1	76 y	67 y	1.1 y	22 x	11 x	1.9 x	25	5	5.0
Bhutan	100	100	1.0	90	54	1.6	11	14	1.3	64	60	1.1	96	90	1.1	32	15	2.1	74	29	2.5
Bolivia (Plurinational State of)	79 y	72 y	1.1 y	88	51	1.7	3	6	2.3	38	32	1.2	98	96	1.0	32	9	3.5	57	24	2.4
Bosnia and Herzegovina	99	100	1.0	100	100	1.0	2	1	0.7	34 x	35 x	1.0 x	97	98	1.0	50	47	1.1	100	92	1.1
Botswana	78	67	1.2	99 x	90 x	1.1 x	–	–	–	47 x	51 x	0.9 x	89 x	85 x	1.0 x	–	–	–	78	42	1.9
Brazil	–	–	–	98 x	94 x	1.0 x	2 x	2 x	1.0 x	–	–	–	–	–	–	–	–	–	87	48	1.8
Brunei Darussalam	–	–	–	–	–	–	–	–	–	–	–	–	–	–	–	–	–	–	–	–	–
Bulgaria	–	–	–	–	–	–	–	–	–	–	–	–	–	–	–	–	–	–	100	100	1.0
Burkina Faso	93	74	1.3	93	61	1.5	–	–	–	31	19	1.6	83	45	1.8	–	–	–	50	6	7.8
Burundi	87	74	1.2	88	58	1.5	18	30	1.7	33	38	0.9	87	73	1.2	–	–	–	45	51	0.9
Cabo Verde	–	–	–	91 x	64 x	1.4 x	–	–	–	–	–	–	–	–	–	–	–	–	74	45	1.6
Cambodia	74	60	1.2	95	67	1.4	19	30	1.6	33	34	1.0	96	93	1.0	55	41	1.3	76	22	3.4
Cameroon	81	48	1.7	87	47	1.9	7	20	2.8	27	12	2.2	94	78	1.2	–	–	–	58	36	1.6
Canada	–	–	–	–	–	–	–	–	–	–	–	–	–	–	–	–	–	–	100	99	1.0
Central African Republic	78	52	1.5	83	38	2.2	23	24	1.0	23	12	2.0	86	66	1.3	21 x	13 x	1.6 x	43	28	1.5
Chad	42	9	4.9	60	12	5.1	22	30	1.4	27	10	2.8	71	47	1.5	18	7	2.6	31	6	4.8
Chile	–	–	–	100 x	99 x	1.0 x	–	–	–	–	–	–	–	–	–	–	–	–	100	89	1.1
China	–	–	–	100	100	1.0	1	4	3.3	–	–	–	–	–	–	–	–	–	74	56	1.3
Colombia	97	95	1.0	98	86	1.1	3	5	1.6	57	49	1.2	91	91	1.0	26	17	1.5	82	65	1.3
Comoros	90 x	87 x	1.0 x	92	79	1.2	12	17	1.4	40	37	1.1	41 x	29 x	1.4 x	–	–	–	–	–	–
Congo	95	85	1.1	98	86	1.1	8 x	15 x	1.9 x	38	27	1.4	–	–	–	16	10	1.6	19	15	1.3
Cook Islands	–	–	–	–	–	–	–	–	–	–	–	–	–	–	–	–	–	–	95	95	1.0
Costa Rica	–	–	–	100	99	1.0	–	–	–	–	–	–	96	96	1.0	–	–	–	95	92	1.0

TABLE 12 | DISPARITIES BY RESIDENCE >>

TABLE 12

Countries and areas	Birth registration (%)++ 2005–2012*			Skilled attendant at birth (%) 2008–2012*			Underweight prevalence in children under 5 (%) 2008–2012*			Diarrhoea treatment with oral rehydration salts (ORS) (%) 2008–2012*			Primary school net attendance ratio 2008–2012*			Comprehensive knowledge of HIV (%) Females 15–24 2008–2012*			Use of improved sanitation facilities (%) 2011		
	urban	rural	ratio of urban to rural	urban	rural	ratio of urban to rural	urban	rural	ratio of rural to urban	urban	rural	ratio of urban to rural	urban	rural	ratio of urban to rural	urban	rural	ratio of urban to rural	urban	rural	ratio of urban to rural
Côte d'Ivoire	85	54	1.6	84	45	1.9	12	17	1.5	22	14	1.5	73 y	65 y	1.1 y	22	8	2.7	36	11	3.1
Croatia	–	–	–	–	–	–	–	–	–	–	–	–	–	–	–	–	–	–	99	98	1.0
Cuba	100 y	100 y	1.0 y	–	–	–	–	–	–	54	37	1.4	–	–	–	55	49	1.1	94	87	1.1
Cyprus	–	–	–	–	–	–	–	–	–	–	–	–	–	–	–	–	–	–	100	100	1.0
Czech Republic	–	–	–	–	–	–	–	–	–	–	–	–	–	–	–	–	–	–	100	100	1.0
Democratic People's Republic of Korea	100	100	1.0	100	100	1.0	13	27	2.0	75	73	1.0	100	99	1.0	11	4	2.8	88	73	1.2
Democratic Republic of the Congo	24	29	0.8	96	75	1.3	17	27	1.6	26	27	1.0	86	70	1.2	21	12	1.7	29	31	0.9
Denmark	–	–	–	–	–	–	–	–	–	–	–	–	–	–	–	–	–	–	100	100	1.0
Djibouti	92	84	1.1	95 x	40 x	2.3 x	27 y	27 y	1.0 y	–	–	–	67 x	49 x	1.4 x	18 x	9 x	2.0 x	73	22	3.4
Dominica	–	–	–	–	–	–	–	–	–	–	–	–	–	–	–	–	–	–	–	–	–
Dominican Republic	–	–	–	98 x	97 x	1.0 x	3 x	4 x	1.2 x	34	27	1.3	95	95	1.0	42 x	37 x	1.2 x	86	74	1.2
Ecuador	89	92	1.0	98 x	99 x	1.0 x	–	–	–	–	–	–	–	–	–	–	–	–	96	86	1.1
Egypt	99 y	99 y	1.0 y	90	72	1.2	6	6	1.0	28	29	1.0	90 y	87 y	1.0 y	7	3	2.3	97	93	1.0
El Salvador	99	99	1.0	97	94	1.0	4 y	7 y	2.0 y	60	56	1.1	–	–	–	–	–	–	79	53	1.5
Equatorial Guinea	49 x	28 x	1.8 x	87 x	49 x	1.8 x	–	–	–	43 x	19 x	2.2 x	–	–	–	–	–	–	–	–	–
Eritrea	–	–	–	65 x	10 x	6.2 x	23 x	40 x	1.7 x	59 x	39 x	1.5 x	–	–	–	–	–	–	–	4	–
Estonia	–	–	–	–	–	–	–	–	–	–	–	–	–	–	–	–	–	–	100	94	1.1
Ethiopia	29	5	5.9	51	4	12.7	16	30	1.9	45	24	1.9	86	61	1.4	38	19	2.0	27	19	1.4
Fiji	–	–	–	–	–	–	–	–	–	–	–	–	–	–	–	–	–	–	92	82	1.1
Finland	–	–	–	–	–	–	–	–	–	–	–	–	–	–	–	–	–	–	100	100	1.0
France	–	–	–	–	–	–	–	–	–	–	–	–	–	–	–	–	–	–	100	100	1.0
Gabon	89	91	1.0	93	69	1.3	6	9	1.6	27	21	1.3	87 y	89 y	1.0 y	32	15	2.2	33	30	1.1
Gambia	54	52	1.0	77	41	1.9	12	21	1.8	39	39	1.0	75	54	1.4	41	24	1.7	70	65	1.1
Georgia	99	98	1.0	99 x	98 x	1.0 x	1	1	1.6	44 x	36 x	1.2 x	97	95	1.0	–	–	–	96	91	1.1
Germany	–	–	–	–	–	–	–	–	–	–	–	–	–	–	–	–	–	–	100	100	1.0
Ghana	72	55	1.3	88	54	1.6	11	16	1.5	37	34	1.1	80	68	1.2	42	30	1.4	19	8	2.4
Greece	–	–	–	–	–	–	–	–	–	–	–	–	–	–	–	–	–	–	99	97	1.0
Grenada	–	–	–	–	–	–	–	–	–	–	–	–	–	–	–	–	–	–	–	–	–
Guatemala	96	97	1.0	77	37	2.1	8 y	16 y	1.9 y	38	37	1.0	–	–	–	32	14	2.2	88	72	1.2
Guinea	78	33	2.4	84	32	2.7	15	23	1.5	46	30	1.5	–	–	–	–	–	–	32	11	2.9
Guinea-Bissau	30	21	1.4	69	29	2.4	13	21	1.6	28	13	2.1	84	57	1.5	22	8	2.8	33	8	4.1
Guyana	91	87	1.0	98	90	1.1	7	12	1.7	42 x	38 x	1.1 x	96	94	1.0	72	47	1.5	88	82	1.1
Haiti	85	77	1.1	59	25	2.4	8	13	1.6	56	51	1.1	86 y	73 y	1.2 y	41	29	1.4	34	17	1.9
Holy See	–	–	–	–	–	–	–	–	–	–	–	–	–	–	–	–	–	–	–	–	–
Honduras	95	93	1.0	94	73	1.3	5	9	2.0	59	61	1.0	94 y	92 y	1.0 y	42	23	1.9	86	74	1.2
Hungary	–	–	–	–	–	–	–	–	–	–	–	–	–	–	–	–	–	–	100	100	1.0
Iceland	–	–	–	–	–	–	–	–	–	–	–	–	–	–	–	–	–	–	100	100	1.0
India	59	35	1.7	76	43	1.7	33 x	46 x	1.4 x	33 x	24 x	1.4 x	–	–	–	33 x	14 x	2.4 x	60	24	2.5
Indonesia	76	58	1.3	92	75	1.2	15	21	1.4	41	37	1.1	91 y	91 y	1.0 y	14	9	1.6	73	44	1.7
Iran (Islamic Republic of)	99 y	98 y	1.0 y	98	93	1.1	–	–	–	64	58	1.1	97	95	1.0	–	–	–	100	99	1.0

TABLE 12 | DISPARITIES BY RESIDENCE >>

Countries and areas	Birth registration (%)++ 2005–2012* urban	rural	ratio of urban to rural	Skilled attendant at birth (%) 2008–2012* urban	rural	ratio of urban to rural	Underweight prevalence in children under 5 (%) 2008–2012* urban	rural	ratio of rural to urban	Diarrhoea treatment with oral rehydration salts (ORS) (%) 2008–2012* urban	rural	ratio of urban to rural	Primary school net attendance ratio 2008–2012* urban	rural	ratio of urban to rural	Comprehensive knowledge of HIV (%) Females 15–24 2008–2012* urban	rural	ratio of urban to rural	Use of improved sanitation facilities (%) 2011 urban	rural	ratio of urban to rural
Iraq	99	99	1.0	94	85	1.1	8	9	1.0	25	19	1.3	94	84	1.1	4	1	3.7	86	80	1.1
Ireland	–	–	–	–	–	–	–	–	–	–	–	–	–	–	–	–	–	–	100	98	1.0
Israel	–	–	–	–	–	–	–	–	–	–	–	–	–	–	–	–	–	–	100	100	1.0
Italy	–	–	–	–	–	–	–	–	–	–	–	–	–	–	–	–	–	–	–	–	–
Jamaica	97	99	1.0	99	98	1.0	–	–	–	–	–	–	97 x	98 x	1.0 x	–	–	–	78	82	1.0
Japan	–	–	–	–	–	–	–	–	–	–	–	–	–	–	–	–	–	–	100	100	1.0
Jordan	99	100	1.0	100	100	1.0	3	2	0.7	20	23	0.9	–	–	–	–	–	–	98	98	1.0
Kazakhstan	100	100	1.0	100	100	1.0	4	3	0.8	–	–	–	99	99	1.0	40	31	1.3	97	98	1.0
Kenya	76	57	1.3	75	37	2.0	10	17	1.7	40	39	1.0	81	72	1.1	57	45	1.3	31	29	1.1
Kiribati	95	93	1.0	84	77	1.1	–	–	–	–	–	–	81 y	86 y	0.9 y	45	43	1.1	51	30	1.7
Kuwait	–	–	–	–	–	–	–	–	–	–	–	–	–	–	–	–	–	–	100	100	1.0
Kyrgyzstan	97	95	1.0	100	99	1.0	3	6	1.7	37	35	1.1	93 x	92 x	1.0 x	23 x	18 x	1.3 x	94	93	1.0
Lao People's Democratic Republic	88	71	1.2	80	31	2.6	16	29	1.8	65	40	1.6	95	83	1.1	39	18	2.2	87	48	1.8
Latvia	–	–	–	–	–	–	–	–	–	–	–	–	–	–	–	–	–	–	–	–	–
Lebanon	–	–	–	–	–	–	–	–	–	–	–	–	–	–	–	–	–	–	100	–	–
Lesotho	43	46	1.0	88	54	1.6	12	13	1.1	57	50	1.1	93	88	1.0	44	36	1.2	32	24	1.3
Liberia	5 y	3 y	1.9 y	79 x	32 x	2.4 x	17 x	20 x	1.2 x	57 x	52 x	1.1 x	46 x	21 x	2.2 x	26 x	15 x	1.8 x	30	7	4.2
Libya	–	–	–	–	–	–	–	–	–	–	–	–	–	–	–	–	–	–	97	96	1.0
Liechtenstein	–	–	–	–	–	–	–	–	–	–	–	–	–	–	–	–	–	–	–	–	–
Lithuania	–	–	–	–	–	–	–	–	–	–	–	–	–	–	–	–	–	–	95	–	–
Luxembourg	–	–	–	–	–	–	–	–	–	–	–	–	–	–	–	–	–	–	100	100	1.0
Madagascar	92	78	1.2	82	39	2.1	31 x	37 x	1.2 x	32	14	2.2	93	77	1.2	40	19	2.1	19	11	1.7
Malawi	–	–	–	84	69	1.2	10	13	1.3	72	69	1.0	93	84	1.1	56	38	1.5	50	53	0.9
Malaysia	–	–	–	–	–	–	10	15	1.5	–	–	–	–	–	–	–	–	–	96	95	1.0
Maldives	93	92	1.0	99	93	1.1	11	20	1.8	–	–	–	83	83	1.0	43 y	32 y	1.4 y	97	98	1.0
Mali	92	77	1.2	86	47	1.8	14	20	1.4	17	10	1.8	80	50	1.6	19	12	1.5	35	14	2.5
Malta	–	–	–	–	–	–	–	–	–	–	–	–	–	–	–	–	–	–	100	100	1.0
Marshall Islands	96	96	1.0	97 x	68 x	1.4 x	–	–	–	39 x	37 x	1.1 x	–	–	–	33 x	12 x	2.7 x	84	55	1.5
Mauritania	75	49	1.5	88	49	1.8	–	–	–	26 x	14 x	2.0 x	72	55	1.3	9	4	2.7	51	9	5.5
Mauritius	–	–	–	–	–	–	–	–	–	–	–	–	–	–	–	–	–	–	92	90	1.0
Mexico	98 y	82 y	1.2 y	98	87	1.1	–	–	–	54	48	1.1	–	–	–	–	–	–	87	77	1.1
Micronesia (Federated States of)	–	–	–	–	–	–	–	–	–	–	–	–	–	–	–	–	–	–	83	47	1.8
Monaco	–	–	–	–	–	–	–	–	–	–	–	–	–	–	–	–	–	–	100	–	–
Mongolia	99	99	1.0	99	98	1.0	3	4	1.4	35	26	1.4	97	94	1.0	36	21	1.7	64	29	2.2
Montenegro	99	99	1.0	100 x	98 x	1.0 x	2 x	1 x	0.5 x	–	–	–	97 x	98 x	1.0 x	–	–	–	92	87	1.1
Morocco	97 y	91 y	1.1 y	92	55	1.7	2	4	2.5	28 x	18 x	1.5 x	96 x	83 x	1.2 x	–	–	–	83	52	1.6
Mozambique	51	47	1.1	80	44	1.8	10	17	1.7	65	50	1.3	86 y	74 y	1.2 y	40	24	1.6	41	9	4.5
Myanmar	94	64	1.5	90	63	1.4	19	24	1.3	72	56	1.3	93	89	1.0	–	–	–	84	74	1.1
Namibia	–	–	–	94 x	73 x	1.3 x	12 x	19 x	1.6 x	67 x	60 x	1.1 x	94 x	91 x	1.0 x	65 x	65 x	1.0 x	57	17	3.4
Nauru	–	–	–	–	–	–	–	–	–	–	–	–	–	–	–	–	–	–	66	–	–

TABLE 12 | DISPARITIES BY RESIDENCE >>

TABLE 12

Countries and areas	Birth registration (%)++ 2005–2012*			Skilled attendant at birth (%) 2008–2012*			Underweight prevalence in children under 5 (%) 2008–2012*			Diarrhoea treatment with oral rehydration salts (ORS) (%) 2008–2012*			Primary school net attendance ratio 2008–2012*			Comprehensive knowledge of HIV (%) Females 15–24 2008–2012*			Use of improved sanitation facilities (%) 2011		
	urban	rural	ratio of urban to rural	urban	rural	ratio of urban to rural	urban	rural	ratio of rural to urban	urban	rural	ratio of urban to rural	urban	rural	ratio of urban to rural	urban	rural	ratio of urban to rural	urban	rural	ratio of urban to rural
Nepal	44	42	1.0	73	32	2.3	17	30	1.8	44	39	1.1	97	93	1.0	40	24	1.7	50	32	1.5
Netherlands	–	–	–	–	–	–	–	–	–	–	–	–	–	–	–	–	–	–	100	100	1.0
New Zealand	–	–	–	–	–	–	–	–	–	–	–	–	–	–	–	–	–	–	–	–	–
Nicaragua	–	–	–	92 x	56 x	1.7 x	4 x	7 x	1.8 x	64 x	55 x	1.2 x	76 y	64 y	1.2 y	–	–	–	63	37	1.7
Niger	71	25	2.9	83	21	3.9	23	38	1.7	47	44	1.1	71 x	32 x	2.2 x	31 x	8 x	3.8 x	34	4	7.9
Nigeria	63	32	2.0	74	37	2.0	17	28	1.6	45	21	2.2	87	62	1.4	29	19	1.5	33	28	1.2
Niue	–	–	–	–	–	–	–	–	–	–	–	–	–	–	–	–	–	–	100	100	1.0
Norway	–	–	–	–	–	–	–	–	–	–	–	–	–	–	–	–	–	–	100	100	1.0
Oman	–	–	–	–	–	–	–	–	–	–	–	–	–	–	–	–	–	–	97	95	1.0
Pakistan	32	24	1.3	66	33	2.0	27	33	1.3	44 x	40 x	1.1 x	78 x	62 x	1.3 x	–	–	–	72	34	2.1
Palau	–	–	–	–	–	–	–	–	–	–	–	–	–	–	–	–	–	–	100	100	1.0
Panama	–	–	–	99	84	1.2	–	–	–	–	–	–	–	–	–	–	–	–	77	54	1.4
Papua New Guinea	–	–	–	88 x	48 x	1.9 x	12 x	20 x	1.6 x	–	–	–	–	–	–	–	–	–	57	13	4.3
Paraguay	82 y	69 y	1.2 y	–	–	–	–	–	–	–	–	–	89	87	1.0	–	–	–	–	–	–
Peru	96 y	94 y	1.0 y	96	70	1.4	2	8	4.3	35	23	1.5	97	94	1.0	–	–	–	81	38	2.1
Philippines	–	–	–	78	48	1.6	–	–	–	58	36	1.6	–	–	–	23	17	1.4	79	69	1.1
Poland	–	–	–	–	–	–	–	–	–	–	–	–	–	–	–	–	–	–	96	–	–
Portugal	–	–	–	–	–	–	–	–	–	–	–	–	–	–	–	–	–	–	100	100	1.0
Qatar	–	–	–	–	–	–	–	–	–	–	–	–	–	–	–	–	–	–	100	100	1.0
Republic of Korea	–	–	–	–	–	–	–	–	–	–	–	–	–	–	–	–	–	–	100	100	1.0
Republic of Moldova	100	100	1.0	100 x	99 x	1.0 x	2 x	4 x	2.0 x	9 x	6 x	1.6 x	–	–	–	–	–	–	89	83	1.1
Romania	–	–	–	100 x	98 x	1.0 x	3 x	4 x	1.3 x	–	–	–	–	–	–	–	–	–	–	–	–
Russian Federation	–	–	–	–	–	–	–	–	–	–	–	–	–	–	–	–	–	–	74	59	1.3
Rwanda	60	64	0.9	82	67	1.2	6	12	1.9	26	30	0.9	92	87	1.1	66	50	1.3	61	61	1.0
Saint Kitts and Nevis	–	–	–	–	–	–	–	–	–	–	–	–	–	–	–	–	–	–	–	–	–
Saint Lucia	–	–	–	–	–	–	–	–	–	–	–	–	–	–	–	–	–	–	70	64	1.1
Saint Vincent and the Grenadines	–	–	–	–	–	–	–	–	–	–	–	–	–	–	–	–	–	–	–	–	–
Samoa	62	44	1.4	94	78	1.2	–	–	–	–	–	–	89 y	88 y	1.0 y	5	2	2.4	93	91	1.0
San Marino	–	–	–	–	–	–	–	–	–	–	–	–	–	–	–	–	–	–	–	–	–
Sao Tome and Principe	76	74	1.0	89	75	1.2	12	14	1.1	45	52	0.9	86	85	1.0	47	38	1.3	41	23	1.8
Saudi Arabia	–	–	–	–	–	–	–	–	–	–	–	–	–	–	–	–	–	–	100	100	1.0
Senegal	89	66	1.4	91	49	1.8	12	21	1.8	24	21	1.2	81	50	1.6	–	–	–	68	39	1.7
Serbia	99	99	1.0	100	100	1.0	2	1	0.7	50	22	2.3	99	98	1.0	63	41	1.5	98	96	1.0
Seychelles	–	–	–	–	–	–	–	–	–	–	–	–	–	–	–	–	–	–	97	97	1.0
Sierra Leone	78	78	1.0	72	59	1.2	20	22	1.1	66	75	0.9	80	72	1.1	30	19	1.6	22	7	3.4
Singapore	–	–	–	–	–	–	–	–	–	–	–	–	–	–	–	–	–	–	100	–	–
Slovakia	–	–	–	–	–	–	–	–	–	–	–	–	–	–	–	–	–	–	100	100	1.0
Slovenia	–	–	–	–	–	–	–	–	–	–	–	–	–	–	–	–	–	–	100	100	1.0
Solomon Islands	–	–	–	95 x	84 x	1.1 x	8 x	12 x	1.5 x	40 x	37 x	1.1 x	72 x,y	65 x,y	1.1 x,y	34 x	28 x	1.2 x	81	15	5.4
Somalia	6	2	3.7	65 x	15 x	4.5 x	20 x	38 x	1.9 x	25 x	9 x	2.9 x	30 x	9 x	3.3 x	7 x	2 x	4.1 x	52	6	8.3
South Africa	–	–	–	94 x	85 x	1.1 x	10 x	9 x	0.9 x	41 x	32 x	1.3 x	–	–	–	–	–	–	84	57	1.5

TABLE 12 | DISPARITIES BY RESIDENCE >>

Countries and areas	Birth registration (%)++ 2005–2012*			Skilled attendant at birth (%) 2008–2012*			Underweight prevalence in children under 5 (%) 2008–2012*			Diarrhoea treatment with oral rehydration salts (ORS) (%) 2008–2012*			Primary school net attendance ratio 2008–2012*			Comprehensive knowledge of HIV (%) Females 15–24 2008–2012*			Use of improved sanitation facilities (%) 2011		
	urban	rural	ratio of urban to rural	urban	rural	ratio of urban to rural	urban	rural	ratio of rural to urban	urban	rural	ratio of urban to rural	urban	rural	ratio of urban to rural	urban	rural	ratio of urban to rural	urban	rural	ratio of urban to rural
South Sudan	45	32	1.4	31	15	2.0	23	29	1.3	44	37	1.2	47	23	2.0	16	7	2.3	16	7	2.1
Spain	–	–	–	–	–	–	–	–	–	–	–	–	–	–	–	–	–	–	100	100	1.0
Sri Lanka	97	98	1.0	99 x	99 x	1.0 x	–	–	–	57 x	50 x	1.1 x	97 x	98 x	1.0 x	–	–	–	83	93	0.9
State of Palestine	99	99	1.0	99 x	98 x	1.0 x	–	–	–	–	–	–	–	–	–	8	6	1.3	95	93	1.0
Sudan	85	50	1.7	41	16	2.5	24	35	1.5	23	22	1.1	89	69	1.3	10	3	3.4	44	13	3.3
Suriname	100	98	1.0	95	86	1.1	6	6	1.1	33	55	0.6	97	94	1.0	45	33	1.4	90	66	1.4
Swaziland	62	47	1.3	89	80	1.1	4	6	1.5	65	55	1.2	97	96	1.0	70	55	1.3	63	55	1.1
Sweden	–	–	–	–	–	–	–	–	–	–	–	–	–	–	–	–	–	–	100	100	1.0
Switzerland	–	–	–	–	–	–	–	–	–	–	–	–	–	–	–	–	–	–	100	100	1.0
Syrian Arab Republic	97	95	1.0	99	93	1.1	9 x	9 x	1.0 x	56 x	44 x	1.3 x	89 x	85 x	1.0 x	7 x	7 x	1.0 x	96	94	1.0
Tajikistan	88	89	1.0	93	86	1.1	11	13	1.2	58	61	0.9	97 x,y	97 x,y	1.0 x,y	–	–	–	95	94	1.0
Thailand	100	99	1.0	100	100	1.0	5 x	8 x	1.6 x	50 x	59 x	0.9 x	98 x	98 x	1.0 x	43 x	47 x	0.9 x	89	96	0.9
The former Yugoslav Republic of Macedonia	100	100	1.0	97	95	1.0	1	2	2.3	19 x	30 x	0.6 x	99	98	1.0	33 x	18 x	1.8 x	97	83	1.2
Timor-Leste	50	57	0.9	59	20	2.9	35	47	1.4	65	74	0.9	79	70	1.1	14	12	1.2	68	27	2.5
Togo	93	71	1.3	91	43	2.1	10	20	1.9	15	10	1.5	94	86	1.1	39	27	1.4	26	3	9.3
Tonga	–	–	–	–	–	–	–	–	–	–	–	–	–	–	–	–	–	–	99	89	1.1
Trinidad and Tobago	–	–	–	–	–	–	–	–	–	–	–	–	–	–	–	–	–	–	92	92	1.0
Tunisia	100	98	1.0	100	97	1.0	–	–	–	69	59	1.2	99	97	1.0	22	13	1.7	97	75	1.3
Turkey	95	92	1.0	96	80	1.2	1	3	2.1	–	–	–	94 y	91 y	1.0 y	–	–	–	97	75	1.3
Turkmenistan	96	95	1.0	100 x	99 x	1.0 x	7 x	9 x	1.3 x	32 x	45 x	0.7 x	–	–	–	7 x	4 x	2.0 x	100	98	1.0
Tuvalu	60	38	1.6	–	–	–	1 x	2 x	1.7 x	–	–	–	98 x,y	99 x,y	1.0 x,y	38 x	41 x	0.9 x	86	80	1.1
Uganda	38	29	1.3	89	52	1.7	7	15	2.3	46	43	1.1	85	81	1.1	48	35	1.4	34	35	1.0
Ukraine	100	100	1.0	99 x	98 x	1.0 x	–	–	–	–	–	–	71 x	76 x	0.9 x	48 x	37 x	1.3 x	96	89	1.1
United Arab Emirates	–	–	–	–	–	–	–	–	–	–	–	–	–	–	–	–	–	–	98	95	1.0
United Kingdom	–	–	–	–	–	–	–	–	–	–	–	–	–	–	–	–	–	–	100	100	1.0
United Republic of Tanzania	44	10	4.6	83	40	2.0	11	17	1.5	44	44	1.0	91	77	1.2	55	45	1.2	24	7	3.3
United States	–	–	–	–	–	–	–	–	–	–	–	–	–	–	–	–	–	–	100	99	1.0
Uruguay	–	–	–	–	–	–	–	–	–	–	–	–	–	–	–	–	–	–	99	98	1.0
Uzbekistan	100	100	1.0	100 x	100 x	1.0 x	4 x	4 x	1.0 x	34 x	31 x	1.1 x	97 x	95 x	1.0 x	33 x	30 x	1.1 x	100	100	1.0
Vanuatu	53	41	1.3	87 x	72 x	1.2 x	11 x	11 x	1.0 x	–	–	–	85 x	80 x	1.1 x	23 x	13 x	1.8 x	65	55	1.2
Venezuela (Bolivarian Republic of)	–	–	–	–	–	–	–	–	–	–	–	–	–	–	–	–	–	–	–	–	–
Viet Nam	97	94	1.0	99	91	1.1	6	14	2.3	47	46	1.0	98	98	1.0	58	48	1.2	93	67	1.4
Yemen	42 y	11 y	4.0 y	62 x	26 x	2.3 x	–	–	–	30 x	34 x	0.9 x	83 x	64 x	1.3 x	4 x	1 x	6.7 x	93	34	2.7
Zambia	28	9	3.2	83 x	31 x	2.7 x	13 x	15 x	1.2 x	59 x	60 x	1.0 x	91 x	77 x	1.2 x	–	–	–	56	33	1.7
Zimbabwe	65	43	1.5	86	58	1.5	8	10	1.3	26	18	1.4	89	88	1.0	59	47	1.3	52	33	1.6

TABLE 12

TABLE 12 | DISPARITIES BY RESIDENCE

Countries and areas	Birth registration (%)[++] 2005–2012* urban	rural	ratio of urban to rural	Skilled attendant at birth (%) 2008–2012* urban	rural	ratio of urban to rural	Underweight prevalence in children under 5 (%) 2008–2012* urban	rural	ratio of rural to urban	Diarrhoea treatment with oral rehydration salts (ORS) (%) 2008–2012* urban	rural	ratio of urban to rural	Primary school net attendance ratio 2008–2012* urban	rural	ratio of urban to rural	Comprehensive knowledge of HIV (%) Females 15–24 2008–2012* urban	rural	ratio of urban to rural	Use of improved sanitation facilities (%) 2011 urban	rural	ratio of urban to rural
SUMMARY INDICATORS[#]																					
Sub-Saharan Africa	61	35	1.7	78	40	2.0	15	24	1.6	38	30	1.3	85	68	1.3	33	24	1.4	42	24	1.8
Eastern and Southern Africa	49	29	1.7	75	35	2.1	12	21	1.8	44	36	1.2	86	72	1.2	47	31	1.5	53	26	2.0
West and Central Africa	64	40	1.6	82	47	1.8	15	26	1.7	37	24	1.6	85	63	1.4	28	16	1.7	35	22	1.6
Middle East and North Africa	95	78	1.2	89	63	1.4	–	–	–	39	31	1.3	93	82	1.1	–	3	–	93	69	1.3
South Asia	53	34	1.6	72	40	1.8	31	43	1.4	38	31	1.2	–	–	–	32	14	2.3	61	29	2.1
East Asia and Pacific	–	–	–	96	88	1.1	5	10	2.0	49 **	41 **	1.2 **	93 **	92 **	1.0 **	23 **	22 **	1.0 **	76	58	1.3
Latin America and Caribbean	96	88	1.1	96	76	1.3	–	–	–	–	–	–	–	–	–	–	–	–	86	63	1.4
CEE/CIS	98	97	1.0	–	–	–	–	–	–	–	–	–	–	–	–	–	–	–	84	82	1.0
Least developed countries	54	34	1.6	75	38	2.0	17	27	1.5	46	40	1.2	84	71	1.2	32	22	1.5	48	31	1.6
World	80 **	51 **	1.6 **	87	54	1.6	14	27	1.9	42 **	32 **	1.3 **	–	–	–	–	18 **	–	80	47	1.7

\# For a complete list of countries and areas in the regions, subregions and country categories, see page 26.

DEFINITIONS OF THE INDICATORS

Birth registration – Percentage of children under age 5 who were registered at the moment of the survey. This includes children whose birth certificate was seen by the interviewer or whose mother or caretaker says the birth has been registered.

Skilled attendant at birth – Percentage of births attended by skilled health personnel (doctor, nurse or midwife).

Underweight prevalence in children under 5 – Percentage of children under age 5 who are below minus two standard deviations from median weight-for-age of the World Health Organization (WHO) Child Growth Standards.

Diarrhoea treatment with oral rehydration salts (ORS) – Percentage of children under age 5 who had diarrhoea in the two weeks preceding the survey and who received oral rehydration salts (ORS packets or pre-packaged ORS fluids).

Primary school net attendance ratio – Number of children attending primary or secondary school who are of official primary school age, expressed as a percentage of the total number of children of official primary school age. Because of the inclusion of primary-school-aged children attending secondary school, this indicator can also be referred to as a primary adjusted net attendance ratio.

Comprehensive knowledge of HIV – Percentage of young women (aged 15–24) who correctly identify the two major ways of preventing the sexual transmission of HIV (using condoms and limiting sex to one faithful, uninfected partner), who reject the two most common local misconceptions about HIV transmission and who know that a healthy-looking person can be HIV-positive.

Use of improved sanitation facilities – Percentage of the population using any of the following sanitation facilities, not shared with other households: flush or pour-flush latrine connected to a piped sewerage system, septic tank or pit latrine; ventilated improved pit latrine; pit latrine with a slab; covered pit; composting toilet.

MAIN DATA SOURCES

Birth registration – Demographic and Health Surveys (DHS), Multiple Indicator Cluster Surveys (MICS), other national household surveys, censuses and vital registration systems.

Skilled attendant at birth – DHS, MICS and other nationally representative sources.

Underweight prevalence in children under 5 – DHS, MICS, other national household surveys, WHO and UNICEF.

Diarrhoea treatment with oral rehydration salts (ORS) – DHS, MICS and other national household surveys.

Primary school net attendance ratio – DHS, MICS and other national household surveys.

Comprehensive knowledge of HIV – AIDS Indicator Surveys (AIS), DHS, MICS and other national household surveys; HIV/AIDS Survey Indicators Database, <www.measuredhs.com/hivdata>.

Use of improved sanitation facilities – UNICEF and WHO Joint Monitoring Programme.

Italicized disparity data are from different sources than the data presented for the same indicators in other tables of the report: Table 2 (Nutrition – Underweight prevalence), Table 3 (Health – Diarrhoea treatment), Table 4 (HIV/AIDS – Comprehensive knowledge of HIV), Table 5 (Education – Primary school participation) and Table 8 (Women – Skilled attendant at birth).

NOTES

– Data not available.

x Data refer to years or periods other than those specified in the column heading. Such data are not included in the calculation of regional and global averages, with the exception of 2005–2006 data from India and 2006 skilled attendant at birth data from Brazil. Estimates from data years prior to 2000 are not displayed.

y Data differ from the standard definition or refer to only part of a country. If they fall within the noted reference period, such data are included in the calculation of regional and global averages.

++ Changes in the definition of birth registration were made from the second and third rounds of MICS (MICS2 and MICS3) to the fourth round (MICS4). In order to allow for comparability with later rounds, data from MICS2 and MICS3 on birth registration were recalculated according to the MICS4 indicator definition. Therefore, the recalculated data presented here may differ from estimates included in MICS2 and MICS3 national reports.

* Data refer to the most recent year available during the period specified in the column heading.

** Excludes China.

TABLE 13 | DISPARITIES BY HOUSEHOLD WEALTH

Countries and areas	Birth registration (%)++ 2005–2012*			Skilled attendant at birth (%) 2008–2012*			Underweight prevalence in children under 5 (%) 2008–2012*			Diarrhoea treatment with oral rehydration salts (ORS) (%) 2008–2012*			Primary school net attendance ratio 2008–2012*			Comprehensive knowledge of HIV (%) 2008–2012*					
																females 15–24			males 15–24		
	poorest 20%	richest 20%	ratio of richest to poorest	poorest 20%	richest 20%	ratio of richest to poorest	poorest 20%	richest 20%	ratio of poorest to richest	poorest 20%	richest 20%	ratio of richest to poorest	poorest 20%	richest 20%	ratio of richest to poorest	poorest 20%	richest 20%	ratio of richest to poorest	poorest 20%	richest 20%	ratio of richest to poorest
Afghanistan	31	58	1.9	16	76	4.9	–	–	–	56	52	0.9	40	79	2.0	0	5	23.0	–	–	–
Albania	98	99	1.0	98	100	1.0	8	4	2.0	–	–	–	89	91	1.0	20	60	3.0	10	38	3.8
Algeria	99	100	1.0	88 x	98 x	1.1 x	5 x	2 x	2.5 x	15 x	19 x	1.2 x	93 x	97 x	1.0 x	5 x	20 x	3.7 x	–	–	–
Andorra	–	–	–	–	–	–	–	–	–	–	–	–	–	–	–	–	–	–	–	–	–
Angola	24 x	53 x	2.2 x	–	–	–	–	–	–	–	–	–	63	90	1.4	–	–	–	–	–	–
Antigua and Barbuda	–	–	–	–	–	–	–	–	–	–	–	–	–	–	–	–	–	–	–	–	–
Argentina	–	–	–	–	–	–	–	–	–	–	–	–	–	–	–	–	–	–	–	–	–
Armenia	100	100	1.0	99	100	1.0	8	2	5.3	–	–	–	98	97	1.0	–	–	–	–	–	–
Australia	–	–	–	–	–	–	–	–	–	–	–	–	–	–	–	–	–	–	–	–	–
Austria	–	–	–	–	–	–	–	–	–	–	–	–	–	–	–	–	–	–	–	–	–
Azerbaijan	92	97	1.1	76 x	100 x	1.3 x	15 x	2 x	7.5 x	3 x	36 x	13.3 x	72 x	78 x	1.1 x	1 x	12 x	10.3 x	2 x	14 x	6.3 x
Bahamas	–	–	–	–	–	–	–	–	–	–	–	–	–	–	–	–	–	–	–	–	–
Bahrain	–	–	–	–	–	–	–	–	–	–	–	–	–	–	–	–	–	–	–	–	–
Bangladesh	24	41	1.7	12	64	5.5	50	21	2.4	81	82	1.0	72	81	1.1	–	–	–	–	–	–
Barbados	–	–	–	–	–	–	–	–	–	–	–	–	–	–	–	–	–	–	–	–	–
Belarus	–	–	–	100	100	1.0	2 x	0 x	5.0 x	–	–	–	93	93	1.0	–	–	–	–	–	–
Belgium	–	–	–	–	–	–	–	–	–	–	–	–	–	–	–	–	–	–	–	–	–
Belize	95	97	1.0	89	98	1.1	9	3	2.9	–	–	–	88	98	1.1	20	53	2.7	–	–	–
Benin	61	95	1.6	52 x	96 x	1.9 x	–	–	–	15 x	32 x	2.1 x	53 y	79 y	1.5 y	9 x	26 x	3.1 x	17 x	52 x	3.0 x
Bhutan	100	100	1.0	34	95	2.8	16	7	2.2	60	56	0.9	85	97	1.1	7	32	4.4	–	–	–
Bolivia (Plurinational State of)	68 y	90 y	1.3 y	38	99	2.6	8	2	3.8	31	35	1.1	95	99	1.0	5	40	8.4	11	45	4.3
Bosnia and Herzegovina	100	99	1.0	100	100	1.0	1	4	0.2	–	–	–	95	97	1.0	37	44	1.2	38	45	1.2
Botswana	–	–	–	84 x	100 x	1.2 x	16 x	4 x	4.0 x	–	–	–	–	–	–	–	–	–	–	–	–
Brazil	–	–	–	–	–	–	–	–	–	–	–	–	–	–	–	–	–	–	–	–	–
Brunei Darussalam	–	–	–	–	–	–	–	–	–	–	–	–	–	–	–	–	–	–	–	–	–
Bulgaria	–	–	–	–	–	–	–	–	–	–	–	–	–	–	–	–	–	–	–	–	–
Burkina Faso	62	95	1.5	46	92	2.0	–	–	–	13	31	2.5	31	85	2.8	–	–	–	–	–	–
Burundi	64	87	1.4	51	81	1.6	41	17	2.4	35	42	1.2	64	87	1.4	–	–	–	–	–	–
Cabo Verde	–	–	–	–	–	–	–	–	–	–	–	–	–	–	–	–	–	–	–	–	–
Cambodia	48	78	1.6	49	97	2.0	35	16	2.2	32	34	1.1	87	98	1.1	28	58	2.1	30	64	2.1
Cameroon	28	89	3.2	19	97	5.1	–	–	–	8	36	4.7	60	99	1.6	–	–	–	–	–	–
Canada	–	–	–	–	–	–	–	–	–	–	–	–	–	–	–	–	–	–	–	–	–
Central African Republic	46	85	1.8	33	87	2.6	26	19	1.4	11	28	2.5	57	90	1.6	14 x	23 x	1.6 x	19 x	33 x	1.7 x
Chad	5	46	9.2	8	61	7.6	33	21	1.6	5	29	5.3	40	74	1.8	6	18	2.9	–	–	–
Chile	–	–	–	–	–	–	–	–	–	–	–	–	–	–	–	–	–	–	–	–	–
China	–	–	–	–	–	–	–	–	–	–	–	–	–	–	–	–	–	–	–	–	–
Colombia	–	–	–	84	99	1.2	6	2	3.1	47	61	1.3	90	93	1.0	15	32	2.2	–	–	–
Comoros	76 x	96 x	1.3 x	49 x	77 x	1.6 x	–	–	–	16 x	24 x	1.5 x	25 x	39 x	1.6 x	–	–	–	–	–	–
Congo	80	99	1.2	40 x	95 x	2.4 x	16 x	5 x	3.2 x	13 x	18 x	1.4 x	–	–	–	–	–	–	12	27	2.3

TABLE 13 | DISPARITIES BY HOUSEHOLD WEALTH >>

TABLE 13

Countries and areas	Birth registration (%)** 2005–2012*			Skilled attendant at birth (%) 2008–2012*			Underweight prevalence in children under 5 (%) 2008–2012*			Diarrhoea treatment with oral rehydration salts (ORS) (%) 2008–2012*			Primary school net attendance ratio 2008–2012*			Comprehensive knowledge of HIV (%) 2008–2012* females 15–24			males 15–24		
	poorest 20%	richest 20%	ratio of richest to poorest	poorest 20%	richest 20%	ratio of richest to poorest	poorest 20%	richest 20%	ratio of poorest to richest	poorest 20%	richest 20%	ratio of richest to poorest	poorest 20%	richest 20%	ratio of richest to poorest	poorest 20%	richest 20%	ratio of richest to poorest	poorest 20%	richest 20%	ratio of richest to poorest
Cook Islands	–	–	–	–	–	–	–	–	–	–	–	–	–	–	–	–	–	–	–	–	–
Costa Rica	–	–	–	–	–	–	–	–	–	–	–	–	–	–	–	–	–	–	–	–	–
Côte d'Ivoire	44	90	2.0	35	91	2.6	21	10	2.1	6	24	3.7	57 y	80 y	1.4 y	–	–	–	–	–	–
Croatia	–	–	–	–	–	–	–	–	–	–	–	–	–	–	–	–	–	–	–	–	–
Cuba	–	–	–	–	–	–	–	–	–	–	–	–	–	–	–	–	–	–	–	–	–
Cyprus	–	–	–	–	–	–	–	–	–	–	–	–	–	–	–	–	–	–	–	–	–
Czech Republic	–	–	–	–	–	–	–	–	–	–	–	–	–	–	–	–	–	–	–	–	–
Democratic People's Republic of Korea	–	–	–	–	–	–	–	–	–	–	–	–	–	–	–	–	–	–	–	–	–
Democratic Republic of the Congo	25	27	1.1	69	99	1.4	29	12	2.3	28	26	0.9	65	92	1.4	8	24	2.8	–	–	–
Denmark	–	–	–	–	–	–	–	–	–	–	–	–	–	–	–	–	–	–	–	–	–
Djibouti	–	–	–	–	–	–	–	–	–	–	–	–	–	–	–	–	–	–	–	–	–
Dominica	–	–	–	–	–	–	–	–	–	–	–	–	–	–	–	–	–	–	–	–	–
Dominican Republic	–	–	–	95 x	99 x	1.0 x	5 x	1 x	4.4 x	26	46	1.8	92	98	1.1	31 x	46 x	1.5 x	21 x	41 x	2.0 x
Ecuador	–	–	–	99 x	98 x	1.0 x	–	–	–	–	–	–	–	–	–	–	–	–	–	–	–
Egypt	99 y	100 y	1.0 y	55	97	1.8	8	5	1.4	34	23	0.7	83 y	93 y	1.1 y	2	9	4.9	9	28	3.1
El Salvador	98	99	1.0	91	98	1.1	12 y	1 y	12.9 y	–	–	–	–	–	–	–	–	–	–	–	–
Equatorial Guinea	29 x	53 x	1.9 x	47 x	85 x	1.8 x	–	–	–	24 x	37 x	1.5 x	–	–	–	–	–	–	–	–	–
Eritrea	–	–	–	7 x	81 x	12.1 x	–	–	–	–	–	–	–	–	–	–	–	–	–	–	–
Estonia	–	–	–	–	–	–	–	–	–	–	–	–	–	–	–	–	–	–	–	–	–
Ethiopia	3	18	7.0	2	46	26.8	36	15	2.4	18	45	2.5	52	86	1.7	–	–	–	–	–	–
Fiji	–	–	–	–	–	–	–	–	–	–	–	–	–	–	–	–	–	–	–	–	–
Finland	–	–	–	–	–	–	–	–	–	–	–	–	–	–	–	–	–	–	–	–	–
France	–	–	–	–	–	–	–	–	–	–	–	–	–	–	–	–	–	–	–	–	–
Gabon	92	86	0.9	74	95	1.3	10	2	5.5	24	19	0.8	85 y	86 y	1.0 y	–	–	–	–	–	–
Gambia	46	61	1.3	34	58	1.7	24	10	2.5	43	32	0.7	47	82	1.7	20	48	2.4	–	–	–
Georgia	99	98	1.0	95 x	99 x	1.0 x	–	–	–	–	–	–	92	96	1.0	–	–	–	–	–	–
Germany	–	–	–	–	–	–	–	–	–	–	–	–	–	–	–	–	–	–	–	–	–
Ghana	47	82	1.7	39	98	2.5	20	6	3.2	44	27	0.6	61	86	1.4	18	53	2.9	19	49	2.6
Greece	–	–	–	–	–	–	–	–	–	–	–	–	–	–	–	–	–	–	–	–	–
Grenada	–	–	–	–	–	–	–	–	–	–	–	–	–	–	–	–	–	–	–	–	–
Guatemala	–	–	–	20	95	4.7	21 y	3 y	6.5 y	39	51	1.3	–	–	–	5	41	7.8	–	–	–
Guinea	21	83	4.0	26 x	57 x	2.2 x	24	19	1.3	18 x	59 x	3.3 x	–	–	–	–	–	–	–	–	–
Guinea-Bissau	17	35	2.0	23	82	3.6	22	11	2.1	16	37	2.3	52	87	1.7	6	25	4.3	–	–	–
Guyana	84	92	1.1	81	96	1.2	16	4	3.8	–	–	–	91	97	1.1	37	72	2.0	25	65	2.6
Haiti	71	92	1.3	10	78	8.1	18	4	4.7	52	62	1.2	66 y	92 y	1.4 y	–	–	–	–	–	–
Holy See	–	–	–	–	–	–	–	–	–	–	–	–	–	–	–	–	–	–	–	–	–
Honduras	92	95	1.0	58	98	1.7	13	3	4.1	63	52	0.8	89 y	94 y	1.1 y	–	–	–	–	–	–
Hungary	–	–	–	–	–	–	–	–	–	–	–	–	–	–	–	–	–	–	–	–	–

TABLE 13 | DISPARITIES BY HOUSEHOLD WEALTH >>

Countries and areas	Birth registration (%)++ 2005–2012*			Skilled attendant at birth (%) 2008–2012*			Underweight prevalence in children under 5 (%) 2008–2012*			Diarrhoea treatment with oral rehydration salts (ORS) (%) 2008–2012*			Primary school net attendance ratio 2008–2012*			Comprehensive knowledge of HIV (%) 2008–2012*					
																females 15–24			males 15–24		
	poorest 20%	richest 20%	ratio of richest to poorest	poorest 20%	richest 20%	ratio of richest to poorest	poorest 20%	richest 20%	ratio of poorest to richest	poorest 20%	richest 20%	ratio of richest to poorest	poorest 20%	richest 20%	ratio of richest to poorest	poorest 20%	richest 20%	ratio of richest to poorest	poorest 20%	richest 20%	ratio of richest to poorest
Iceland	–	–	–	–	–	–	–	–	–	–	–	–	–	–	–	–	–	–	–	–	–
India	24	72	3.0	24	85	3.6	57 x	20 x	2.9 x	19 x	43 x	2.3 x	–	–	–	4 x	45 x	11.7 x	15 x	55 x	3.8 x
Indonesia	41	88	2.2	58	97	1.7	23	10	2.2	39	34	0.9	–	–	–	–	–	–	2 x	27 x	12.2 x
Iran (Islamic Republic of)	–	–	–	–	–	–	–	–	–	–	–	–	–	–	–	–	–	–	–	–	–
Iraq	98	100	1.0	82	96	1.2	9	8	1.1	19	22	1.1	79	98	1.2	1	8	7.2	–	–	–
Ireland	–	–	–	–	–	–	–	–	–	–	–	–	–	–	–	–	–	–	–	–	–
Israel	–	–	–	–	–	–	–	–	–	–	–	–	–	–	–	–	–	–	–	–	–
Italy	–	–	–	–	–	–	–	–	–	–	–	–	–	–	–	–	–	–	–	–	–
Jamaica	96	99	1.0	97	98	1.0	–	–	–	–	–	–	–	–	–	–	–	–	–	–	–
Japan	–	–	–	–	–	–	–	–	–	–	–	–	–	–	–	–	–	–	–	–	–
Jordan	–	–	–	98 x	100 x	1.0 x	3	0	26.0	18 x	30 x	1.6 x	–	–	–	–	–	–	–	–	–
Kazakhstan	100	100	1.0	100	100	1.0	4	4	1.2	–	–	–	99	100	1.0	25	44	1.8	13	49	3.8
Kenya	48	80	1.7	20	81	4.0	25	9	2.8	40	37	0.9	58	85	1.5	29	61	2.1	42	68	1.6
Kiribati	93	94	1.0	76	93	1.2	–	–	–	–	–	–	84 y	87 y	1.0 y	42	49	1.2	38	51	1.3
Kuwait	–	–	–	–	–	–	–	–	–	–	–	–	–	–	–	–	–	–	–	–	–
Kyrgyzstan	97	97	1.0	93 x	100 x	1.1 x	–	–	–	–	–	–	94 x	94 x	1.0 x	17 x	29 x	1.7 x	–	–	–
Lao People's Democratic Republic	66	93	1.4	11	91	8.4	37	12	3.0	35	69	2.0	71	97	1.4	6	41	6.5	12	43	3.6
Latvia	–	–	–	–	–	–	–	–	–	–	–	–	–	–	–	–	–	–	–	–	–
Lebanon	–	–	–	–	–	–	–	–	–	–	–	–	–	–	–	–	–	–	–	–	–
Lesotho	42	49	1.2	35	90	2.6	18	9	1.9	35 x	39 x	1.1 x	83	94	1.1	26	48	1.8	14	45	3.3
Liberia	1 y	7 y	6.1 y	26 x	81 x	3.2 x	21 x	13 x	1.6 x	41 x	64 x	1.6 x	15 x	56 x	3.7 x	14 x	29 x	2.1 x	17 x	37 x	2.2 x
Libya	–	–	–	–	–	–	–	–	–	–	–	–	–	–	–	–	–	–	–	–	–
Liechtenstein	–	–	–	–	–	–	–	–	–	–	–	–	–	–	–	–	–	–	–	–	–
Lithuania	–	–	–	–	–	–	–	–	–	–	–	–	–	–	–	–	–	–	–	–	–
Luxembourg	–	–	–	–	–	–	–	–	–	–	–	–	–	–	–	–	–	–	–	–	–
Madagascar	61	93	1.5	22	90	4.1	40 x	24 x	1.7 x	12	29	2.4	59	96	1.6	10	42	4.3	8	49	6.5
Malawi	–	–	–	63	89	1.4	17	13	1.3	67	73	1.1	75	96	1.3	34	55	1.6	35	54	1.5
Malaysia	–	–	–	–	–	–	–	–	–	–	–	–	–	–	–	–	–	–	–	–	–
Maldives	92	94	1.0	89	99	1.1	24	11	2.3	–	–	–	82	82	1.0	23	48	2.0	–	–	–
Mali	65	96	1.5	31	90	2.9	22	11	2.0	8	16	2.1	36	85	2.4	9	19	2.0	–	–	–
Malta	–	–	–	–	–	–	–	–	–	–	–	–	–	–	–	–	–	–	–	–	–
Marshall Islands	92	98	1.1	68 x	99 x	1.5 x	–	–	–	–	–	–	–	–	–	12 x	39 x	3.3 x	37 x	58 x	1.6 x
Mauritania	33	84	2.6	27	96	3.6	–	–	–	9	33	3.8	45	83	1.9	2	12	7.9	–	–	–
Mauritius	–	–	–	–	–	–	–	–	–	–	–	–	–	–	–	–	–	–	–	–	–
Mexico	–	–	–	–	–	–	–	–	–	–	–	–	–	–	–	–	–	–	–	–	–
Micronesia (Federated States of)	–	–	–	–	–	–	–	–	–	–	–	–	–	–	–	–	–	–	–	–	–
Monaco	–	–	–	–	–	–	–	–	–	–	–	–	–	–	–	–	–	–	–	–	–
Mongolia	99	99	1.0	98	99	1.0	5	1	5.6	24	50	2.1	93	98	1.1	17	42	2.5	12	48	4.1

TABLE 13

TABLE 13 | DISPARITIES BY HOUSEHOLD WEALTH >>

Countries and areas	Birth registration (%)++ 2005–2012*			Skilled attendant at birth (%) 2008–2012*			Underweight prevalence in children under 5 (%) 2008–2012*			Diarrhoea treatment with oral rehydration salts (ORS) (%) 2008–2012*			Primary school net attendance ratio 2008–2012*			Comprehensive knowledge of HIV (%) 2008–2012*					
																females 15–24			males 15–24		
	poorest 20%	richest 20%	ratio of richest to poorest	poorest 20%	richest 20%	ratio of richest to poorest	poorest 20%	richest 20%	ratio of poorest to richest	poorest 20%	richest 20%	ratio of richest to poorest	poorest 20%	richest 20%	ratio of richest to poorest	poorest 20%	richest 20%	ratio of richest to poorest	poorest 20%	richest 20%	ratio of richest to poorest
Montenegro	96	100	1.0	98 x	100 x	1.0 x	4 x	1 x	4.0 x	–	–	–	92 x	100 x	1.1 x	–	–	–	–	–	–
Morocco	–	–	–	30 x	95 x	3.2 x	–	–	–	18 x	25 x	1.4 x	77 x	97 x	1.3 x	–	–	–	–	–	–
Mozambique	42	60	1.4	32	90	2.8	23	6	3.6	41	70	1.7	67 y	91 y	1.4 y	–	–	–	–	–	–
Myanmar	50	96	1.9	51	96	1.9	33	14	2.5	52	75	1.4	81	95	1.2	–	–	–	–	–	–
Namibia	–	–	–	60 x	98 x	1.6 x	22 x	7 x	3.1 x	50 x	59 x	1.2 x	88 x	97 x	1.1 x	61 x	69 x	1.1 x	55 x	67 x	1.2 x
Nauru	71	88	1.2	97 x	98 x	1.0 x	7 x	3 x	2.7 x	–	–	–	82 x,y	90 x,y	1.1 x,y	13 x,y	10 x,y	0.8 x,y	–	25 x,y	–
Nepal	36	52	1.5	11	82	7.6	40	10	4.0	39	36	0.9	91	99	1.1	–	–	–	–	–	–
Netherlands	–	–	–	–	–	–	–	–	–	–	–	–	–	–	–	–	–	–	–	–	–
New Zealand	–	–	–	–	–	–	–	–	–	–	–	–	–	–	–	–	–	–	–	–	–
Nicaragua	–	–	–	42 x	99 x	2.4 x	9 x	1 x	9.0 x	53 x	64 x	1.2 x	–	–	–	–	–	–	–	–	–
Niger	20	67	3.3	5 x	59 x	11.8 x	–	–	–	14 x	32 x	2.3 x	26 x	70 x	2.7 x	5 x	30 x	6.5 x	6 x	34 x	5.8 x
Nigeria	12	76	6.2	11	90	8.2	38	10	4.0	12	56	4.7	34	94	2.8	–	–	–	–	–	–
Niue	–	–	–	–	–	–	–	–	–	–	–	–	–	–	–	–	–	–	–	–	–
Norway	–	–	–	–	–	–	–	–	–	–	–	–	–	–	–	–	–	–	–	–	–
Oman	–	–	–	–	–	–	–	–	–	–	–	–	–	–	–	–	–	–	–	–	–
Pakistan	18	38	2.1	16 x	77 x	4.8 x	–	–	–	41 x	44 x	1.1 x	42 x	88 x	2.1 x	–	–	–	–	–	–
Palau	–	–	–	–	–	–	–	–	–	–	–	–	–	–	–	–	–	–	–	–	–
Panama	–	–	–	–	–	–	–	–	–	–	–	–	–	–	–	–	–	–	–	–	–
Papua New Guinea	–	–	–	–	–	–	–	–	–	–	–	–	–	–	–	–	–	–	–	–	–
Paraguay	67 y	89 y	1.3 y	–	–	–	–	–	–	–	–	–	–	–	–	–	–	–	–	–	–
Peru	93 y	99 y	1.1 y	60	99	1.7	10	1	11.0	24	34	1.4	92	97	1.1	–	–	–	–	–	–
Philippines	–	–	–	26	94	3.7	–	–	–	37	55	1.5	–	–	–	14	26	1.8	–	–	–
Poland	–	–	–	–	–	–	–	–	–	–	–	–	–	–	–	–	–	–	–	–	–
Portugal	–	–	–	–	–	–	–	–	–	–	–	–	–	–	–	–	–	–	–	–	–
Qatar	–	–	–	–	–	–	–	–	–	–	–	–	–	–	–	–	–	–	–	–	–
Republic of Korea	–	–	–	–	–	–	–	–	–	–	–	–	–	–	–	–	–	–	–	–	–
Republic of Moldova	99	100	1.0	99 x	100 x	1.0 x	6 x	1 x	6.0 x	–	–	–	–	–	–	–	–	–	–	–	–
Romania	–	–	–	–	–	–	–	–	–	–	–	–	–	–	–	–	–	–	–	–	–
Russian Federation	–	–	–	–	–	–	–	–	–	–	–	–	–	–	–	–	–	–	–	–	–
Rwanda	58	64	1.1	61	86	1.4	16	5	3.0	22	37	1.7	80	94	1.2	–	–	–	–	–	–
Saint Kitts and Nevis	–	–	–	–	–	–	–	–	–	–	–	–	–	–	–	–	–	–	–	–	–
Saint Lucia	–	–	–	–	–	–	–	–	–	–	–	–	–	–	–	–	–	–	–	–	–
Saint Vincent and the Grenadines	–	–	–	–	–	–	–	–	–	–	–	–	–	–	–	–	–	–	–	–	–
Samoa	31	63	2.1	66	95	1.4	–	–	–	–	–	–	85 y	91 y	1.1 y	3	3	1.0	3	9	2.7
San Marino	–	–	–	–	–	–	–	–	–	–	–	–	–	–	–	–	–	–	–	–	–
Sao Tome and Principe	74	86	1.1	74	93	1.3	18	7	2.6	29 x	34 x	1.2 x	75	95	1.3	27	56	2.0	39	55	1.4
Saudi Arabia	–	–	–	–	–	–	–	–	–	–	–	–	–	–	–	–	–	–	–	–	–
Senegal	50	94	1.9	30	96	3.2	24	10	2.4	21	31	1.5	47	78	1.7	–	–	–	–	–	–
Serbia	97	100	1.0	99	100	1.0	3	2	1.4	–	–	–	96	98	1.0	28	69	2.4	28	66	2.4

TABLE 13 | DISPARITIES BY HOUSEHOLD WEALTH >>

Countries and areas	Birth registration (%)++ 2005–2012*			Skilled attendant at birth (%) 2008–2012*			Underweight prevalence in children under 5 (%) 2008–2012*			Diarrhoea treatment with oral rehydration salts (ORS) (%) 2008–2012*			Primary school net attendance ratio 2008–2012*			Comprehensive knowledge of HIV (%) 2008–2012*					
																females 15–24			males 15–24		
	poorest 20%	richest 20%	ratio of richest to poorest	poorest 20%	richest 20%	ratio of richest to poorest	poorest 20%	richest 20%	ratio of poorest to richest	poorest 20%	richest 20%	ratio of richest to poorest	poorest 20%	richest 20%	ratio of richest to poorest	poorest 20%	richest 20%	ratio of richest to poorest	poorest 20%	richest 20%	ratio of richest to poorest
Seychelles	–	–	–	–	–	–	–	–	–	–	–	–	–	–	–	–	–	–	–	–	–
Sierra Leone	74	88	1.2	44	85	1.9	22	15	1.4	75	70	0.9	59	88	1.5	14	36	2.6	–	–	–
Singapore	–	–	–	–	–	–	–	–	–	–	–	–	–	–	–	–	–	–	–	–	–
Slovakia	–	–	–	–	–	–	–	–	–	–	–	–	–	–	–	–	–	–	–	–	–
Slovenia	–	–	–	–	–	–	–	–	–	–	–	–	–	–	–	–	–	–	–	–	–
Solomon Islands	–	–	–	74 x	95 x	1.3 x	14 x	10 x	1.4 x	–	–	–	58 x,y	78 x,y	1.3 x,y	17 x	37 x	2.1 x	35 x	50 x	1.5 x
Somalia	1	7	6.6	11 x	77 x	7.2 x	42 x	14 x	3.0 x	7 x	31 x	4.8 x	3 x	40 x	12.5 x	1 x	8 x	13.5 x	–	–	–
South Africa	–	–	–	–	–	–	–	–	–	–	–	–	–	–	–	–	–	–	–	–	–
South Sudan	21	57	2.7	8	41	5.1	32	21	1.6	27	52	1.9	12 x	58 x	4.7 x	3	18	6.1	–	–	–
Spain	–	–	–	–	–	–	–	–	–	–	–	–	–	–	–	–	–	–	–	–	–
Sri Lanka	97	98	1.0	97 x	99 x	1.0 x	29 x	11 x	2.6 x	–	–	–	97 x	99 x	1.0 x	–	–	–	–	–	–
State of Palestine	99	100	1.0	98 x	100 x	1.0 x	–	–	–	–	–	–	–	–	–	5	10	2.1	–	–	–
Sudan	26	98	3.8	6	59	10.5	40	17	2.4	21	16	0.7	55	97	1.8	1	11	13.6	–	–	–
Suriname	98	100	1.0	84	95	1.1	6	4	1.5	–	–	–	92	96	1.1	26	52	2.0	–	–	–
Swaziland	39	73	1.9	65	94	1.4	8	4	2.3	58	60	1.0	95	99	1.0	49	72	1.5	44	64	1.5
Sweden	–	–	–	–	–	–	–	–	–	–	–	–	–	–	–	–	–	–	–	–	–
Switzerland	–	–	–	–	–	–	–	–	–	–	–	–	–	–	–	–	–	–	–	–	–
Syrian Arab Republic	93	99	1.1	78 x	99 x	1.3 x	10 x	7 x	1.4 x	45 x	59 x	1.3 x	–	–	–	4 x	10 x	2.9 x	–	–	–
Tajikistan	86	90	1.0	90 x	90 x	1.0 x	–	–	–	52 x	50 x	1.0 x	96 x,y	98 x,y	1.0 x,y	–	–	–	–	–	–
Thailand	99	100	1.0	93 x	100 x	1.1 x	11 x	3 x	3.7 x	56 x	54 x	1.0 x	97 x	99 x	1.0 x	47 x	43 x	0.9 x	–	–	–
The former Yugoslav Republic of Macedonia	99	100	1.0	92	97	1.1	2	0	–	–	–	–	97	99	1.0	9 x	45 x	5.0 x	–	–	–
Timor-Leste	50	56	1.1	10	69	6.9	49	35	1.4	70	71	1.0	60	83	1.4	9	16	1.8	11	35	3.0
Togo	59	97	1.7	28	94	3.4	21	9	2.4	8	19	2.5	80	96	1.2	18	42	2.3	20	55	2.7
Tonga	–	–	–	–	–	–	–	–	–	–	–	–	–	–	–	–	–	–	–	–	–
Trinidad and Tobago	96	99	1.0	98 x	100 x	1.0 x	–	–	–	–	–	–	95 x	98 x	1.0 x	48 x	62 x	1.3 x	–	–	–
Tunisia	98	100	1.0	94	100	1.1	–	–	–	–	–	–	96	98	1.0	10	29	2.8	–	–	–
Turkey	89	99	1.1	73	100	1.4	4	1	8.4	–	–	–	87 y	97 y	1.1 y	–	–	–	–	–	–
Turkmenistan	94	97	1.0	99 x	100 x	1.0 x	8 x	2 x	4.0 x	45 x	30 x	0.7 x	–	–	–	3 x	8 x	2.8 x	–	–	–
Tuvalu	39	71	1.8	99 x	98 x	1.0 x	1 x	0 x	–	–	–	–	99 x,y	100 x,y	1.0 x,y	34 x,y	39 x,y	1.2 x,y	–	67 x,y	–
Uganda	27	44	1.6	43	88	2.0	18	8	2.2	43	45	1.1	73	87	1.2	–	–	–	–	–	–
Ukraine	100	99	1.0	97 x	99 x	1.0 x	–	–	–	–	–	–	78 x	75 x	1.0 x	33 x	45 x	1.4 x	28 x	42 x	1.5 x
United Arab Emirates	–	–	–	–	–	–	–	–	–	–	–	–	–	–	–	–	–	–	–	–	–
United Kingdom	–	–	–	–	–	–	–	–	–	–	–	–	–	–	–	–	–	–	–	–	–
United Republic of Tanzania	4	56	12.7	31	90	2.9	22	9	2.3	41	38	0.9	68	93	1.4	39	55	1.4	34	56	1.7
United States	–	–	–	–	–	–	–	–	–	–	–	–	–	–	–	–	–	–	–	–	–
Uruguay	–	–	–	–	–	–	–	–	–	–	–	–	–	–	–	–	–	–	–	–	–
Uzbekistan	100	100	1.0	100 x	100 x	1.0 x	5 x	3 x	1.7 x	–	–	–	94 x	97 x	1.0 x	25 x	33 x	1.3 x	–	–	–
Vanuatu	27	55	2.0	55 x	90 x	1.6 x	12 x	10 x	1.2 x	–	–	–	74 x	89 x	1.2 x	9 x	23 x	2.7 x	–	–	–

TABLE 13

TABLE 13 | DISPARITIES BY HOUSEHOLD WEALTH >>

Countries and areas	Birth registration (%)++ 2005–2012*			Skilled attendant at birth (%) 2008–2012*			Underweight prevalence in children under 5 (%) 2008–2012*			Diarrhoea treatment with oral rehydration salts (ORS) (%) 2008–2012*			Primary school net attendance ratio 2008–2012*			Comprehensive knowledge of HIV (%) 2008–2012*					
																females 15–24			males 15–24		
	poorest 20%	richest 20%	ratio of richest to poorest	poorest 20%	richest 20%	ratio of richest to poorest	poorest 20%	richest 20%	ratio of poorest to richest	poorest 20%	richest 20%	ratio of richest to poorest	poorest 20%	richest 20%	ratio of richest to poorest	poorest 20%	richest 20%	ratio of richest to poorest	poorest 20%	richest 20%	ratio of richest to poorest
Venezuela (Bolivarian Republic of)	–	–	–	95 x	92 x	1.0 x	–	–	–	–	–	–	86 x	99 x	1.2 x	–	–	–	–	–	–
Viet Nam	87	98	1.1	72	99	1.4	21	3	6.6	–	–	–	95	99	1.0	38	68	1.8	–	–	–
Yemen	3 y	51 y	15.5 y	17 x	74 x	4.3 x	–	–	–	31 x	37 x	1.2 x	44 x	87 x	2.0 x	0 x	4 x	–	–	–	–
Zambia	5	31	5.8	27 x	91 x	3.4 x	16 x	11 x	1.5 x	61 x	61 x	1.0 x	73 x	96 x	1.3 x	–	–	–	–	–	–
Zimbabwe	35	75	2.1	48	91	1.9	12	6	2.1	18	28	1.6	84	91	1.1	–	–	–	–	–	–
SUMMARY INDICATORS#																					
Sub-Saharan Africa	26	63	2.4	27	83	3.1	29	11	2.6	24	41	1.7	55	90	1.6	–	–	–	–	–	–
Eastern and Southern Africa	24	50	2.1	27	75	2.8	26	11	2.3	33	45	1.4	64	89	1.4	–	–	–	–	–	–
West and Central Africa	27	71	2.6	29	91	3.2	32	11	2.9	17	41	2.4	46	90	1.9	–	–	–	–	–	–
Middle East and North Africa	76	94	1.2	–	–	–	–	–	–	–	–	–	–	–	–	–	–	–	–	–	–
South Asia	24	65	2.6	22	82	3.8	56	20	2.8	27	47	1.7	–	–	–	4	43	11.7	15	55	3.8
East Asia and Pacific	–	–	–	50 **	96 **	1.9 **	24 **	10 **	2.5 **	40 **	45 **	1.1 **	–	–	–	–	–	–	–	–	–
Latin America and Caribbean	–	–	–	–	–	–	–	–	–	–	–	–	–	–	–	–	–	–	–	–	–
CEE/CIS	96	99	1.0	–	–	–	–	–	–	–	–	–	–	–	–	–	–	–	–	–	–
Least developed countries	28	55	2.0	29	78	2.7	32	14	2.3	38	47	1.2	63	88	1.4	–	–	–	–	–	–
World	51 **	79 **	1.6 **	32 **	86 **	2.7 **	37 **	14 **	2.7 **	28 **	44 **	1.6 **	–	–	–	–	–	–	–	–	–

For a complete list of countries and areas in the regions, subregions and country categories, see page 26

DEFINITIONS OF THE INDICATORS

Birth registration – Percentage of children under age 5 who were registered at the moment of the survey. This includes children whose birth certificate was seen by the interviewer or whose mother or caretaker says the birth has been registered.

Skilled attendant at birth – Percentage of births attended by skilled health personnel (doctor, nurse or midwife).

Underweight prevalence in children under 5 – Percentage of children under age 5 who are below minus two standard deviations from median weight-for-age of the World Health Organization (WHO) Child Growth Standards.

Diarrhoea treatment with oral rehydration salts (ORS) – Percentage of children under age 5 who had diarrhoea in the two weeks preceding the survey and who received oral rehydration salts (ORS packets or pre-packaged ORS fluids).

Primary school net attendance ratio – Number of children attending primary or secondary school who are of official primary school age, expressed as a percentage of the total number of children of official primary school age. Because of the inclusion of primary-school-aged children attending secondary school, this indicator can also be referred to as a primary adjusted net attendance ratio.

Comprehensive knowledge of HIV – Percentage of young men and women (aged 15–24) who correctly identify the two major ways of preventing the sexual transmission of HIV (using condoms and limiting sex to one faithful, uninfected partner), who reject the two most common local misconceptions about HIV transmission and who know that a healthy-looking person can be HIV-positive.

MAIN DATA SOURCES

Birth registration – Demographic and Health Surveys (DHS), Multiple Indicator Cluster Surveys (MICS), other national household surveys, censuses and vital registration systems.

Skilled attendant at birth – DHS, MICS and other nationally representative sources.

Underweight prevalence in children under 5 – DHS, MICS, other national household surveys, WHO and UNICEF.

Diarrhoea treatment with oral rehydration salts (ORS) – DHS, MICS and other national household surveys.

Primary school net attendance ratio – DHS, MICS and other national household surveys.

Comprehensive knowledge of HIV – AIDS Indicator Surveys (AIS), DHS, MICS and other national household surveys; HIV/AIDS Survey Indicators Database, <www.measuredhs.com/hivdata>.

Italicized disparity data are from different sources than the data presented for the same indicators in other tables of the report: Table 2 (Nutrition – Underweight prevalence), Table 3 (Health – Diarrhoea treatment), Table 4 (HIV/AIDS – Comprehensive knowledge of HIV), Table 5 (Education — Primary school participation) and Table 8 (Women – Skilled attendant at birth).

NOTES

– Data not available.

x Data refer to years or periods other than those specified in the column heading. Such data are not included in the calculation of regional and global averages, with the exception of 2005–2006 data from India. Estimates from data years prior to 2000 are not displayed.

y Data differ from the standard definition or refer to only part of a country. If they fall within the noted reference period, such data are included in the calculation of regional and global averages.

++ Changes in the definition of birth registration were made from the second and third rounds of MICS (MICS2 and MICS3) to the fourth round (MICS4). In order to allow for comparability with later rounds, data from MICS2 and MICS3 on birth registration were recalculated according to the MICS4 indicator definition. Therefore, the recalculated data presented here may differ from estimates included in MICS2 and MICS3 national reports.

* Data refer to the most recent year available during the period specified in the column heading.

** Excludes China.

TABLE 14 | EARLY CHILDHOOD DEVELOPMENT

Countries and areas	Attendance in early childhood education 2005–2012*					Adult support for learning++ 2005–2012*					Father's support for learning++ 2005–2012*	Learning materials at home 2005–2012*						Children left in inadequate care 2005–2012*				
												Children's books			Playthings++							
	total	male	female	poorest 20%	richest 20%	total	male	female	poorest 20%	richest 20%		total	poorest 20%	richest 20%	total	poorest 20%	richest 20%	total	male	female	poorest 20%	richest 20%
Afghanistan	1	1	1	0	4	73	74	73	72	80	62	2	1	5	53	52	57	40	42	39	43	27
Albania	40	39	42	26	60	86	85	87	68	96	53	32	16	52	53	57	48	13	14	11	9	16
Bangladesh	15	14	15	11	16	61	61	60	42	85	53	–	–	–	–	–	–	–	–	–	–	–
Belarus	88	86	89	75	91	96	94	97	90	99	68	92	83	96	79	77	79	4	4	4	4	5
Belize	32	30	34	16	59	86	88	83	73	94	50	40	17	73	57	55	58	2	3	2	4	1
Bhutan	10	10	10	3	27	54	52	57	40	73	51	6	1	24	52	36	60	14	13	15	17	7
Bosnia and Herzegovina	13	12	14	2	31	95	95	96	87	100	76	56	39	73	56	58	60	2	2	2	3	1
Botswana	18	–	–	–	–	–	–	–	–	–	–	–	–	–	–	–	–	–	–	–	–	–
Burkina Faso	2	3	1	0	9	14	14	14	12	26	24	–	–	–	–	–	–	–	–	–	–	–
Burundi	5	5	5	4	10	34	35	34	32	38	20	–	–	–	–	–	–	–	–	–	–	–
Cameroon	30	29	31	4	67	62	64	61	47	72	35	4	0	13	41	30	57	31	30	32	38	19
Central African Republic	5	5	6	2	17	74	74	74	70	78	42	1	0	3	49	41	51	61	60	62	58	60
Chad	5	5	4	1	16	70	69	70	64	71	29	1	0	2	43	38	50	56	57	56	58	56
Côte d'Ivoire	5	5	5	1	15	50	50	51	55	57	40	5	3	13	39	44	35	59	60	58	62	51
Democratic People's Republic of Korea	98	98	97	–	–	91	88	93	–	–	75	79	–	–	47	–	–	17	17	16	–	–
Democratic Republic of the Congo	5	5	5	2	18	61	61	62	62	76	36	1	0	2	29	21	40	60	60	60	69	39
Djibouti	14	12	16	–	–	36	36	35	–	–	23	15	–	–	24	–	–	12	11	13	–	–
Gambia	18	17	19	12	32	48	49	47	50	55	21	1	0	4	42	28	50	21	22	19	25	18
Georgia	43	44	42	17	70	93	93	93	85	99	61	72	48	91	38	41	41	8	8	8	7	8
Ghana	68	65	72	42	97	40	38	42	23	78	30	6	1	23	41	31	51	21	21	21	27	15
Guinea-Bissau	10	10	10	4	26	–	–	–	–	–	–	–	–	–	–	–	–	–	–	–	–	–
Guyana	49	48	50	33	78	89	88	89	77	99	52	54	28	86	65	67	60	11	13	10	19	6
Honduras	19	17	21	13	28	48	47	49	28	75	59	11	1	34	78	74	81	4	5	4	8	2
Iran (Islamic Republic of)	20 y	19 y	22 y	–	–	70 y	69 y	70 y	–	–	60 y	36 y	–	–	67 y	–	–	15 y	15 y	15 y	–	–
Iraq	4	4	4	1	10	58	58	59	40	78	55	5	1	16	34	34	32	8	8	7	9	8
Jamaica	86	84	88	–	–	94	95	93	–	–	41	57	–	–	71	–	–	4	4	3	–	–
Kazakhstan	37	36	38	19	61	92	92	91	84	96	49	48	24	76	45	40	49	4	4	4	5	4
Kyrgyzstan	19	21	17	7	47	88	90	85	86	99	54	76	76	85	57	59	54	11	12	9	11	6
Lao People's Democratic Republic	23	21	25	5	73	57	58	57	42	87	52	5	1	24	41	29	50	14	15	13	20	8
Lebanon	62	63	60	–	–	56 y	58 y	54 y	–	–	74 y	29	–	–	16 y	–	–	9	8	10	–	–
Mali	10	10	10	1	40	29	27	30	28	44	14	0	0	2	40	33	49	33	33	33	33	36
Mauritania	14	14	14	2	41	55	54	55	55	64	28	–	–	–	40	42	39	26	27	26	24	25
Mongolia	58	56	60	25	80	57	54	60	42	71	39	23	6	48	68	74	62	9	9	8	10	6
Montenegro	29	28	30	6	62	97	96	98	88	100	79	77	50	92	39	49	33	6	8	5	11	3
Morocco	39	36	41	6	78	35 y	34 y	35 y	16 y	59 y	58 y	21 y	9 y	52 y	14 y	19 y	7 y	9	9	9	11	6
Mozambique	–	–	–	–	–	47	45	48	48	50	20	3	2	10	–	–	–	33	33	32	–	–
Myanmar	23	23	23	8	46	58 y	58 y	58 y	42 y	76 y	44 y	–	–	–	–	–	–	–	–	–	–	–

TABLE 14

TABLE 14 | EARLY CHILDHOOD DEVELOPMENT >>

Countries and areas	Attendance in early childhood education 2005–2012*					Adult support for learning++ 2005–2012*					Father's support for learning++ 2005–2012*	Learning materials at home 2005–2012*						Children left in inadequate care 2005–2012*				
												Children's books			Playthings++							
	total	male	female	poorest 20%	richest 20%	total	male	female	poorest 20%	richest 20%		total	poorest 20%	richest 20%	total	poorest 20%	richest 20%	total	male	female	poorest 20%	richest 20%
Nepal	30 y	29 y	31 y	14 y	61 y	–	–	–	–	–	–	–	–	–	–	–	–	–	–	–	–	–
Nigeria	43	42	43	10	84	65	66	64	48	89	37	6	0	19	38	29	48	40	40	40	40	34
Sao Tome and Principe	27	29	26	18	51	–	–	–	–	–	–	–	–	–	–	–	–	–	–	–	–	–
Senegal	22 y	23 y	21 y	7 y	43 y	–	–	–	–	–	–	–	–	–	–	–	–	–	–	–	–	–
Serbia	44	41	47	22	75	95	96	95	84	98	78	76	49	86	63	65	60	1	1	1	2	1
Sierra Leone	14	13	15	5	42	54	53	55	45	79	42	2	0	10	35	24	50	32	33	32	29	28
Somalia	2	2	2	1	6	79	80	79	76	85	48	–	–	–	–	–	–	–	–	–	–	–
South Sudan	6	6	6	2	13	–	–	–	–	–	–	–	–	–	–	–	–	–	–	–	–	–
State of Palestine	15	16	15	9	26	58	58	57	49	69	77	12	–	–	64	–	–	13	13	14	12	15
Sudan	20	20	21	10	48	–	–	–	–	–	–	–	–	–	–	–	–	–	–	–	–	–
Suriname	34	33	35	16	63	73	71	75	56	91	26	25	4	61	59	61	60	7	7	7	9	8
Swaziland	33	32	34	36	50	50	50	50	35	71	10	4	1	12	69	64	74	15	15	15	20	9
Syrian Arab Republic	8	8	7	4	18	70	70	69	52	84	62	30	12	53	52	52	51	17	17	17	22	15
Tajikistan	10	11	10	1	29	74	73	74	56	86	23	17	4	33	46	43	44	13	13	12	15	11
Thailand	61	60	61	55	78	89	90	89	86	98	57	43	25	71	55	58	49	13	14	13	18	7
The former Yugoslav Republic of Macedonia	22	25	19	0	56	92	92	91	81	96	71	52	18	81	71	70	79	5	5	5	11	1
Togo	29	27	31	10	52	62	61	63	55	68	38	2	0	7	31	26	41	41	42	41	45	35
Trinidad and Tobago	75	74	76	65	87	98	98	98	96	100	63	81	66	93	65	63	72	1	1	1	2	0
Tunisia	44	42	47	13	81	71	68	74	44	90	71	18	3	40	53	46	56	13	13	14	18	9
Ukraine	63	63	63	30	74	–	–	–	–	–	–	97	93	99	47	36	47	10	11	10	15	4
Uzbekistan	20	20	19	5	46	91	91	90	83	95	54	43	32	59	67	74	62	5	5	5	6	7
Viet Nam	72	71	73	59	91	77	74	80	63	94	61	20	3	49	49	41	54	9	10	9	17	4
Yemen	3	3	3	0	8	33	34	32	16	56	37	10	4	31	49	45	49	34	36	33	46	22
SUMMARY INDICATORS#																						
Sub-Saharan Africa	26	26	26	8	53	–	–	–	–	–	–	–	–	–	–	–	–	–	–	–	–	–
Eastern and Southern Africa	–	–	–	–	–	–	–	–	–	–	–	–	–	–	–	–	–	–	–	–	–	–
West and Central Africa	28	28	28	8	57	58	58	58	48	77	35	4	0	13	37	29	46	43	43	43	46	35
Middle East and North Africa	17	17	18	–	–	–	–	–	–	–	–	–	–	–	–	–	–	–	–	–	–	–
South Asia	–	–	–	–	–	–	–	–	–	–	–	–	–	–	–	–	–	–	–	–	–	–
East Asia and Pacific	–	–	–	–	–	–	–	–	–	–	–	–	–	–	–	–	–	–	–	–	–	–
Latin America and Caribbean	–	–	–	–	–	–	–	–	–	–	–	–	–	–	–	–	–	–	–	–	–	–
CEE/CIS	–	–	–	–	–	–	–	–	–	–	–	–	–	–	–	–	–	–	–	–	–	–
Least developed countries	12	12	12	6	25	–	–	–	–	–	–	–	–	–	–	–	–	–	–	–	–	–
World	–	–	–	–	–	–	–	–	–	–	–	–	–	–	–	–	–	–	–	–	–	–

For a complete list of countries and areas in the regions, subregions and country categories, see page 26.

TABLE 14 | EARLY CHILDHOOD DEVELOPMENT